AF717245

# SOLDIERS ON INTERNATIONAL MISSIONS

# SOLDIERS ON INTERNATIONAL MISSIONS: THERE AND BACK AGAIN

BY

**STÉPHANIE VINCENT LYK-JENSEN**
*VIVE – The Danish Center for Social Science Research, Denmark*

**PEDER J. PEDERSEN**
*Department of Economics, Aarhus University & VIVE – The Danish Center for Social Science Research, Denmark*

emerald PUBLISHING

United Kingdom – North America – Japan – India – Malaysia – China

Emerald Publishing Limited
Howard House, Wagon Lane, Bingley BD16 1WA, UK

First edition 2019

Copyright © Stéphanie Vincent Lyk-Jensen and Peder J. Pedersen. Published under exclusive license.

**Reprints and permissions service**
Contact: permissions@emeraldinsight.com

No part of this book may be reproduced, stored in a retrieval system, transmitted in any form or by any means electronic, mechanical, photocopying, recording or otherwise without either the prior written permission of the publisher or a licence permitting restricted copying issued in the UK by The Copyright Licensing Agency and in the USA by The Copyright Clearance Center. Any opinions expressed in the chapters are those of the authors. Whilst Emerald makes every effort to ensure the quality and accuracy of its content, Emerald makes no representation implied or otherwise, as to the chapters' suitability and application and disclaims any warranties, express or implied, to their use.

**British Library Cataloguing in Publication Data**
A catalogue record for this book is available from the British Library

ISBN: 978-1-78973-032-6 (Print)
ISBN: 978-1-78973-031-9 (Online)
ISBN: 978-1-78973-033-3 (Epub)

Printed and bound by CPI Group (UK) Ltd, Croydon, CR0 4YY

ISOQAR certified Management System, awarded to Emerald for adherence to Environmental standard ISO 14001:2004.

ISOQAR REGISTERED
Certificate Number 1985
ISO 14001

INVESTOR IN PEOPLE

# Contents

# List of Figures

# List of Tables

# List of Abbreviations

| | |
|---|---|
| **BPP** | Børge Prien-prøven is the Danish Armed Forces intelligence test |
| **DIB** | Danish International Brigade was a peacekeeping force established in 1994. It was officially disbanded on 15 February 2005 |
| **FPT** | Danish Ministry of Defence Personnel Agency (*Forsvarets Personeltjeneste*) |
| **HBU** | Basic military education (Hærens Basisuddannelse) |
| **HOK** | Army Operational Command (*Haerens Operative Kommando*, HOK) |
| **HRU** | Military reaction forces education (*Hærens Reaktionsstyrkeuddannelse*) |
| **IFOR** | NATO Implementation Force (December 1995, December 1996) in Bosnia Herzegovina |
| **IMP** | Institute for Military Psychology (*Institut for Militærpsykologi*), since 1 January 2011: The Military Psychological Department (*Militærpsykologisk Afdeling*, MPA) |
| **INTOPS** | International Operation |
| **IRAQ** | Coalition in Iraq (2003–2007). The coalition forces was a military command during the 2003 invasion of Iraq, led by the United States of America, United Kingdom, Australia, Spain and Poland |
| **ISAF** | International Security Assistance Force (2002–2014) in Afghanistan. Denmark has had deployed soldiers under the NATO-command since January 2002 |
| **KFOR** | NATO Kosovo Force, in Kosovo, since June 1999 |
| **MPA** | The Military Psychological Department (*Militærpsykologisk Afdeling*, MPA), before 2011: Institute for Military Psychology (*Institut for Militærpsykologi*, IMP) |
| **NATO** | The North Atlantic Treaty Organisation |
| **SFI** | The Danish National Centre for Social Research. Since 1July 2007, SFI and KORA (the Danish Institute for Local and Regional Government Research) were merged into VIVE – The Danish Centre for Social Science Research. In the book, we refer to SFI for the source of data and some previous analyses |
| **SFOR** | Stabilisation Force, in Bosnia Herzegovina (December 1996 to 2004) |

| | |
|---|---|
| **SRS** | Army Standing Reaction Force (*Haerens Staaende ReaktionsStyrke,* SRS) |
| **UNCRO** | United Nations Confidence Restoration Operation in Croatia (March 1995 to January 1996) |
| **UNIFIL** | United Nations Interim Force in Lebanon, since 1978, and enhanced in 2006 |
| **UNIKOM** | United Nations Iraq-Kuwait Observation Mission, in Iraq and Kuwait (April 1991 to October 2003) |
| **UN** | United Nations |
| **UNPROFOR** | United Nations Protection Forces, in Bosnia and Herzegovina, Croatia, Serbia, Montenegro and Macedonia (February 1992 to March 1995) |
| **VIVE** | The Danish Centre for Social Science Research |

# About the Authors

**Stéphanie Vincent Lyk-Jensen** is Senior Researcher at VIVE – The Danish Center for Social Science Research. She holds a PhD in Economics. Her work focuses on quantitative methods to measure the impact of policies and interventions. Her research areas include behavioural economics, economics of health, labour economics and applied econometrics. She has studied the motivations to sign up for a military deployment, the effect of military deployment on mental health and the impact of military service on men's income and crime. Her work is published in journals such as *Defence and Peace Economics*, *Economics and Human Biology* and *Labour Economics.*

**Peder J. Pedersen** has a Doctorate in Economics and is Professor Emeritus at Aarhus University, Denmark. Currently he is Consultant at VIVE – The Danish Centre for Social Science Research and Research Fellow at IZA, the Institute for the Study of Labour, Bonn, Germany. His research focuses on labour economics, international mobility, income distribution and poverty. He has published in books and in such journals as *International Journal of Manpower, Scandinavian Journal of Economics, Empirical Economics, Review of Income and Wealth* and *Industrial and Labour Relations Review.*

# Acknowledgements

The analyses reported in this book were supported by *Soldaterlegatet* with financial support from Tryg, Lundbeck, Novo Nordisk and Aase and Ejnar Danielsen's funds. We are grateful to the Danish Armed Forces for facilitating data collection. We also thank Ann Fenger Benwell, Malene Damgaard, Ane Glad, Julie Heideman, Jens Kofod, Agnete Aslaug Kjær and Cecilie Dohlmann Weatherall for their contributions to the whole project.

Chapter 1

# Introduction

In the first half of the twentieth century, the two world wars sent millions of soldiers into battle. Since the Cold War, military action has increasingly involved deployment of professional soldiers to regional conflicts in either peacekeeping (PK) missions or peace-enforcing (PE) missions – that is, soldiers fighting in a 'distant' war. Millions of men and women have been deployed to such missions and have returned with experiences that may greatly affect their lives and the lives of their families, in both the short and the long run.

The experiences of the Danish Armed Forces, who participate in more and more international deployments, provide an excellent case study for the transformation of the military – from mass armies built on conscription during the Cold War to much smaller professional units that can be deployed to international missions. Gilroy and Williams (2006) provide a general introduction to and description of the shift towards all-volunteer forces (AVFs) in Europe. In Denmark, the military situation changed from being a 'front-line' situation during the Cold War to a situation characterised by the ambition to participate in international missions with allied forces (Heurlin, 2006). The timing of this change coincides precisely with the period of the data used for the analyses in this book (1992–2009). Denmark also constitutes an exception to the international trend towards AVFs, as it has kept conscription (Heurlin, 2006). While only a small share of a cohort has to serve in the military, this group of conscripts is a pool of potential recruitment to the group of voluntary professional soldiers.

In another comprehensive survey of the transformation to AVF with deployment capabilities, Tresch and Leuprecht (2010) provide a broad European coverage and emphasise how the strategy shift creates a great demand for soldiers qualified for international deployments. Sørensen (2010) illustrates some of the Danish aspects of this shift, with a special focus on policies that are relative for veterans. King (2011) describes and analyses this transformation using case studies of the UK, Germany and France and illustrates the multinational military cooperation with the planning and implementation of the mission in Afghanistan. Petersson (2011) uses the Scandinavian countries to exemplify this change in a setting with a partial denationalisation of the national defence forces. He contrasts the strong Danish engagement in sharp missions in southern Afghanistan with the engagement of another NATO member, Norway, in the northern part of the country, where there are fewer combat situations. Despite these differences in strategy, Petersson (2011) also emphasises the common need in the Scandinavian countries to ensure that the population at large see this transformation as justified.

In a collective volume, Caforio (2013) focuses on the new form of warfare, that is, irregular groups in non-state wars, where the parties in conflict deploy regular troops within large coalitions. Caforio (2013) encompasses all the nine national contributions analysing interview-based surveys in the participating countries.

Kold and Sørensen (2013a) report the results from interviews of 542 Danish respondents with questions about separation from the family, psychological problems and stress during deployment and adaptation to a normal life after returning home. Kold and Sørensen (2013b) describe the mission types and destinations involved in deployments of Danish Armed Forces, with a focus on the public opinion regarding these deployments.

Thus, the literature provides hypotheses and analyses of challenges and experiences of this form of deployment of soldiers to 'distant' wars and our analyses build on this relevant literature. To our knowledge, this book is the first to investigate the impact of deployment on the soldiers' lives when they return home to family, work and civilian life in general. As an illustrative study, this book uses the full population of Danish soldiers deployed to international PK and PE missions between 1992 and 2009 – a total of 26,000 men and women. These soldiers were deployed in PK missions in the former Yugoslavia or PE missions in Iraq and Afghanistan – or a combination of these.

While PK missions are predominant in the beginning of the period, PE missions are predominant towards the end. Both types of mission presented challenges for the deployed soldiers. The missions in the former Yugoslavia were likely to cause frustration, with the risk of later psychological reactions, for example when soldiers had to witness brutal and humiliating treatment of civilians without being able to interfere. In contrast, the missions to Iraq and Afghanistan contained the clear possibility of involvement in combat situations, with the risk of being wounded or killed.

The total sum of experiences of the 26,000 deployed soldiers and the problems that may result from these deployments lie far beyond the scope of a book such as this. Our ambition here is to focus on the central topics and issues involved in being deployed in an international mission and returning home.

The analyses answer the following questions:

- Who are the men and women who choose to be deployed?
- Why do they choose to be deployed?
- Which challenges do soldiers face *before*, *during* and *after* returning home from a mission?
- What are the consequences of deployment on soldiers' individual lives?

To answer the central questions about the deployed soldiers, we draw relevant data from administrative registers, data following all the deployed soldiers over 18 years and covering both their pre-deployment lives and their experiences after returning home. A number of data sets are specifically developed to present a unique possibility of analysing the impact of deployment on important issues, such as the financial situation of the soldiers before and after a mission, their post-deployment career in the labour market, criminal activity, smoking and drinking, and overall health. Moreover, the analyses provide a portrait of the men and the women who choose to be deployed and explain their motives as well as the challenges they face before and during deployment and after returning home. The analyses also compare these soldiers with relevant control groups, also constructed from administrative registers.

To explore in greater depth the soldiers' motivations, feelings and emotional reactions, we supplemented the registered data with a broad survey of approximately 3,200 present and former soldiers, a before-and-after deployment survey of 600 soldiers and qualitative in-depth interviews of 44 individuals (veterans, parents, relatives and support group professionals).

The unique contribution is that the data to which we have access provide us with an opportunity to compare a number of life conditions among the deployed soldiers before and after deployment. As a rule, investigations of this kind are usually limited to accessing data after the soldiers return home. This book is the first to provide a longitudinal perspective covering the participants in these missions before, during and after deployment, on a large range of life outcomes. In addition, the comprehensive data material consists of the results of in-depth qualitative interviews, comprehensive telephone interviews and questionnaire surveys carried out among a large representative group of veterans.

Our analyses of these rich data sets have also dismissed some myths or disproved hypotheses. For example, we found that veterans have a *lower* crime rate and a *better* financial situation than the control group. Moreover, the various sources of data – interviews, surveys and administrative records – complement one another. To the objective information from the administrative records, we add more subjective information from interviews and questionnaires. For example, we used questionnaires to study the motivation of soldiers to sign up voluntarily for the military training qualifying them for deployment in a mission. We designed the study as a before-and-after questionnaire, as soldiers' original motivation for choosing deployment may have changed after the deployment. While the scope of change in motivations differs, the veterans generally have a positive experience of their deployment.

As soldiers sent on an international mission do not represent a random sample of the population, investigations of this kind face a methodological challenge. Clearly, a process of self-selection is involved, as the soldiers' volunteering for deployment is followed by the selection process that the military undertakes to select soldiers for missions. Although the deployed soldiers belong to a physically and mentally relatively strong group, being deployed does not come without costs: the risk of being wounded during deployment and coming home with physical injuries or psychological problems. For example, when we observe the first three years after returning home, we find a sharp rise in psychiatric diagnoses and the purchase of mental health medication – a tendency we do not find in the control group.

The 26,000 soldiers were studied over an 18-year period, during which they were deployed on very different missions. Given this wealth of data, our study contributes important new knowledge about and insights into how PK or PE deployment on international military missions affects soldiers and their lives, as no other study had access the data necessary to analyse so many aspects of a deployment.

This book is structured as follows. Chapter 2 gives a brief summary of the entire investigation. Chapter 3 presents an overview of the sources of data and methods used in this book. Chapter 4 provides a statistical portrait of the soldiers before their deployment. Chapter 5 presents the results of in-depth qualitative interviews with a group comprising the deployed soldiers, their relatives and representatives from the military and other institutions. Chapter 6 presents the results of a large representative interview investigation of veterans. The chapter focuses on the path into – and for some out of – the military, social relationships and self-assessed health, as well as the experiences during a mission. Chapter 7 investigates whether the deployment itself has an independent effect on soldiers' motivation to volunteer for a mission, on the financial situation of the soldiers and on soldiers' criminal behaviour. Chapter 8 analyses the central elements in the soldiers' health profile before and after deployment, with a focus on psychiatric diagnoses, purchase of medication for psychological problems, work-related injuries and mortality among the deployed soldiers after they return home. Chapter 9 concludes with some perspectives arising from the study.

Chapter 2

# Summary of Contents

The chapters in this book contain descriptions and analyses of a great many factors connected with deployment on international missions. The objective of this summary is to provide a brief overview of the content of book (Chapters 3–8), in which we draw on different data sets to comprehensively describe all soldiers sent on international military missions for the Danish army over a period of 18 years. These data sets are uniquely suited for analysing and explaining soldiers' lives and experiences from a before-and-after perspective.

The fundamental question here is whether deployment on a peacekeeping (PK) or a peace-enforcing (PE) mission has an independent effect on a series of important beliefs, decisions and behaviours in the soldiers' individual lives. The basic methodological challenge in answering this question is that, by their very nature, the deployed cannot be observed as if they had not been deployed (the 'counterfactual situation'). Moreover, as soldiers themselves have volunteered for deployment, they constitute a select group. In each of these six particular chapters, we deal with this self-selection issue in various ways – descriptively, analytically and with a control group comprising comparable non-deployed persons.

*Chapter 3* summarises the data sets and methods that chapters 4–8 apply in different ways for different purposes. The data are derived from administrative registers, qualitative interviews, a large telephone survey and a smaller questionnaire survey. Military records are the source of data about the deployed soldiers between 1992 and 2009. Personal data for 1980–2010 also come from the Statistics Denmark registers for all those deployed. Information from these sources therefore covers a number of years before the actual deployment. Other sources include data from the Danish Health Authority (*Sundhedsstyrelsen*) records both before and after deployment and from the National Board of Industrial Injuries (*Arbejdsskadestyrelsen* (ASK)). We use personal identity numbers (*centrale personregister* (CPR)) for combining information from the various data sources. These data are, of course, anonymised for research purposes.

From the administrative registers, we build a general population that we use primarily to analyse the socio-demographic characteristics of the deployed and their financial, health and criminal status. We focus on the before-and-after aspects of deployment. The social statistical records provide socio-demographic profiles, as well as criminal records, health status and the current job market status of those who have left the military.

As the registers do not contain subjective information for all those deployed, we carried out *qualitative interviews* with 44 individuals to both elicit and elucidate their motivations and experiences before and after deployment. These individuals included deployed soldiers, their relatives, people from the military and support group professionals. Qualitative interviews yield insights and information that cannot be obtained from the administrative records alone (e.g. relationships with family during and after a deployment).

One further source of data is a telephone interview survey of a random sample of 4,000 deployed soldiers, a survey with an unusually high response rate of 80 per cent. It included questions on socio-economic background, experiences during missions, type of employment contract (for those still in the military), the employment situation for veterans and smoking and drinking habits.

In addition, we obtained data from another questionnaire survey of those deployed on two specific missions, one PK and one PE. Central to the survey were the soldiers' motivations before and after deployment, broken down into 12 categories.

The methods vary throughout the chapters. Results from both the qualitative interviews and other interviews, as well as from the questionnaires, are presented in the form of *descriptive analyses.* Other chapters use econometric analyses, with logistic regressions explaining the probability of specific outcomes, and difference-in-differences methods applied to the before-and-after analyses with a control group. The control group, which constitutes an important methodological instrument, consists of men (in a relevant age interval) who are deemed eligible for military service but who have never been deployed. Registered data are used for both groups.

*Chapter 4* presents a statistical portrait of the deployed. On average, although the soldiers were deployed on two missions, the variation is great, as half have been deployed only once. We cover changes that have occurred in both mission types, from PK to predominantly PE, and mission destination. In terms of numbers of deployments, the former Yugoslavia is the dominant destination area, with the greatest weight in the first years of the period we study, whereas Iraq and Afghanistan dominate in the later years. Moreover, from around 2000, the number of deployed soldiers starts increasing.

The statistical portrait starts with the socio-demographic background factors. The dominant age group is 21–24 years old. The proportion of women among the deployed increases throughout the period from two per cent to 10 per cent, and while the proportion of immigrant and their descendants is low, it also increases from one per cent to two per cent. The proportion of those with a further education (i.e. higher secondary or tertiary) increases, whereas the proportion of those with a vocational training decreases. Results of intelligence tests show that the deployed are at least at the same level as those not deployed.

A look at income and socio-economic status before deployment reveals that the soldiers have a higher relative income than other similar groups in the year before deployment. At that time, they also had better labour force attachment than other similar groups.

As for convictions for property crimes, a sharp drop occurs in the three years before deployment, starting at the same level as the general population. While the same drop occurs for violent crimes in pre-deployment period, this drop starts at a lower level than that for the general population.

Data for the repatriated soldiers are available only for 2005–2009, during which time most repatriations were from Afghanistan, chiefly because of illness and social problems. The main causes of injuries and death were roadside bombs, combat or explosions.

*Chapter 5* focuses on the qualitative interviews with previous deployed soldiers and their relatives, as well as with representatives from the military and other institutions. The interview structure emphasises soldiers' experiences and needs *before*, *during* and *after* returning home from a mission. The central elements *before* deployment are the transition to another life situation, the change in close relationships and soldiers' motivations for choosing to take part in a deployment. *During* deployment, the focus is on comradeship and personal development. The significant elements *after* returning home are personal change, reintegration into the previous life situation and meetings with the military and other institutions, as well as whether veterans feel that they are valued by society.

The qualitative interviews show that the significant motivational factors before the deployment are self-realisation, new experiences, ideology, comradeship, need for money and military professionalism. During a mission, the most important issues are the problematic nature of powerlessness, occurring within a limited mandate. The quality of leadership, 'the military family' and communication with the soldiers' own families also appear important. Media coverage is generally perceived as one-sided and negative, with a strong negative effect on the deployed. After returning home, soldiers appear changed: they miss the comradeship they experienced during deployment, and they mention the absence of social recognition from the media. Psychological after-reactions also appear in the first months after they return home. Soldiers generally refer to their personal growth as a positive consequence of deployment.

Although the military and other organisations offer post-deployment help, two problems emerge: one is that contact may be lost with soldiers whose psychological after-effects appear much later and the other is that help is given only to those soldiers who request it. More broadly, the large number of people deployed on missions constitutes a group of new citizens with special needs.

*Chapter 6* presents the results of a telephone survey of 4,000 randomly selected deployed soldiers. The focus is on socio-demographic background factors, the path into and out of the military, later work experience and mission experience, especially on which conditions were either enriching or stressful for the veterans. The survey also focuses on social relationships, self-assessed health and contact with the military's support organisations, with an emphasis on the veterans' smoking habits and use of drugs.

The chapter starts with a short overview of the respondents' demographic profiles, including the number of adults in the family of origin and current family and housing situations. Then, it follows a brief review of the path into – and, for some, out of – the military, including the type of military contract, educational level before enlisting and the number of deployments at the time of the survey. Finally, the chapter examines the employment situation of those who have left the military: about five per cent are retired or took early retirement and five per cent are unemployed, regardless of when they left the military.

As for mission experiences, 75 per cent of respondents were deployed once, to the former Yugoslavia, whereas the many-time deployed were more often (or also) sent to Afghanistan. Only a very small share of respondents turned into 'mission bums', that is, those who choose deployment a great many times. The study also reveals that deployment is an important family tradition for one of every three deployed soldiers.

About seven per cent of respondents were repatriated, mostly for health or social problems. Overall about three per cent were wounded in combat, and another nine per cent had non-combat-related injuries. Respondents also self-assessed whether they had psychological or physical problems after deployment. In all, 17 per cent felt that they had psychological problems, and four per cent considered these problems serious. Another seven per cent reported physical problems, with two per cent considering them serious.

For self-assessed social relationships, the experience of being lonely is more widespread among veterans than in the general population. The self-assessment of illness is on a par with that of the general population – a surprising finding given the self-selection and screening that take place before a deployment.

Although veterans have lower weekly alcohol consumption than the general population, they engage in more binge-drinking. Smoking is more widespread among the younger veterans than in the general population. Although fewer veterans have used cannabis, a greater proportion of veterans younger than 45 years have had experiences with other illegal substances.

*Chapter 7* focuses on the important issue of whether research can show that deployment in itself has an independent effect in three areas: motivations for deployment, financial situation and probability of committing crimes. The analyses of motivation are based on a questionnaire survey carried out with 447 respondents who had been deployed on either a PE mission to Afghanistan or a PK mission to Lebanon in the spring of 2011, thus representing both a PK and a PE deployment. The questionnaire investigates soldiers' motivations with a 12-item typology of possible specific motivations, divided into four categories: self-oriented gain, dignity, other-oriented gain and fidelity.

The analysis shows that motivation changes during deployment. The more idealistic motivations became less important after the soldiers return home. The first-time deployed are generally more positive than the more experienced (many-time deployed), who put greater emphasis on financial motivation. Women who are deployed place a high value on making a difference for the people needing help in the mission areas and on the idea of performing a challenging job. Moreover, privates rate comradeship the highest, whereas officers choose having a challenging job. We analyse both whether the soldiers' financial situation before deployment may have influenced their decision to go on a mission and whether the soldiers' financial situation (especially their net debt) after deployment – a good indicator of how they manage other areas of their lives – is affected.

Financial data with information about income, loans and bank accounts first became available in 1997, thereby allowing us to investigate the soldiers' financial situation from two years before to up to five years after returning home. We find that deployment sharply increased disposable income during the years of deployment. The soldiers' net debt is measured as bank debt minus savings. The proportion of soldiers with savings greater than loans increases from 40 per cent before deployment to 50 per cent during deployment, falling to 30 per cent five years after returning home. This profile reflects, among other things, a life cycle with an increasing share of veterans owning their own house or apartment.

The analysis indicates that the soldiers' debt before deployment was not sufficiently high as to constitute an important motivation for deployment. Statistical analyses of change in net debt from before to after deployment show a significant correlation with socio-economic characteristics such as age, marital status, gender and ownership of property. However, our findings do not indicate that wages during deployment were used primarily for paying off debts. Finally, we compared those deployed with a control group from the same birth cohort (1975–1982), finding that the deployed had both lower net debt and higher disposable income.

The before-and-after factors are critical, when we study criminality. We focus on soldiers who had no previous criminal record or compare the deployed and the control group for criminality. While, in Chapter 4, we find a notable drop in criminality until the year of deployment, in Chapter 7, we see a marked increase one to two years after returning home, followed by a decrease. Violent crimes increase sharply in the first year after returning home among two to six of every 1,000 soldiers. Despite the sharpness of this increase, however, the actual number of crimes is relatively low.

In a statistical analysis, we find that the probability of committing a crime after returning home increases if the soldier had a criminal record before deployment, is between 18 and 24 years old, does not have children, has a relatively low education, was in out-of-home care (foster care) for some of his upbringing, grew up in a one-parent family or was unemployed for some years before deployment. Moreover, in contrast to the control group, we find less property crime and fewer violent crimes among the deployed. Thus, we find no statistical evidence that deployment increases the tendency to commit violent crimes.

*Chapter 8* covers the health of soldiers before and after deployment. The analysis includes four central elements: the first comprises psychiatric diagnoses and contacts with the psychiatric health care system. The data come from administrative registers that, particularly in this area, provide objective, not subjective (e.g. self-assessed) measures. The second element, the purchase of medication for mental diseases, supports the first element. The third element is work-related injuries registered for all the deployed, and the fourth is an analysis of mortality among the deployed after returning home. (Those who were killed while on deployment, primarily as a result of roadside bombs, combat or explosion, are covered in Chapter 4.)

These four elements make Chapter 8 a larger chapter. It begins with a descriptive overview of the different psychiatric diagnoses and the changes before and after deployment. We typically find a shift from nervous and stress-related diagnoses before deployment to affective problems, including depression, upon return. This descriptive part, which covers the period until a diagnosis was made, shows correlations among diagnoses, background factors and types of mission.

In all, as many as five per cent of all deployed were recorded as having a psychiatric diagnosis during 1995–2010. The analyses indicate that psychiatric diagnoses are especially prevalent in soldiers deployed to the former Yugoslavia (PK mission). The probability of receiving such a diagnosis increases, if a soldier had been diagnosed before deployment, was repatriated (in 2005–2009), is between 25 and 44 years, has less education, was in out-of-home care, grew up in a one-parent family, was unemployed during the year before deployment, was last deployed at least six years earlier and was a private. Moreover, although we find a general increase in the number of contacts with the psychiatric health care system after deployment, they are fewer than the number in the control group.

The second element is the purchase of mental health-related medication in 1995–2010, likewise with an emphasis on the before-and-after factors. Evaluating the results calls for understanding that the period after returning home varies greatly, with data for 15 years or more for those first deployed early in that period, and for a very short time for those deployed in 2009. In all, about 20 per cent bought medication, and half of those who made such a purchase did so six years or more after returning home.

The likelihood of buying this type of medication increases after deployment if the soldier had bought it before deployment, was repatriated, had been deployed more than six years earlier, was in out-of-home care for part of his upbringing or grew up in a one-parent family, was unemployed one year before deployment, has either a short or a long education or was above 25 years at the time of first deployment.

The frequency of the purchase of medication among those deployed for the first time in 2002 is below than that in the control group. However, in 2010 – eight years after deployment – the level is the same. About 17 per cent of the deployed have been registered with a psychiatric diagnosis, have purchased mental health-related medication or have been treated for substance abuse.

Work-related injuries, illness and accidents among the deployed are reported to the National Board of Industrial Injuries or the Office of Injury and Compensation for the military. Data are available for 1997–2009. Reporting of work-related injuries and accidents is included in the analysis if their date fell within the time of deployment. As a result of changes in the definition of injuries and accidents and the shift from PK to PE at about the same time, the number of both injuries and accidents increased after 2004.

One of the main results in Chapter 8 is that veterans who report a work-related injury constitute a significantly larger group than those wounded or repatriated during a mission (see Chapter 4). In all, 17 per cent of the veterans have reported such an injury or accident. Among veterans who were wounded, who were repatriated or who reported a work-related injury, 22 per cent were recorded with a psychiatric diagnosis, or they purchased medication for a psychological problem.

In a statistical analysis of the risk of being wounded, being repatriated, or reporting a work-related injury in 2005–2010, the risk is greater if the soldier was older than 44 years on his most recent deployment, was in out-of-home care for part of his upbringing, was deployed to Afghanistan, Iraq, or Kosovo, or was deployed during the latter part of the period.

We analyse mortality among the formerly deployed after they return. In all, 54 soldiers died during deployment and 241 after returning home. Importantly, in the descriptive part of the analysis, we see an obvious increase in mortality within 2–6 years. We find large variation among those dying after returning home in terms of personal, health-related and military characteristics. The risk is greater if the deployed had a psychiatric diagnosis or purchased medication for psychological problems, was deployed either only once or to the former Yugoslavia, was older than 45 years, had a short education or had no children at the time of the most recent deployment. When one excludes soldiers dying during deployment (overwhelmingly in combat situations), the mortality is lower among soldiers than among the control group in the same 1975–1982 birth cohort.

In this chapter, we have summarised the entire investigation and reviewed the main findings. In the next chapter, we present an overview of the sources of data and methods from which we obtained these findings.

Chapter 3

# Overview of Data and Methods

The purpose of this chapter is to provide an overview of the different types of data we have used for describing and analysing the Danish soldiers who participated in international missions between 1992 and 2009. In addition, we also introduce and describe our methods.

Whereas some of the data sets are used in much of the study, others are linked to specific questions in a particular chapter. We begin with an overview of the most general data set, which allowed us to investigate the situation of soldiers in a number of ways before, during and after their deployment on a mission. The single elements in this data set are derived from a range of administrative registers. As these administrative records use the Danish personal identification numbers (CPR), we were able to gather information about the individual soldiers over a relatively long period and for a variety of characteristics such as demographic characteristics, education, social affiliation, health care, death and cause of death, employment, unemployment, income and criminal records. Also included in the study are data derived from qualitative interviews with 44 individuals, together with questionnaire-based data for a large population of soldiers. The combined data and some previous analyses conducted in SFI-reports (10:21; 11:25; 12:01; 12:09; 12:24) are referred to in the source of the figures and tables as SFI.

## Records-based Data

We gathered these data from many different sources with the objective of forming a common data set of the deployed soldiers in 1992–2009, covering a range of socio-demographics and military characteristics. Our administrative records come from six different sources, military as well as civilian:

(1) military personnel service, NATO, INTOPS and Coordination Section data (hereafter called INTOPS data) on soldiers deployed on international missions in 1992–2009;
(2) military recruitment data, which contain information about the Armed Forces Day (AFD) tests in 1994–2010;
(3) administrative records of soldiers repatriated in 2005–2010;
(4) administrative records from the Army Operational Command of soldiers who were wounded or who died in 2005–2010;

(5) administrative records on individual characteristics from Statistics Denmark (*Danmark Statistik*); and
(6) data from Statistics Denmark for the entire Danish population covering a large range of socio-demographics background.

Data obtained from the military form the main population for the study, with data on the 53,861 deployments of all 26,028 soldiers on international military missions.

Using personal identification numbers (CPR), we were able to match the main population from the extensive military data with records-based data from Statistics Denmark. No identifying information is linked to the data used for analysis. Data were remotely anonymised and analysed securely.

Through the administrative records from Statistics Denmark, we also had access to information for the entire period from 1980 to 2009/2010 on all soldiers deployed on international missions between 1992 and 2009, covering at least 12 years before deployment for all soldiers. For some soldiers deployed earlier, we also have observations over periods of many years. However, the periods covered decrease, the closer one comes to the final year 2009.

Data from Statistics Denmark for 1980–2009 were arranged in a panel data set in which subjects can be followed over a number of years. These data come from the following records:

- population, household and family records containing such information as gender, age, type of family and number of children;
- the integrated database for job market research, the central register for job market statistics and the records-based workforce statistics;
- education records with information about the highest education achieved and any ongoing education;
- income records;
- child and youth records with information about any preventive social measures;
- records from the comprehensive social statistics registers;
- records for emigrants, immigrants and their descendants, with data on times of emigration and immigration; and
- criminal register, with data on convictions and type of crime

## Interview Data

*Qualitative interviews* are used primarily for revealing motivations, experiences during deployment and any resulting effects of deployment. These data encompass information that are not available from administrative records. These qualitative interviews include 44 respondents: 20 deployed, seven relatives and 17 people from the military and different support organisations. These interviews, carried out in the first half of 2010 as semi-structured interviews, included an important element of openness. An in-depth analysis was done for evaluating the validity and reliability of the data. Although these data can provide relevant and important information not available in the registers, care should be used when generalising from such data. The number of respondents is very small in comparison with the main population of deployed soldiers. In addition, the respondents voluntary chose to participate in this survey, participation was voluntary. Thus, the sample might be positively self-selected; for example, veterans suffering severe after-effects of deployment or post-deployment effects might choose not to participate in such an interview.

*Telephone interviews* were undertaken with 4,000 veterans randomly chosen from among those previously deployed. The interviews last approximately 40 minutes, and the response rate was high (80%). Because both the sensitivity and the formulation of the questions were suitable to a telephone interview, we chose this format to reach a large number of respondents. The interviews were carried out during March–May 2011.

An analysis of the drop-out rate shows only small discrepancies, for example, slightly more older respondents and more of those 'not alone' (married or cohabiting). Completion of the survey and the reasons for dropping out are shown in Table 3.1. Only six per cent refused to participate.

In Table 3.2, the respondents are divided in terms of background factors. Table 3.2 shows the small over-representation of veterans who were older and veterans in a relationship.

Likewise, studying the response rate by military characteristics does not show large discrepancies. Slightly more officers replied, and there was a slight increase with age at the time of first deployment. Finally, when we consider the specific missions, we find no discrepancies. The 3,198 respondents are not significantly different from the other 24,470 deployed.

Table 3.1. Completion and Drop-out Rate in the Interview Survey of Previously Deployed Veterans.

| | *N* | % |
|---|---|---|
| Completed interviews | 3,198 | 80 |
| Partly completed interviews | 13 | 0 |
| No contact | 460 | 12 |
| Refused to participate | 248 | 6 |
| Sick or in hospital | 54 | 1 |
| Other | 27 | 1 |
| Total | 4,000 | 100 |

*Source*: SFI Survey.

Table 3.2. Total Response Rate in Terms of Background Factors.

| Background Factors | Response Rate |
|---|---|
| Gender[a] | 80 |
| Female | 83 |
| Male | 80 |
| Ethnicity[a] | 80 |
| Danish | 81 |
| Other | 75 |
| Age groups | 80 |
| 20–24 years | 75 |
| 25–29 years | 78 |
| 30–44 years | 80 |
| 45–59 years | 82 |
| ≥60 years | 85 |
| Civil status measured at the survey | 80 |
| Single/divorced | 82 |
| Not single (cohabiting, married) | 83 |

*Source*: SFI survey.
*Note*: [a]Answer bias significant at five per cent level.

The questions in the interview fall into the following categories:

- *Socio-demographic background*: age, gender, civilian status, number of children or step-children, parents divorced or not, housing, highest current civilian and military education, level of education when they joined the military and volunteer or draftee;
- *Terms of employment for those still employed in the military:* the current, whether they have taken or are taking a civilian education funded by the military, seniority in the military, sick leave, personnel group, their duties any plans for another deployment, and military evaluation result (i.e. eligible for deployment or not);
- *Terms of employment for those no longer in the military*: length of employment, type of armed forces during that time (e.g. Army, Air Force), reasons for leaving the military, personnel group when they left, last type of contract, receipt of financing for a civilian education from a military education grant or not and, if so, whether they took up that option, and current main occupation;
- *Family members who have been deployed*;
- *Previous missions*: these questions are phrased differently depending on whether the veteran was deployed either once or more. The purpose of these

questions was to obtain further deployment information that is not available from the military database. This information allowed us to check whether the deployed were on more missions than were registered and, in particular, to what extent the deployments were as a team or as an individual (not sent out as part of a team). We asked whether they had leadership duties, what their primary area of work was and how often they left the camp during a deployment;

- *Questions about being wounded, being repatriated, having physical and mental problems, experiencing combat situations and receiving possible compensation.* We also asked about contact with the military's support organisations and the veterans' satisfaction with these;
- *Experiences during a mission:* soldiers who were deployed only once were asked 15 detailed questions about their experiences. For those deployed several times, we ask for a more general evaluation, as distinguishing between different missions may be difficult;
- *Drinking, smoking and drug use*: to provide a comparison group with the deployed, we based these questions on a population study from Kristiansen, Ekholm, Grønbæk and Schurmann Tolstrup (2008); and
- *Social relationships, recreational activities and illness*: these questions were inspired by population studies from Ekholm et al. (2006) and the Danish Health Authority (2011), (Sundhedsstyrelsen), also with the aim of forming a comparison group.

## Questionnaire Study of Motivation

A smaller collection of data is based on a survey of two missions: to Afghanistan (the ISAF11 team) and Lebanon (the UNIFIL4 team) in the spring of 2011. The two missions differed in that the one to Afghanistan was peace-enforcing (PE) and the one to Lebanon was peacekeeping (PK). The focus of the questionnaire study was on the soldiers' motivation both before and after the missions, based on the 12 motives listed below. The soldiers were asked before and after their deployment which of the following motivations was important to them in relation to the missions, rated on a scale from 1 to 10:

(1) to have a challenging job;
(2) to have a job with responsibilities;
(3) to work with people whom I respect;
(4) to do something for my country;
(5) to make a positive difference for the people needing help in the mission area;
(6) to have a once-in-a-lifetime experience;
(7) to prevent a terrorist attack in Denmark;
(8) to build democracy in the mission area;
(9) to be a part of an elite team;
(10) to experience comradeship during deployment;
(11) to earn good wages; and
(12) to practise my military training.

Table 3.3. The 12 Statements of Motivation in the Analysis, Classified According to Eighmey's (2006) Typology.

| | **Tangible** | **Intangible** |
|---|---|---|
| Self-oriented | *Gain for self* | *Dignity* |
| | 1. To have a challenging job | 2. To have a job with responsibilities |
| | 11. To earn good wages | 3. To work with people whom I respect |
| | 12. To practise my military training | 6. To have a once-in-a-lifetime experience |
| | | 9. To be a part of an elite team |
| Other-oriented | *Gain for other* | *Fidelity* |
| | 5. To make a positive difference for the people needing help in the mission area | 4. To do something for my country |
| | 8. To build democracy in the mission area | 7. To prevent a terrorist attack in Denmark |
| | | 10. To experience comradeship during deployment |

Using Eighmey's (2006) typology, we classified the 12 motives on the basis of two criteria: (1) whether they were tangible or intangible and (2) whether they could be understood as being primarily directed towards the individual himself or towards others. The differences in motives of the various groups of soldiers are analysed with a descriptive approach and standard statistical methods. Table 3.3 shows the classification based on Eighmey (2006).

## Data and Methods Used in Analysing the Financial Situation and Criminality of Soldiers before and after Deployment

The data come primarily from the general records-based data set as previously described. As a basis for comparison, or benchmark, we also constructed a control group from the administrative records to match the characteristics of the deployed soldiers as much as possible. The control group consists of men who were deemed eligible for military service at the Armed Forces Day (AFD) tests in 1994–2010 but who were never deployed. The Armed Forces Day is the compulsory meeting young Danish male are called to when they turn 18. At this meeting, the eligibility of men called up for military service is determined. In the analyses in which the control group is used as a counterfactual comparison, we use the 1975–1982 birth cohorts for both the deployed and the control group. Some of the analyses further focus on those deployed in 2002, whose missions were representative of the entire deployed population. The period studied is before-and-after *the first* deployment.

The methodological starting point in the before-and-after analyses, which the panel data make possible, is that the deployed also constitute their own 'control group' by comparing them before and after. Of interest are any effects of having been deployed on debt and finances and criminal offences. Using a before-and-after analysis of the soldiers, we focus on the relationship technically referred to as 'ATET' (average treatment effect on the treated, or the average effect on the 'treated') – in this case, those deployed on a mission. The methodological challenge is that non-observed personal characteristics (e.g. motivation) can change over time and that distinct types of behaviour (e.g. criminality) can vary with age.

The alternative to a before-and-after analysis is the difference-in-differences (DID) method, whereby one compares differences in the outcome variables between the deployed and the control group. This method has been described by Angrist and Pischke (2008). An important assumption with this method is that the variables one is interested in, the outcome variable, for example debt or criminality, would have developed in the same way in the treatment group, the deployed in our case, as in the control group – in our case, the comparison group illustrating the counterfactual situation if the veterans had not been deployed.

## Analysis of the Health Profile of Soldiers before and after Deployment

Data that explain the health profile of soldiers and that we use to analyse any influence on the health of deployed soldiers on a mission are derived from the following sources:

- the records-based data set on all the deployed described earlier;
- data on those wounded in combat, killed during deployment, and repatriated. For the repatriated, the data cover only the period of 2005–2009;
- board of health administrative records with information on diagnoses. Administrative records from the drug database (*Laegemiddeldatabasen*), first available from 2005;
- administrative records from the National Board of Industrial Health (ASK, *Arbejdsskadestyrelsen*) for the entire period 1992–2009;
- administrative records from the Office of Industrial Injury and Compensation for the Military (*Forsvarets Arbejdsskade- og Erstatningskontor* (FAEK));
- crisis and catastrophe psychiatric centre;

- administrative records for the control group, described earlier; and
- derived data source, organised in panels, allowing us to conduct before-and-after analyses.

We emphasise that the analyses of the health profiles are descriptive and that causal interpretation must be considered with great care. For example, in relation to the control group, both self-selection and screening of the deployed must be considered; that is, comparisons must be evaluated with caution. However, if the veteran had no contact with the psychiatric health care system before deployment but did after deployment, we cannot exclude that deployment might be the cause. The outcomes studied in the analysis of the health profile are as follows:

- psychiatric diagnoses;
- contact with the psychiatric health care system;
- purchase of medication for psychological problems;
- treatment for substance abuse;
- reported work-related injuries; and
- work-related accidents registered with the military.

In terms of methodology, the analysis has three phases:

(1) we describe the central health variables, before and after deployment, for all soldiers sent on missions in 2002–2009;
(2) we investigate changes in the health profile before and after deployment; and
(3) we compare changes concerning the health profile with changes in the control group.

Three populations of deployed are studied:

(1) all soldiers deployed from 1992 to 2009, with data from the different sources not accessible for the entire period;
(2) soldiers born between 1975 and 1982, regardless of year of deployment; and
(3) soldiers born between 1975 and 1982 who were deployed for the first time in 2002.

The control groups in the analysis consist of the following:

- the deployed themselves in the before-and-after analysis; and
- the control group of men born in 1975–1982 who were deemed eligible for military service but who were never deployed.

In terms of standard statistics, tests and logistical regressions are used in the analysis of the probability of realising one of the outcome variables. For the explanatory variables in the logistic regressions, the odds ratio is used, where values over one imply that the respective variable increases the probability for the respective outcome, whereas values below one decrease the probability.

After this presentation of the sources of data and methods used, we turn to the first results of this book illustrated by a statistical portrait of the soldiers before their deployment in Chapter 4.

Chapter 4

# Soldiers before and during Deployments

This chapter provides a statistical portrait of soldiers sent on international military missions between 1992 and 2009. We begin with a short discussion of the types of missions and the areas of conflict. During those 18 years, the type of mission changed gradually from peacekeeping (PK) to peace-enforcing (PE) operations, with the latter including active combat situations.

We focus on the missions for which the Army Operational Command (*Haerens Operative Kommando* (HOK)) has been responsible. The population we are describing comprises 26,028 soldiers sent on a total of 53,681 missions, that is, an average of two deployments per soldier. However, there are large variations, as almost half of these soldiers were sent on only one mission. Since 2010, the Army continued its engagement in Afghanistan, with almost 11,000 personnel deployments up to 2014.

The very comprehensive data that form the basis for our descriptions and analyses do not cover missions after 2009, and we focus primarily on deployments to the former Yugoslavia, Iraq and Afghanistan. The great analytical advantage of this data set is access to observations covering both several years after the soldiers return home and several years before deployment, thereby allowing us to compare the soldier's situation before and after the deployment. The observation span is clearly reduced for the more recent deployments. However, we can use the experiences of the returning soldiers in 1992–2009, with caution, for evaluating the opportunities available to soldiers on their return home and the problems they encountered after the latest mission in our observation period, deployment to Afghanistan after 2009.

The main content of the rest of the chapter consists of a statistical portrait of a soldier before deployment on his or her first mission. We use anonymised data from the administrative register to illustrate the following:

- demographic conditions, such as age, gender, ethnic background, family type and childhood conditions;
- qualifications, measured by education and the results of an intelligence test taken on Armed Forces Day (AFD) (draft day);
- income and economic status before military deployment; and
- criminal records before deployment, comparing the incidence among the soldiers being deployed with that of a representative control group.

This chapter mainly uses data on the situation before deployment and during the mission. The end of this chapter contains material on incidents during deployments. For these incidents, we consider three groups of soldiers: those who died, those who were wounded and those who for various reasons were sent home (repatriated) during their deployment. Later chapters will focus predominately on the valuable and relevant information we assembled about the situation of the previously deployed soldiers after their return from a mission.

## Types of Missions and Number of Deployments, 1992–2009

In this introductory section, the focus is on all military deployments, whereas in the following sections, the description of the soldiers' backgrounds covers only their first deployment. During 1992–2009, several changes in type of mission and recruitment of soldiers to these missions occurred, as well as in the countries that were the primary destinations. In this period, missions changed from being predominately PK to PE, with the latter involving engagement in combat situations.

In the following analyses and descriptions, we focus on seven missions in chronological order:

(1) UNPROFOR: United Nations Protection Forces (February 1992–March 1995) in Bosnia-Herzegovina, Croatia, Serbia, Montenegro and Macedonia;
(2) UNCRO: United Nations Confidence Restoration Operation in Croatia (March 1995–January 1996);
(3) IFOR: United Nation (Mandated) Implementation Force (December 1995–December 1996) in Bosnia-Herzegovina;
(4) SFOR: Stabilisation Force (December 1996–2004) in Bosnia-Herzegovina;
(5) KFOR: NATO's Kosovo Force (June 1999–);
(6) Iraq (2003–2011): coalition in Iraq not under UN control; and
(7) ISAF: International Security Assistance Force (2002–2014) in Afghanistan, where Denmark has had soldiers stationed under NATO Command since January 2002.

The period for which we have data is dominated by missions to the former Yugoslavia. From 1991 through 2014, there were 33,364 missions (22,632 persons deployed) to the Balkans and Kosovo, and 26,101 missions (15,752 persons deployed) to Afghanistan and Iraq (Ministry of Defence Personnel Administration, *Forsvarsministeriets Personalestyrelse*). Figure 4.1 details the types of missions in 1992–2009.

The change in the type of mission implies a concomitant change in the countries to which the soldiers were deployed. The deployments by country are summarised in Figure 4.2. A similar pie chart illustrating the development since 2010 would be dominated by missions to Afghanistan.

A more detailed illustration of how deployments were divided between the different missions appears in Figure 4.3 for each year from 1992 through 2009.

The recruitment and training of deployed soldiers also changed during this period. Until 2005, the Danish International Brigade (*Den Danske Internationale Brigade*, DIB) was the typical entry point for soldiers who were to be sent on

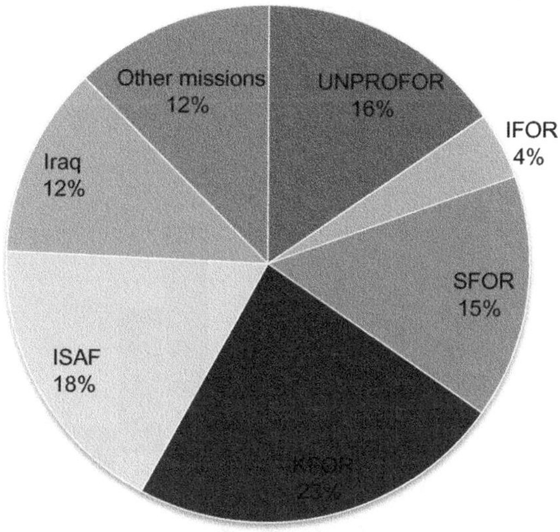


Figure 4.1. Overview of Deployments by Type of Mission, 1992–2009. *Source*: SFI.

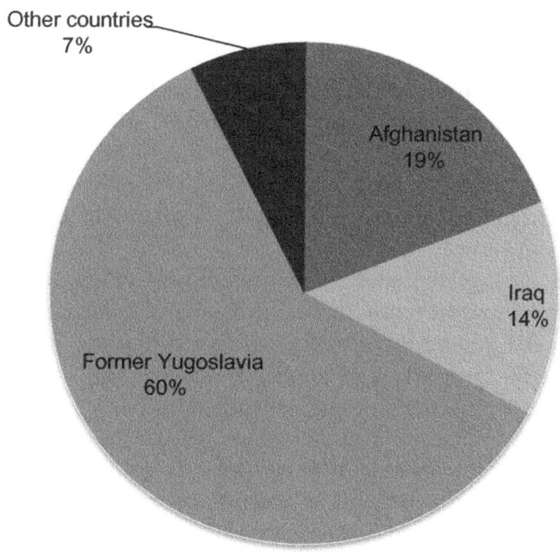


Figure 4.2. Division of Missions by Country, 1992–2009. *Source*: SFI.

deployments. Since 2004–2005, recruits undergo a basic Army training (*Hærens Basisuddannelse*, HBU) for four months (HBU). After this introductory military training, the soldier can continue an eight-month Army Reaction Force Training (*Hærens Reaktionsstyrke Uddannelse*, HRU). This training constitutes

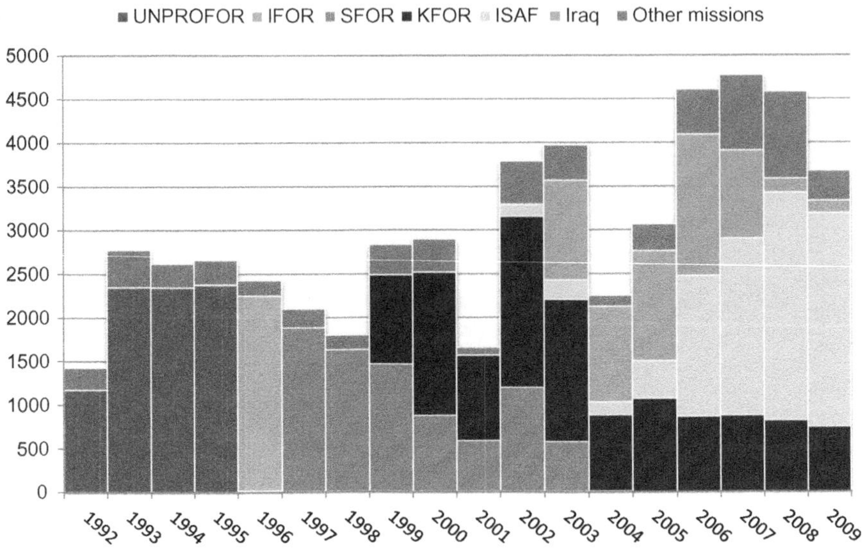


Figure 4.3. Total Number of Deployments by Mission, 1992–2009. *Source*: SFI. *Note*: Total of 53,861 observations. UNCRO and UNPROFOR are merged under UNPROFOR.

the principal foundation for later deployment, which typically lasts six months. Figure 4.4 gives an overview of the deployed soldiers for each year in 1992–2009. There were approximately 1,500 first deployments per year.

Figure 4.4 also shows an increasing trend for soldiers deployed more than once, with a particular increase after 2002. A more detailed distribution of deployments is shown in Figure 4.5.

Slightly over 50% of the soldiers were deployed only once, whereas about 14% were deployed several times, that is, over two years or more. The age distribution has changed among those deployed. In the first deployments to the former Yugoslavia, the proportion of soldiers younger than 25 years was greater than among those deployed to Iraq or Afghanistan.

Soldiers sent on international missions are selected according to several criteria and factors. These include self-selection, as soldiers must volunteer for deployment, as well as the systematic selection process that the military carries out before a soldier is accepted for deployment.

Since 2004, the first selection or screening takes place during AFD (draft day), when the eligibility of men called up for military service is determined; how many are actually conscripted is determined by how many men have volunteered and been selected for service. Although women can now also take part in the AFD, their participation is not compulsory. Since 2004, around 15–20% of recruits have been women (Ministry of Defence Personnel Administration).

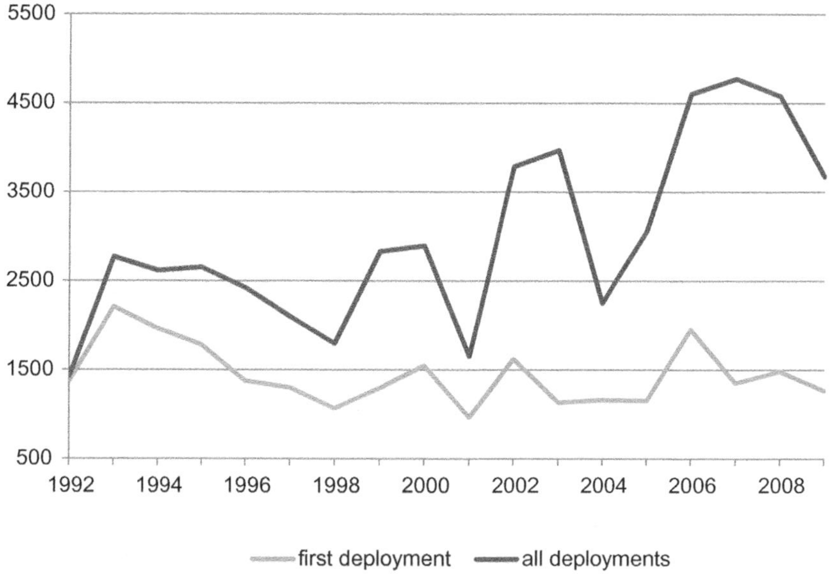


Figure 4.4. Number of First Deployments and All Deployments, 1992–2009. *Source*: SFI.

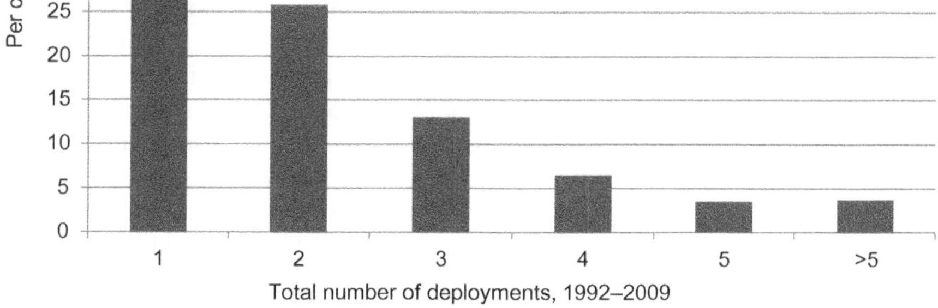


Figure 4.5. Deployments from 1992 to 2009 by Number of Times Each Soldier Was Deployed. *Source*: SFI.

This chapter describes the recruitment until deployment, according to the selection process in place in 2010. After having completed basic training (HBU), the soldier can apply for Army Reaction Force Training (HRU). This first step involves a self-selection, in which a soldier indicates a wish to be accepted into HRU, conditional on an informal screening by the military, that is, a psychological screening, and further screenings during HRU. The intensity and extent of the screening differ according to the groups of personnel – privates, non-commissioned officers (NCO) (e.g. sergeant) and officers. The rest of this chapter focuses on the background – measured in various ways – of the soldiers who were deployed during 1992–2009. In several contexts, we need to compare the soldiers who were deployed with the relevant control groups in the rest of the population. Because of the extensive self-selection and screening that takes place before a soldier can join the group of deployed, these men are not a random sample of the population. We therefore need to take this feature into account in our statistical inference when comparing soldiers with the general population.

## Age, Gender, Ethnic Background, Family Type and Upbringing – Soldiers' Backgrounds before Deployment

In this section, we summarise background characteristics of first-timers, that is, soldiers on their first deployment (based on administrative records from Statistics Denmark). The data on soldiers from before deployment provide a unique opportunity to compare the situation of soldiers both before and after deployment. Most of the background factors refer to the year before military deployment or earlier.

We look now at the age of the first-timers. Comparison of the situation before and after deployment can help to determine the relationship between age and the risk of experiencing stress syndromes or other psychiatric problems. This relationship may also relate to the greater risk that younger soldiers may run of being injured in combat situations. The same applies to women, among whom the risk of consequent problems may be greater for younger women. The average age for all soldiers deployed for the first time is 27.3 years. Despite some variation between years, the average age is clearly increasing in the period, except for privates, for whom the average age is about 24 years throughout the analysis period. The increasing average age over time is also related to the change in mission type, from primarily PK to PE, thus creating a need for soldiers with more comprehensive experience. The distribution of age groups shown in Figure 4.6 shows that the average age of about half of the soldiers is 21–24 years, an age group dominated by privates (not shown).

The distribution by gender among deployed soldiers is shown in Figure 4.7, which shows the large increase in the proportion of women, from 2% in 1992 to almost 12% in 2009.

Compared with the men, a very large proportion of women are in the 'other personnel' group, for example, nurses. The large increases in 2008 and 2009 reflect the establishment of a field hospital in Camp Bastion in Afghanistan.

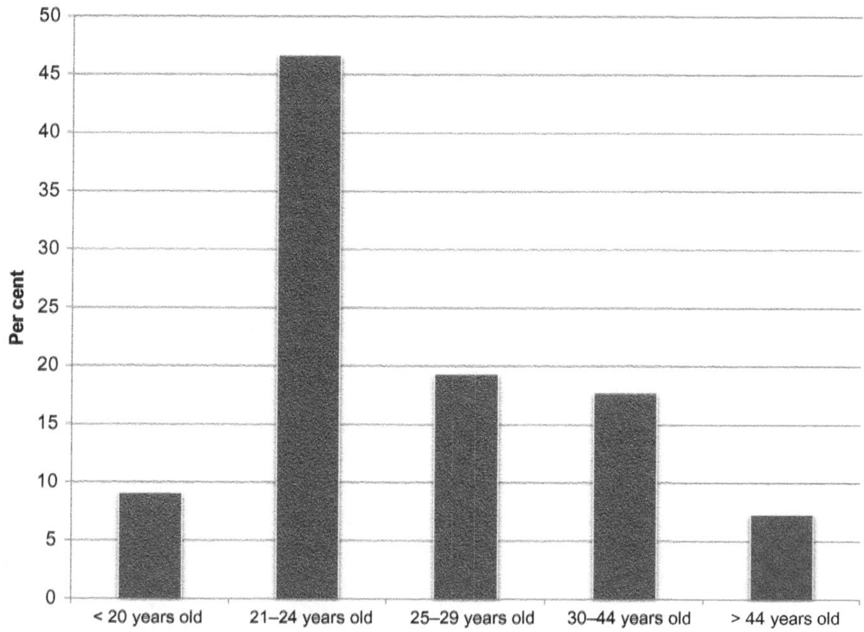


Figure 4.6. Age of Soldiers Deployed for the First Time. *Source*: SFI. *Note*: Total of 26,028 observations.

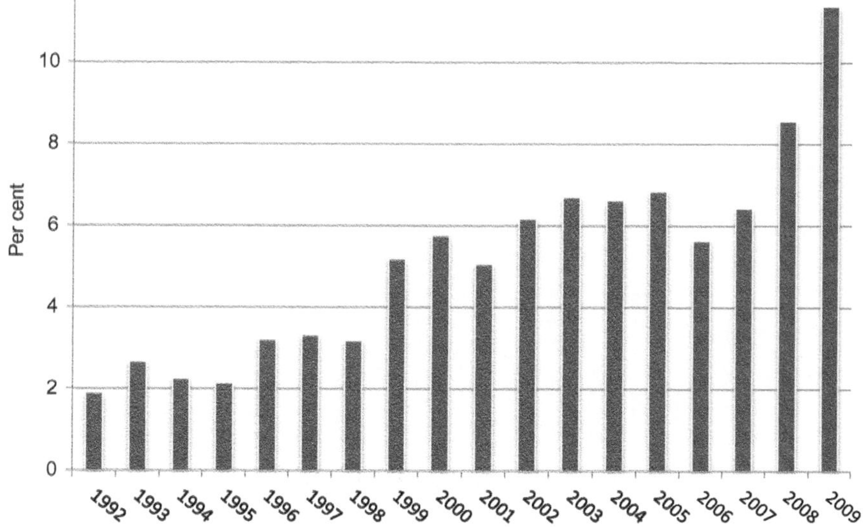


Figure 4.7. Proportion of Women among First-timers by Year of Deployment. *Source*: SFI. *Note*: Total of 26,028 observations.

At least half of the women are privates. At the same time, however, compared with men, there is a relative over-representation of women in the officer group but a strong under-representation in the sergeant group. As the number of women increases greatly during the period, it follows that most of them were deployed to the most recent missions, that is, Afghanistan, Kosovo and Iraq.

Relative to immigrant background, we observe a similar trend as for the women, but with fewer immigrants and their descendants, as Figure 4.8 shows.

When analysing these numbers, we emphasise that only Danish citizens are called up on AFD and that a soldier must have Danish citizenship to be an officer. Thus, immigrants or descendants of immigrants who have been deployed but are not Danish citizens have volunteered for the draft. This group consists of people with backgrounds in many countries. In the distribution of countries of origin, the dominant background is Europe and the Middle East, 53% and 29% of the deployed soldiers in this group, respectively. In the 18- to 25-year-old group in the general population, 15.3% are immigrants or descendants of immigrants. Thus, despite their increasing proportion among the deployed soldiers, this group is clearly under-represented. However, because of its increasing proportion over time, it is most strongly represented in the most recent missions to Kosovo, Iraq and Afghanistan. Some of this group work as interpreters.

An important factor for soldiers and their relatives during deployment is the family situation. Specifically, we look at whether soldiers are married or living with a partner and whether they have children. The year before deployment,

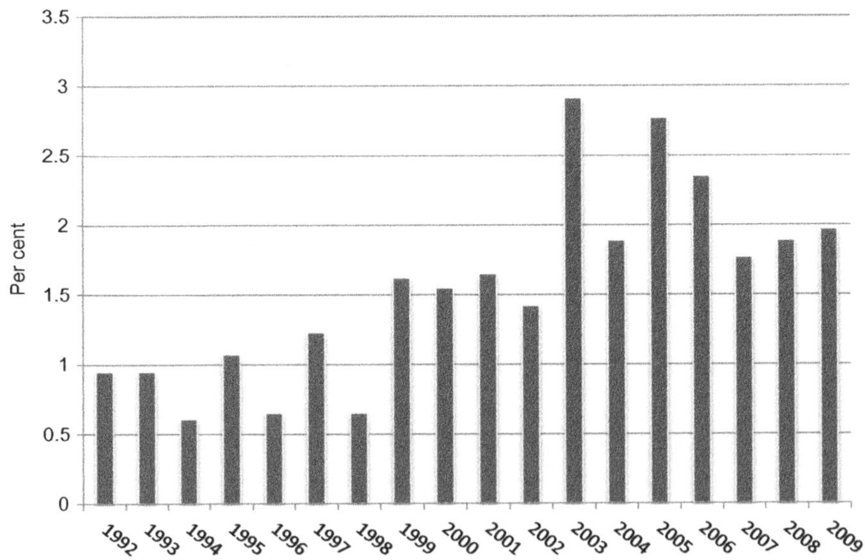


Figure 4.8. Proportion of First-timers Who are Immigrants or Descendants of Immigrants by Year of Deployment. *Source*: SFI. *Note*: Total of 26,028 observations.

83% of first-timers were not married and 80% were childless. Fourteen per cent had one–two children. This relatively low proportion of married soldiers and the low proportion that have children must be viewed in the context of their relatively young age. In terms of the before-and-after perspective, investigating how their deployment would have had a different effect had they had a family becomes very relevant.

The family background of those deployed can also be examined through looking at the type of family in which they lived as 17-year-olds and whether they had been in out-of-home care (foster care) before turning 18. Both family situation and background can influence whether a soldier volunteers for deployment and is indeed deployed. These two factors also affect the before-and-after analyses, as the reaction of family members can influence the situation of the deployed soldier. Another reason for considering these two factors comes from a previous study 'DIB – soldier or not', carried out by the Danish Ministry of Defence, Bache (1998). This study found that soldiers who signed a contract with DIB and were then deployed encountered difficulties in their family home environment more often than did other conscripts.

When comparing soldiers to a control group of all 17-year-old men, we find that slightly more soldiers had moved out of the family home or were living with only one adult: 29% and 23%, respectively. In relation to the distribution among the groups of personnel, the number of soldiers who lived as 17-year-olds with only one adult was the highest among the privates. Similarly, in that same group, a large proportion of the deployed soldiers had left home by the age of 17.

Compared with a control group for the entire male population, the number of soldiers placed in out-of-home care was lower. This lower share can, of course, to a greater or lesser extent, be related to the self-selection and military screening of the soldiers who were deployed. In Figure 4.9, we show the proportion of first-timers who had been placed in care for part of their upbringing. The clearest result shown by the figure is that the number dropped by half between 1992 and 2004. Nonetheless, we cannot draw conclusions about how this drop relates to who volunteers for deployment or whom the military selects through its screening process.

## Educational Background and Intelligence Test Results

Further two factors of interest in both the analysis of who was deployed and the before-and-after analysis are the educational background of the soldiers and the results of the intelligence test that they all take during the AFD. For neither of these is a straightforward comparison with control groups in the rest of the population easy. Educational background reflects the effects of self-selection and military screening, and the intelligence test is a clear selection criterion for eligibility for military service.

Several investigations indicate a correlation between educational background and the probability of choosing a military career path. However, purely idealistic motives for seeking a life in the military may also exist (see Lyk-Jensen & Glad, 2018).

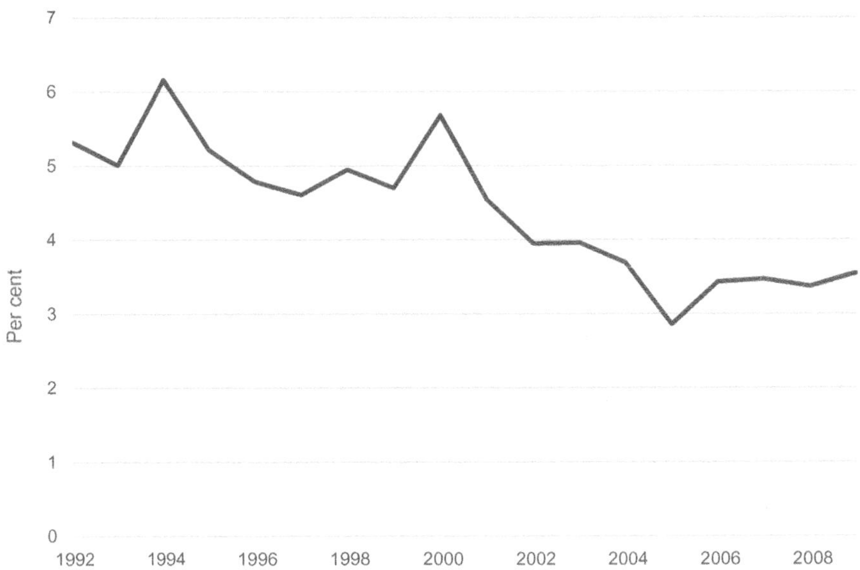


Figure 4.9. Proportion of First-timers Who were in Out-of-home Care during Their Upbringing, by Year of Military Deployment. *Source*: SFI. *Note*: Total of 26,028 observations.

In 1992–2009, the distribution on educational groups was different between deployed soldiers and men aged 15–69 years in the general population. During this period, the number with a higher education increased among both groups. Conversely, the number of deployed soldiers with a vocational education fell, whereas it remained constant in the general population.

An important observation is that deployed women have on average a higher educational level than deployed men. This high educational level reflects differences in the roles they play in the field, where, for example, a substantial proportion of the women have had a longer education within the health care sector.

The average level of education among the deployed soldiers does not show any clear trend over time. In general, however, the average educational level is highest among those sent to Iraq and Afghanistan. This difference may, for example, reflect changes in screening, self-selection or both, with the transition to more PE missions. In many cases, a significantly lower proportion of soldiers who have been deployed on several missions (the 'many-times deployed') have a secondary or vocational education, compared with soldiers who have been on only one mission (the 'one-time deployed'). That the civilian job market has different requirements as to educational background may possibly explain this finding.

The second factor of interest in this section is the score from the intelligence test taken during the AFD, known as the Børge Prien test (*Børge Prien Prøve*, BPP). When evaluating the results, one should consider that data are not available for all the birth cohorts and that, after 1997, the number of tasks to be

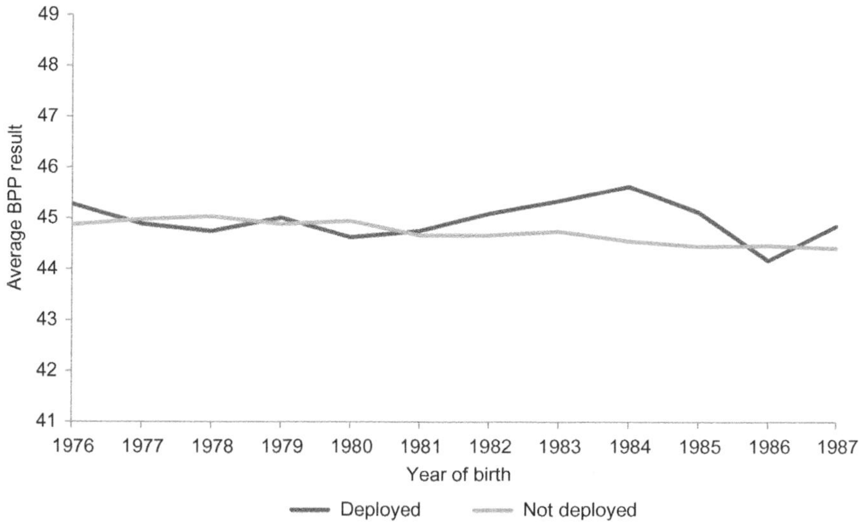


Figure 4.10. Average Results on the BPP Intelligence Test for Deployed and Not-deployed Eligible for Military Service, 1976–1987 (Year of Birth). *Source*: SFI.

solved for being declared eligible for military service increased. In this section, we limit ourselves to the BPP results for 1996–2005. Figure 4.10 presents the average BPP results for soldiers (born in 1976–1987) who were deployed and those who were not. The clearest difference between the two groups occurs among those born in the first half of the 1980s; soldiers who were deployed had consistently, albeit slightly, higher scores than those who were not.

A similar graph for women is shown in Figure 4.11. As the number of observations is relatively small, the average test results according to year rise or fall sharply. However, the results for the deployed women in all 12 birth cohorts are always higher than for those who were not deployed.

All in all, in terms of education and results from the intelligence test, only small differences appear over time and across missions and countries. Yet, as previously mentioned, an element of uncertainty exists when we use control groups from the rest of the population, because of self-selection and the screening of soldiers.

## Income and Socio-economic Status of Soldiers before Their Deployment

The next elements in this portrait of the soldiers concern their income and socio-economic status before being deployed. The income in the year before the first deployment is important in terms of whether a man or a woman chooses military service and deployment and whether income is affected by deployment. In

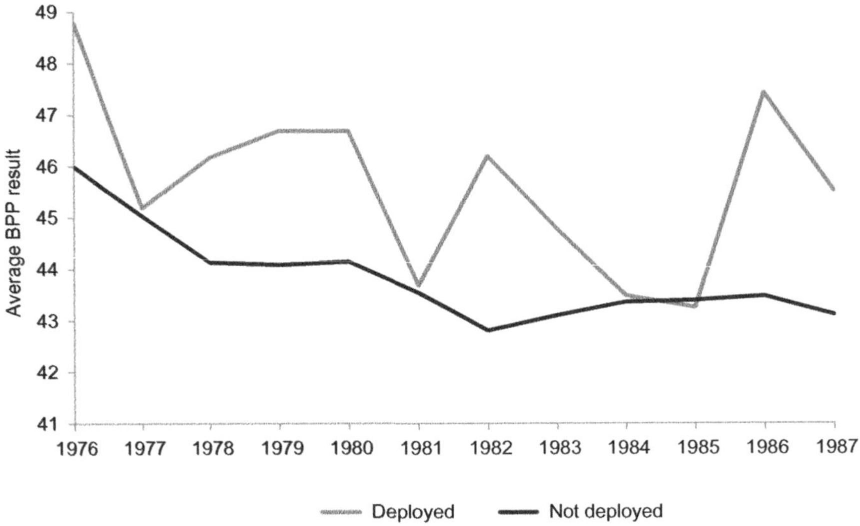


Figure 4.11. Average BPP Results for Deployed and Not-deployed Women Eligible for Military Service, 1976–1987. *Source*: SFI.

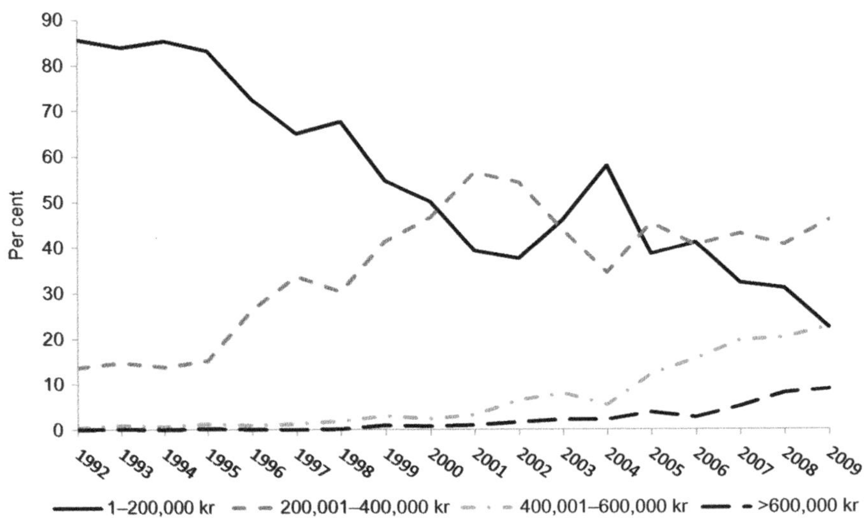


Figure 4.12. First-timers by Income (in 2,000 prices), 1992–2009. *Source*: SFI.

addition to deployment being motivated by purely personal desires and ambitions, financial considerations and expectations could also be involved.

A look at the gross personal income in the year before deployment reveals that the deployed had a higher income than their peer age group the year before deployment. Income in the year before deployment varied markedly with age.

From 1992 to 2009, real income increased, with a particularly strong increase in the five years preceding the financial crisis of 2008. This increase was driven by soldiers with a more comprehensive education being sent to Afghanistan and Iraq. First-timers are on average young, so it is not surprising that most of them had a real income of below 200,000 DKK (in 2,000 prices, 1 EUR = 7.5 DKK) the year before being deployed. While most of the men (58%) have a yearly income below 200,000 DKK, 44% of women had a yearly income, before deployment, of between 200,000 and 400,000 DKK. This difference reflects the older age of the women and their average longer education. The income of privates during their first deployment was at least 455,000 DKK, which is more than what 90% of them earned the year before deployment.

Over time, first-timers were recruited from gradually higher real income groups, as Figure 4.12 shows. Whereas in 1992, 85% of soldiers had an income of less than 200,000 DKK (about 26,667 EUR – 1 EUR = 7.5 DKK) the year before their deployment, this share dropped to only 20% in 2009. This development reflects a change in several factors: (1) a rise in educational level as a result of a change in the character of the missions, (2) increasing compensation for risk during the mission and (3) a change in the composition of personnel groups.

A correlation also exists between income the year before deployment and the missions, destination countries and personnel group. The distribution of income for first-time deployments to various missions is shown in Figure 4.13, which shows that the income before deployment is markedly higher for soldiers deployed to Afghanistan. In addition, and not surprisingly, the distribution of

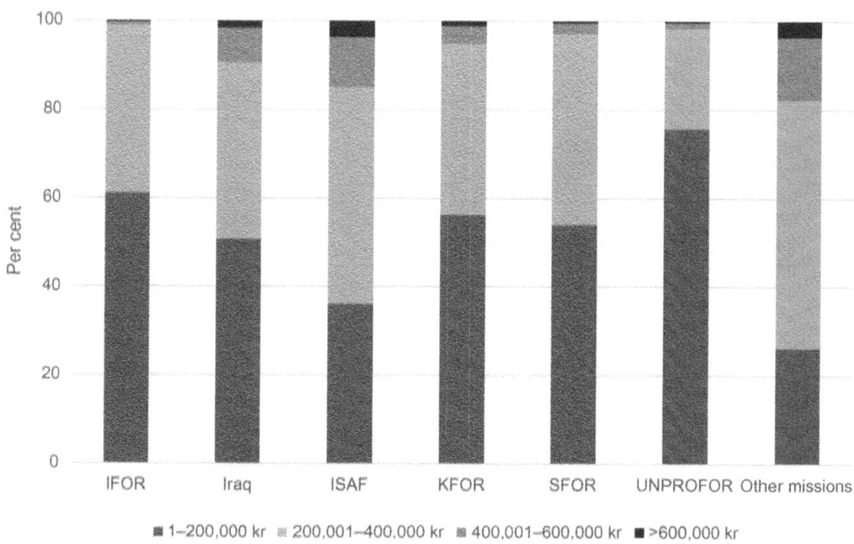


Figure 4.13. Per cent of Income of Soldiers on Their First Deployment, by Mission (in 2,000 Prices), 1992–2009. *Source*: SFI.

income in the previous year is correlated with specific personnel groups, with the lowest pre-deployment income for privates and the highest for the category 'others' (generally comprising more highly trained personnel).

We derive the socio-economic status from administrative records on the income sources the year before deployment. In connection with income, the socio-economic status of soldiers in the year before their first deployment is also important, both for recruitment of the soldiers and as part of the before-and-after analysis. Although socio-economic status can show a person's status only at a given time, being unemployed can clearly provide a motive for applying to a job with the military.

Compared with 18- to 59-year-old men in the general population, soldiers have a significantly better link with the job market during the year before deployment, as some of the deployed were already employed by the military in that year. The socio-economic status of men the year before their first deployment appears in Figure 4.14. Compared with the entire male population aged 18–59, we find a significantly higher degree of participation in the labour market among the deployed soldiers. However, the average age of the soldiers is about 27, and for this reason alone, one would expect a higher degree of labour market participation. During 1992–2009, the proportion of soldiers who had been wage-earners before deployment is consistently around 90%. While unemployment in the year before deployment was 5% for soldiers in the mid-1990s, when unemployment was at its highest level in the general population, during the rest of the period, unemployment was very low among soldiers in the year before deployment.

For the main status of wage-earners in the previous year, Figure 4.15 shows the relative composition of unskilled and employed blue-collar workers. The

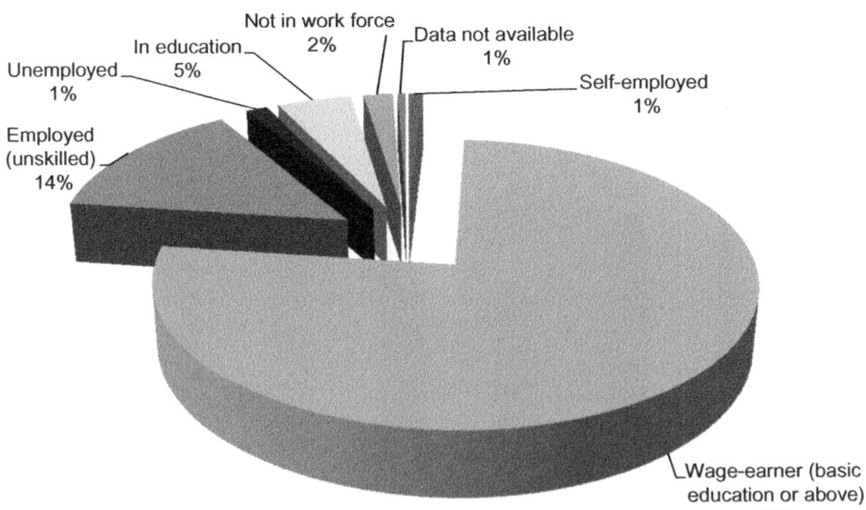


Figure 4.14. Socio-economic Status of Men the Year before the First Field Deployment, 1992–2009.

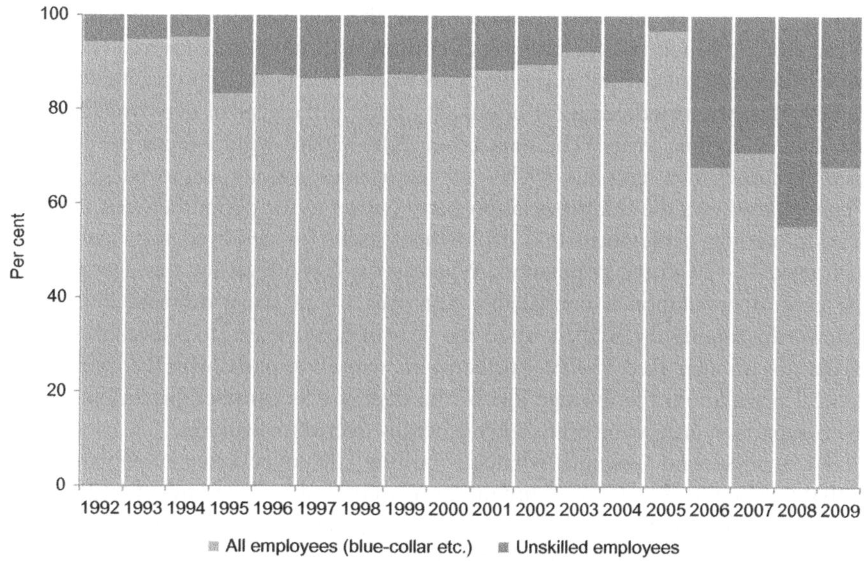


Figure 4.15. Deployed Who Were Employed the Year before Their First Mission. Unskilled and Blue-collar Employees, 1992–2009. *Source*: SFI.

sudden increase in the proportion of unskilled workers in the last years of our analysis period can hardly have been the result of labour market conditions, as these years were characterised by a very strong drop in unemployment. This greater ratio of unskilled to skilled workers is especially true for those deployed to Iraq. However, Figure 4.15 reveals nothing about the relationship between the two groups of wage-earners in the figure and the soldiers who were deployed. Figure 4.15 therefore does not contradict the former hypothesis of an average increased demand for qualifications in more recent PE missions.

Finally, there is a strong correlation between the age of the soldiers and their socio-economic status the year before deployment and, similarly, a strong correlation between that socio-economic status and the personnel group to which the soldiers belonged while deployed.

## Criminality among First-timers

The military screening procedures lead us to expect less criminality among first-timers. Therefore, the primary reason for including criminality is to use data before and after deployment to analyse and evaluate whether military training, the experience of violence and actual fighting lead to later criminality. As there is no consensus from previous studies, reliable data from before and after deployment are thus clearly important.

The data stem from the register-based statistics on criminal convictions. We include the number of those known to be guilty of property crimes and crimes against persons. In this section, we compare the deployed soldiers and the entire population, followed by a description of criminality among the deployed. To evaluate whether a definite criminal profile exists when soldiers are approaching their first deployment, we include data for criminality both in the year of deployment and in the three preceding years. The data cover 2000–2006, with a focus on deployed men, because men commit 99.3% of the crimes among deployed personnel. Figure 4.16 shows the frequency of property crimes in the period between the three years preceding deployment and deployment itself, for deployed men and for all men aged 15–59 in the population. Whereas the crime level for this age group in the general population is consistently just over 1%, a sharp decrease in crime is noteworthy among the soldiers up to the year of deployment, to a level about 20% of that for all men aged 15–59. Furthermore, when compared with the level for the general population, the average age of the deployed is considerably below that in the comparison group and criminality generally decreases with age.

To analyse and evaluate whether training, the experience of violence and actual fighting lead to later criminality, one may find it more important to examine violent crimes. Figure 4.17 shows the frequency of violent crimes. As with the property crimes in Figure 4.16, we find a constant level of violent crime among the 15- to 59-year-olds in the general population but a sharp drop among soldiers the year before deployment.

In contrast to Figure 4.16, the frequency of violent crimes among first-timers three years before deployment is also lower than for men aged 15–59 in the general population. However, the number of all violent crimes is very low.

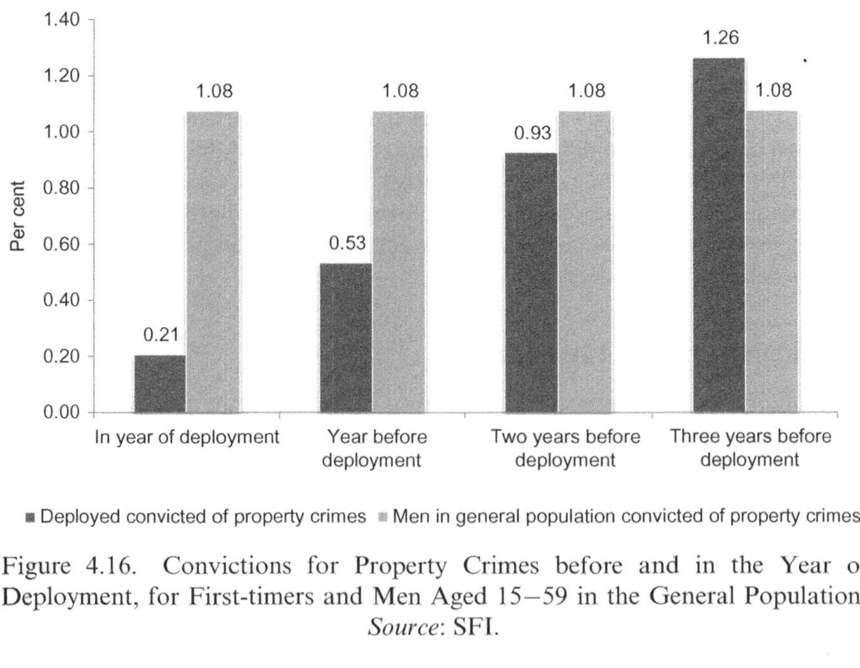


Figure 4.16. Convictions for Property Crimes before and in the Year of Deployment, for First-timers and Men Aged 15–59 in the General Population. *Source*: SFI.

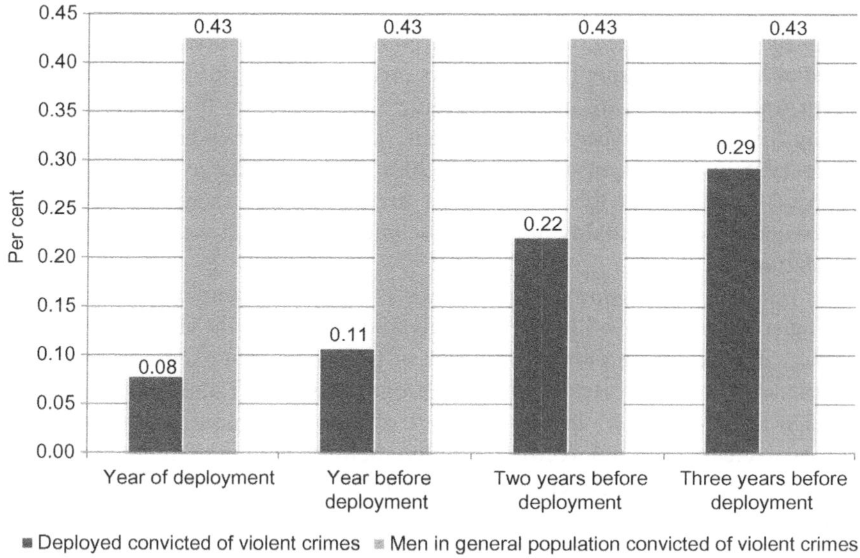


Figure 4.17. Convictions for Violent Crimes by Year of Deployment and Separately for First-timers and Men in the Population Aged 15–59 Years. *Source*: SFI.

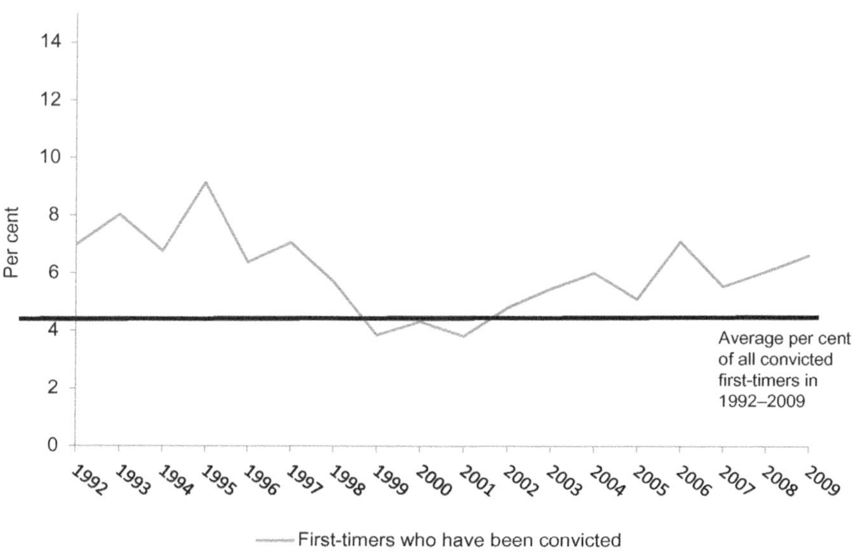


Figure 4.18. Convictions among the Deployed by Year of Deployment, 1992–2009. *Source*: SFI.

To compare criminality within the entire population of deployed soldiers for 1992–2009, we measure criminality as a binary variable if first-timers were convicted at least once during the three years preceding deployment. All convictions except traffic offences are included. Figure 4.18 shows the frequency of crimes among first-timers by year of deployment. The share varies between a high of 9% in 1995 and a low of 4% in 1999–2001. However, the average age of the deployed was lower at the beginning of the period, and there is a clear over-representation of criminality among those younger than 25 years in the general population.

In relation to missions, the number of criminal convictions is highest among soldiers deployed to the Balkans and Afghanistan. However, the differences are barely significant. In terms of personnel groups, despite an over-representation of privates with convictions, this group also has the lowest average age. Moreover, in the group of officers, one requirement for selection is a clean criminal record. Finally, before deployment, no difference in criminality exists between soldiers deployed once and those deployed several times.

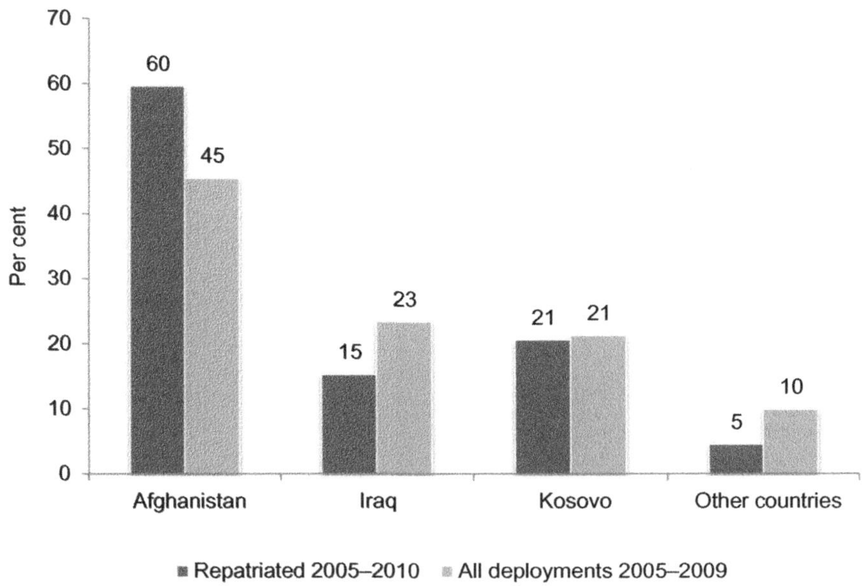


Figure 4.19. Proportion of Repatriated Soldiers and Deployments by Location of Mission. *Notes*: The samples consist of the 399 repatriated soldiers and all 20,292 of the deployments for 2005. Missions before 2005 are not included as we have data on repatriated soldiers only from 2005. Figures for repatriated soldiers in 2010 are only for deployments starting in 2009. *Source*: SFI.

## Repatriated, Wounded and Killed Soldiers

The data to which we have access allow us to identify and investigate who was repatriated (sent home before the end of the mission) and who was wounded during deployment, thereby obtaining a more complete picture of the soldiers, along with insights into some of the long-term human costs of participating in an international military mission. We also include information about the soldiers who were killed during a mission.

In 2005–2009, 399 Danish soldiers were repatriated, predominately from Afghanistan but also from Kosovo and Iraq. Figure 4.19 shows the proportion by country.

Privates are clearly over-represented among those repatriated. However, the data do not allow us to determine the extent to which this over-representation reflects differences in the levels of risk to which the personnel groups are exposed. In relation to missions in Afghanistan, Iraq and Kosovo, no significant differences appear in the proportion of repatriations by personnel group. Moreover, relative to the number of deployments, we found no significant connection between the frequency of repatriation and the number of deployments per soldier.

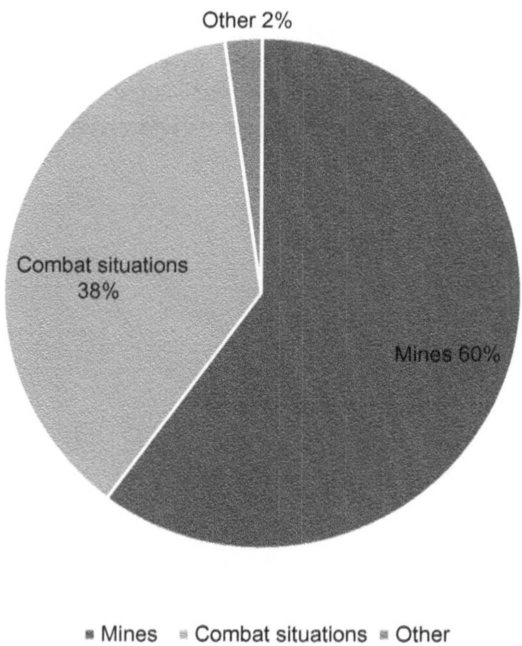


Figure 4.20. Causes of Wounds for All Missions, 1992–2009. *Note*: Figure presents a random sampling of those wounded (in all, 123) under combat conditions, including fighting, artillery, fire attack, fire-fighting and shooting. *Source*: SFI.

The most frequent reasons for repatriation (69% of those in 2005–2010) are social, personal or family problems, and illness or personal injuries. These reasons were responsible for 70% and 76%, respectively, of repatriations from Afghanistan and Iraq, the two largest missions in 2005–2010. These same reasons are also dominant for repatriations among the individual personnel groups. Finally, we found a slight over-representation of the repatriated among those younger than 30.

Data for the wounded are available from the Ministry of Defence for the entire period, 1992–2009. As previously mentioned, some of those wounded (in 2005–2009) are also among the repatriated. Throughout the period, the number being wounded increased as the consequence of the change in type of mission, primarily from PK to PE. However, medical improvements during this period increased the probability of survival for wounded soldiers. In all, 123 soldiers were wounded during the period. Figure 4.20 shows the distribution in terms of the causes of injuries. The largest single cause was mines (improvised explosive devices (IEDs)) (60%), followed by combat situations (38%).

Figure 4.21 shows the distribution of the wounded for the three main mission destinations, with 57% of the wounded soldiers in Afghanistan, followed by the former Yugoslavia and Iraq. A clear over-representation of the wounded and repatriated exists among the privates, a finding apparently linked to their tasks during deployment. The average age of the wounded is barely 25, almost all the wounded are men, most are unmarried and only a few have children.

A total of 51 soldiers were killed in 1992–2009. The causes of death are shown in Figure 4.22, where again mines (IEDs) are the predominant cause

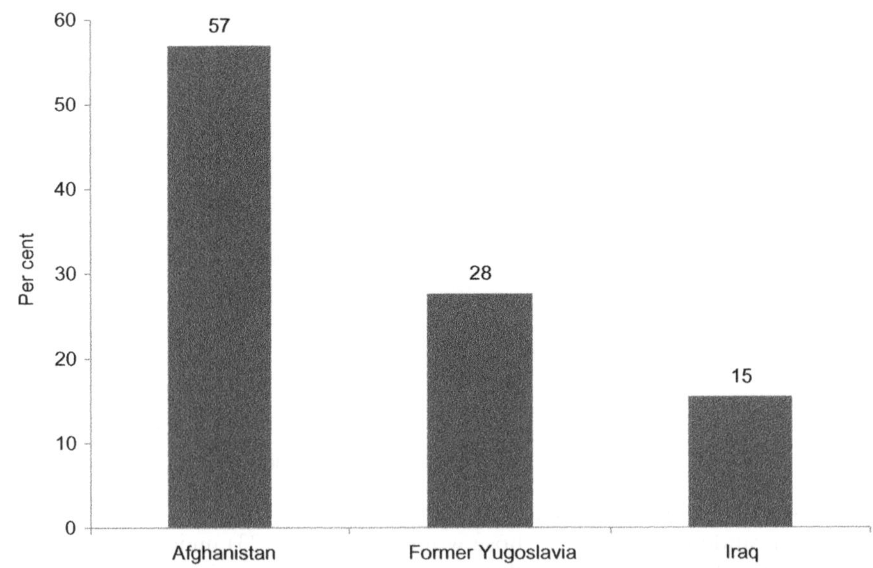


Figure 4.21. Proportion of Wounded by Country of Mission. *Source*: SFI.

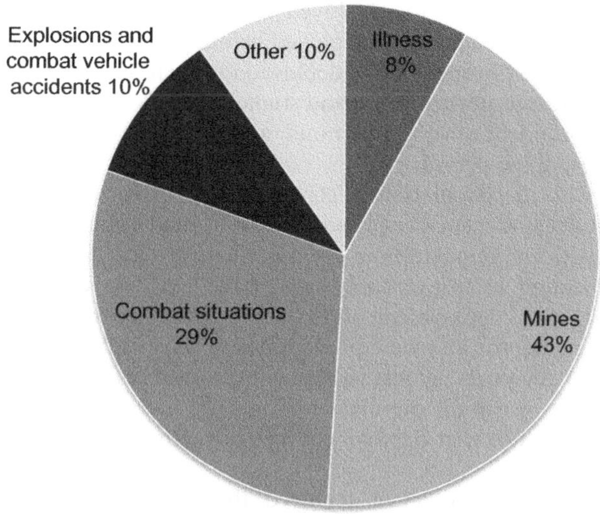


Figure 4.22. Causes of Death. *Source*: SFI.

(43%). Combat situations and combat-related accidents make up 39% of deaths. Most of the deaths occurred in Afghanistan, where more than half took place in the three years 2007–2009. As in the groups of repatriated and wounded soldiers, most of the soldiers killed were privates. However, we found no statistically significant over-representation of deaths in this group. Most of the soldiers killed were between 21 and 24 years old and unmarried, and only a few had children.

## Summary

The main points of this comprehensive portrait of soldiers before and during deployment are as follows:

- The analysis includes all soldiers deployed in 1992–2009.
- The description provides the socio-economic status and characteristics of all soldiers on their first deployment during 1992–2009.
- The portrait is based on administrative records from Statistics Denmark and the Danish Ministry of Defence.
- Differences between the deployed soldiers and the rest of the population may reflect selection differences (both the underlying tendency to choose a military career and the screening carried out by the military in relation to deployment).
- The average age at first deployment is 27, and half of these soldiers are under 24. The large majority are unmarried and have no children (the fairly high

average age is due to all the deployed in 1992 being treated as first-timers, regardless of whether they were deployed before 1992).

- By far, the greatest proportion of deployed are men, although the proportion of women increased during the period studied.
- While the proportion of immigrants and their descendants is small, it increased during the period.
- Compared with the population in general, fewer soldiers grew up in a family with two adults, and a smaller proportion was brought up in out-of-home care.
- Compared with the population in general, relatively few deployed soldiers had a higher education, almost certainly because they are on average younger.
- In the year before deployment, most of those who chose deployment had a relatively high income and were predominately wage-earners.
- Generally, for the years nearest to deployment, soldiers' criminality was lower than that in the rest of the population.
- There is no evidence that deployment was attractive to people with a history of violence.
- Relative to the total number of deployed, the number of wounded and killed was relatively low.
- Privates are over-represented among repatriated and wounded soldiers but not among those killed.
- Social problems and illness were the main reasons for repatriation.
- Most of the wounded, repatriated and killed are ethnic Danish men who lived alone, and only few of them had children.

Chapter 5

# Returning Home from an International Military Mission – An Investigation Based on Qualitative Interviews

## Part 1. Before, during and after Deployment

### *Introduction – Positive and Negative Consequences of Deployment*

This chapter investigates how soldiers experience deployments to international missions and the demands that these deployments make on them and their families. Moreover, this chapter also reviews the support and rehabilitation programmes from the military and other support groups. We investigate these topics through 44 semi-structured qualitative interviews, 20 of which were with individuals who had been deployed. The rest are with families and some of the people with whom the deployed were in contact. Towards the end of the chapter, we evaluate these support and rehabilitation programmes from various angles through these 44 interviews. The citations from the interviews are from SFI-report 10:21.

As the results in this chapter rely on 44 qualitative interviews, it means that the different problems or issues we identify do not necessarily generalise to the 26,000 individuals who have been deployed. We use these interviews to generate some hypotheses we can further investigate in the following quantitative analyses.

This chapter investigates positive and negative consequences of deployment for both the deployed and their families by answering the following questions:

- How do the soldiers experience the consequences of their deployment in their life during and after deployment?
- How do the military and the public authorities in general tackle the soldiers' problems?

Another significant aim of the qualitative interviews was to identify the soldiers' view of which factors are important, so that we could use these factors in the collection of relevant register data. These register data form the basis for the analyses of the financial situation of and criminality among the deployed in Chapter 7 and for the health profile in Chapter 8.

We begin this section with a review of the most recent anthropological and sociological literature related to the deployment situation. Three themes emerge from this literature review on the situation *before* deployment:

(1) deployment as a transition to another life situation;
(2) changes in the deployed soldiers' close relationships; and
(3) motivation to seek deployment.

*During* deployment, the literature focuses especially at two themes:

(1) building up of comradeship and
(2) maturing and masculinity.

Finally, the literature on the period *after* returning home from a deployment reveals four relevant themes in particular:

(1) changes that occur as a result of having been deployed;
(2) re-integration into society;
(3) the significance of support from the military and other organisations after homecoming; and
(4) the recognition – or lack of the same – the returnees receive from society when they return home.

The analysis of the data from the interviews is driven by these substantial themes from the literature. An important element is the transitions from before to after deployment as a passage between states of life (van Gennep, 1960, 1909). Other themes in the literature are motivation (MacCoun, Kier, & Belkin, 2006), homecoming as veterans (Doyle & Peterson, 2005; Dubisch, 2009; Gerber, 1994; and Jonassen, 2009) and changing roles during the transitions (Synnott, 2009).

The analysis uses the interviews to uncover the motivations, the consequences of deployment and the needs of those deployed. Specifically, we explored the motivation of the soldiers before deployment, their experiences during deployment and finally the consequences of deployment, including any need for contact with the health care system. With regard to soldiers' motivations before deployment, as all the interviewed have to remember their original motivations, their answers are probably subject to recall bias. In Chapter 7, we provide results from pre-deployment motivations obtained just before soldiers leave for their mission.

In all, 44 individuals responded to the qualitative interview – 20 from the deployed group, from combat and other units, seven family members and 17 from the military, public authorities or support groups. As most of the interviewees volunteered to participate, we expected an over-representation of positive experiences as opposed to more negative ones. To address this issue, we structured the interview to include questions, inspired from the literature, about both positive and negative experiences.

However, the voluntary participation may also imply that returnees with severe psychological problems, who choose social isolation, were not represented. To compensate for this issue, representatives from the health care and rehabilitating sector were included to provide information about this group of returnees. The families who participated in the interviews cover a large range in terms of their relationship with the deployed.

## Before Deployment – Motivations and Preparation

### *Motivations and Preparation*

This section covers the motivations and the preparations to leave one's former life and become isolated from it for a period of time. Lyk-Jensen and Glad (2018) provide an analysis of changes in the motives among Danish soldiers, while Hedlund (2011) analyse motives among Swedish soldiers.

A group of deployed soldiers typically consists of 40% from the Army Reaction Force Training (*Haerens Reaktionsstyrke Uddannelse* (HRU)) and about 60% from the Army Standing Reaction Force (*Haerens Staaende ReaktionsStyrke* (SRS)). The latter group are professional soldiers under contract until they are 35 or 60 years old. They have chosen a career in the military, and being sent on a specific mission is obligatory (a professional duty).

To investigate the motivations, we therefore focus on the group who, after training in HRU, have chosen to be deployed. The motivational factors that are important for them fall into a variety of categories. The first factors emerging from the answers of the interviewees are self-development and having experiences. A typical answer in this category is: 'It's a cool job. It is something different from the boring daily life I had before.' Or, even more succinctly: 'It's an adventure'. Other soldiers state that they are looking for physical and mental challenges. This answer is connected with a great sense of satisfaction at having a chance to show that one can expand one's boundaries. The intensity one expects – and experiences – during deployment is a part of the motivation. One of the deployed soldiers says: 'Because that is the way it is out there – this is war. It is violent, and it is wild.' That this expected and experienced intensity can itself create complications when returning to a less intense existence is something we will return to.

Maturation and masculinity are other factors cited in the literature. The terms macho and test of manhood are sometimes used to describe masculinity. An increased maturity as a motivation is reflected in the statement: 'I get another perspective on life and can better judge, what is important.' Ideology – or an ideal goal – often is cited as a motivation, 'to make a difference' or expressed more fully, 'making the world a safer place. Or at least a better place. Freeing people down there from the repression they have been living under'.

For another interviewee, an essential motivation was to experience making a difference:

> It was one of the greatest moments in my life. Opening a school in Afghanistan. You should see the children, they were so happy! It was worth everything. And that is what it's like for many of our soldiers.

Although the military points to economic factors as a motivation, the interviewees only mentioned this factor to quite a limited degree. Some also mention being trained for 'military duties' as a motivation factor. Likewise, the chance to receive a civilian education during military service received only a limited mention. A part of the 'military duties' also involves access to 'military hardware'. One veteran expresses this as: 'We are allowed to shoot and to drive around like two small teenagers. And we get paid for it.' Finally, for some, the motivation is the special lifestyle that comes from multiple deployments, in some cases becoming a 'mission bum'. This lifestyle can make it difficult to return to a life outside the military.

### *Risk and the Family*

Obviously, deployment can also have an impact on the soldiers' family relationships. Wadsworth and Riggs (2014) provide a comprehensive contribution in this area. Cesur, Sabia, and Tekin (2013) investigate more specific problems, such as domestic violence, while Skomorovsky and Bullock (2017) focus on children's well-being. The soldiers'motivation can also be coloured by the conception of the risk connected with a deployment, especially for PE missions. To make this risk explicit, the deployed soldiers, as part of their preparations, are encouraged to write a kind of 'testament, goodbye letter'. Representatives of the military's support groups strongly encourage the soldiers to take the time to consider carefully their decision about deployment. 'They have to consider that they may die on the mission, or returning home missing an arm or leg and have to live with that for the rest of their lives.' It is clear that considerations of that type play a role in the relationships with their families. The support and acceptance of their families are very important for the deployed soldiers. However, some soldiers formulate more pointedly, and they were not asking for acceptance, only support. One of the deployed soldiers expressed this point categorically and fatalistically:

> Yes, I am going to Afghanistan, I'm going to be on the front line, yes, I am a combat soldier. If I die, I die; if I survive, I survive.

### *Summary*

A wish for personal experience and ideological reasons are the most important motivations for HRU personnel when choosing deployment. For SRS personnel, comradeship, financial considerations and the desire to carry out military duties are more important motives, without excluding ideological motivations.

## During Deployment – Psychological Well-being

In this section, we focus on the factors which the interviewees name as being important for their psychological well-being during deployment. These main factors are as follows:

- type of mission;
- leadership during the mission;
- comradeship;
- contact with family; and
- recognition by society.

### *Type of Mission*

The missions fall into two different categories. In the 1990s, the missions to the Balkans had a more limited PK mandate, whereas the main category since has been PE missions to Iraq and Afghanistan that include combat situations. A psychological reaction to the missions in the Balkans was a feeling of powerlessness in the face of attacks on civilian populations, expressed by a former soldier deployed to this region as:

> [...] there is a sense of powerlessness seeing people driving in horse-drawn carriages with all their possessions, who were stoned and spat at the whole way [...] it was not easy.

In contrast, the feeling of powerlessness is not the dominant one, in the PE missions to Iraq and Afghanistan, rather there is confrontation with harsh situations, where the deployed or their comrades have themselves been involved in fighting. Again and again in the interviews, there is evidence that this type of mission generates a high adrenaline rush, which many of the deployed find difficult to live without when they come home:

> All your senses are sharpened. It is the same *rush* people feel when they do something extreme, like jumping out of a plane with a parachute. But it is so very extreme.

This type of psychological reaction is not only felt by the combat soldiers but also by other groups of personnel who are not prepared for this type of experience in the same way that combat soldiers are.

### *Leadership*

The leadership of a mission is, like the type of mission, very important for the psychological reactions during deployment. The key points from the interviews about the characteristics of good leadership are the ability to explain why the mission should be carried out and an understanding of the psychological reactions of the soldiers. The opposite, poor leadership, is characterised in the interviews as an absence of personal visibility, leadership that stays 'at the office', a lack of understanding of the soldiers' situation and also a lack of reaction to criticism, for example of training and equipment. Great importance is placed on training and equipment from home that match up with the conditions of the mission. In the words of a former deployed soldier:

> For me, it provides a sense of security to have a great deal of expertise when you are going out into the field. That you know that you can do your work. That is what you fall back on.

### *Comradeship – The Military Family*

Another important factor during deployment is the comradeship in the platoon – typically 30–40 people. The community and comradeship, one belongs to and experiences – 'the military family' – are important part of being deployed. There is an extreme reciprocal dependency, expressed as:

> when one has lain next to a comrade, and it is just a mess everywhere, one has a bond one cannot break, and that one does not have with very many others.

The pressure is so great and the experiences so strong, that what one feels about the tasks carried out cannot be hidden from one's comrades. Intimacy with the 'military family' can in some cases become stronger than that with one's own civilian family: 'Those I was deployed with in 1992, know me better than my wife of 10 years.' A consequence of this intimacy is that a rupture in the group, where some are excluded from the military community, can result in serious psychological problems.

To be sent home – repatriated – from a mission before time, even if it is not one's fault, can nevertheless release a feeling of guilt towards the comrades who remain. This feeling of guilt is exacerbated if the group suffers losses after the soldier has been repatriated. This feeling of guilt occurs even if the repatriated soldier is suffering severe physical, psychological or traumatic injuries. A particularly difficult psychological burden during deployment is to experience the death or wounding of a comrade, whether it affects someone from the Danish forces or from the coalition forces: 'It is hard to see the young boys come in with their lives broken forever one way or another. It is hard to stand by and comfort young boys.'

### *Family Members – The Civilian Family*

Another important factor likely to explain psychological reactions is the kind of contact the soldiers have with their family members during deployment. A general result from the interviews is that the family's tendency to hide their concern and instead support and cheer up the deployed is very important for how the deployed soldiers work and function. The interviews also reveal that modern communications can be a doubled-edged sword. While receiving letters, pictures and packages from the family are generally providing great happiness, direct communication on the telephone may be problematic. For example, one has to stand in a queue for the telephone and has less privacy. Emotional pressure from parents or a partner can also be more important. The soldiers may feel a gap between the new, intense experience they just had and their family sharing details of daily life at home. A special opportunity to physically meet family members during deployment is the leave soldiers are offered in the middle of the half-year deployment. The interviewees were generally satisfied with the possibility of leave, but many found it hard to return to the mission after having been home in a peaceful environment.

The great emphasis that is placed on the family's reactions and attitude is also due to their importance for how the deployed soldier functions on a mission. What the deployed soldier primarily needs is for their family as far as possible to hide their concern and to support him/her, even if they are not in agreement with the decision of being deployed nor sending troops to war. A family member expresses this as: 'A good family member shows interest, has respect for and supports the soldier in the choice he has made. It is his job.' Many families choose not to tell the soldier about their concern and worries, to avoid instilling doubts and anxiety.

### *Recognition from Society*

Another factor influencing on the psychological situation for deployed soldiers is recognition from society, or lack of it, in the form of criticism of the missions the soldier participates in (Canan-Sokullu, 2012; Hines, Gribble, Wessely, Dandeker, & Fear, 2015). The interviewees do not have much trust in the coverage of the missions in the home media. Many of them criticise the media coverage of the mission as one-sided, as it mainly focuses on the tragic occurrences and mistakes made during missions and overlooks the positive results for the civilian population in Afghanistan as an example. While deployed soldiers are frustrated by the scepticism and criticism, they are overall very pleased with the symbols of recognition that gradually have emerged in the form of Flag Day, yellow bow ties from the family network and veterans' parades. We come back to the importance of backup – and criticism – in the following section about returning home from a mission.

### *Summary*

Several factors appear to be of significance for the ability to carry out one's job and for a soldier's psychological state during deployment. A mission with a limited mandate can put stress on the deployed, who experience a sense of powerlessness in the face of attack and actions that appear unfair. Focused leadership that sets a good example, experience with missions, as well as respect for human reactions are important for how a soldier experiences deployment. Leadership is also responsible for relevant training with the right equipment used on a mission. 'The military family', in other words, close comradeship, almost replaces the real/civilian family. But even though relatives (in the civilian family) may recede into the background, they continue to play a relatively important role in the life of the deployed soldier, and communication between the two 'families' has a direct influence of the well-being of the deployed soldier. During deployment, Danish society is primarily represented by the relatives and the media, whose coverage of the war is in general viewed as one-sided and overwhelmingly negative. This attitude from the media has a strong effect on the deployed.

## After Deployment

Once taking into account the small number of veterans in the interviews, the first-timers seems to be more likely personally changed by the deployment.

In general, the interview study also reveals that the families are acutely aware of a change in the soldier who returns home. Most returnees feel that the deployment as a whole has had positive consequences for their lives. It is important to mention this positive aspect as a part of the description below necessarily focuses on problematic areas and negative occurrences. The factors that have a meaning for the time after returning home fall into eight categories:

(1) return to the family;
(2) networks;
(3) recognition by society;
(4) media coverage of the missions the deployed soldiers have been on;
(5) physical injuries;
(6) psychological problems after returning home;
(7) positive consequences of deployment; and
(8) family members.

### *Return Home to the Family*

Returnees describe how it can be difficult to find one's place in the family again. The interviewees describe the first period of time after returning home as characterised by restlessness and difficulties fitting in with the family after having been away. One returnee thinks that the best way to work through intense events that occurred during deployment is to talk about them but found that family members are not always the best listeners. Therefore, some returnees choose to keep relatively quiet about their experiences and only talk about them with their comrades in the military community. For some, it is difficult to recreate the intimacy with the family that existed before deployment. The transition to civilian life with the family can seem very abrupt:

> Suddenly one stands down there and has to take one's machine gun and be ready to drive into enemy territory, and just as suddenly you are home and have to choose what kind of food you want in the supermarket.

### *Networks*

Another factor that emerged from the study was that it was hard to maintain contact with the group one was with, but that it is important, especially for those who need to talk about things that happened during a mission. Support groups such as the Blue Berets (*Blaa Baretter*) help returnees to keep in contact with their former groups, and social media also contributes to maintain it. While for the SRS deployed soldiers who are still employed in the military after their return, it is easier to maintain this network which many returnees value highly, it is typically harder for soldiers who return home to a job outside the military.

### *Recognition by Society*

Many of the respondents in the study attach great importance to the recognition, or lack of it, they receive from society. Others, however, give the impression that this recognition is less important to them, provided the soldier receives recognition from the military and is satisfied with his own contribution. In fact, the interviewees felt a positive change in the recognition they receive from society, especially after the transition to carrying out more PE missions (see also Danish Government, 2010). One respondent from a support organisation characterised this situation as a gradual process and referred, for example to a deployed soldier who was killed in 2007:

> the word hero, and war hero, suddenly was used in the media, and one has to go far back, to the 1850s, before one finds that word used in the media. This example is also a sign of strong support for soldiers in the population.

Another example of this change in attitude is that the population and the politicians while against the war in Afghanistan can at the same time respect the soldiers who are doing a difficult job as a result of a Parliamentary decision.

The returnees have different opinions about the several visible signs of societal recognition. Some think that all visible signs are exaggerated. However, according to the interviews, the soldiers and their families are generally positive concerning initiatives in this area. The parades in particular have a strong emotional appeal. A deployed soldier described a parade in a provincial town: 'It was super cool, for it showed the support of that town. People stood and clapped. I have never experienced anything like it.' The first Flag Day was transmitted on a large screen in a camp in Afghanistan: 'For those of us who were down in Afghanistan on the first Flag Day, it was fantastic [...] to see the official pat on the shoulder from Denmark.'

### *Media Coverage*

A special part of the awareness of the general population is derived from the media coverage of and commentary on the missions. Overall, the deployed soldiers felt that, with a few exceptions, the media coverage was emotional, sensationalistic and negative. Returnees are dissatisfied with the media's morbid fascination with the psychological problems of some returnees after returning home. The media also has expressed scepticism about the usefulness of the missions, which a member of a support organisation found to have an intense negative effect on deployed soldiers. A family member says that the hurtful media coverage 'has an extraordinarily strong impact on the soldiers'. Those interviewed from the military and among deployed soldiers feel that the media has a tendency to overlook the positive things that benefit the local population. A respondent finds it hard to convey good news: 'it is bloody irritating because it also has something to do with support at home.'

### *Physical Injuries*

Soldiers who suffer physical injury often have to go through a long period of treatment and rehabilitation, and some face a life with permanent handicaps. While this situation can be frustrating, the interviewed soldiers say that with time they come to accept the physical injuries and the limits these impose.

One soldier who was wounded is stoical about it:

> I have experienced what I wanted to down there, and I tried. This is just what can happen. I knew the risk. I'm just glad that more didn't go wrong, and that I experienced so much.

Another aspect for soldiers with very visible physical wounds is the reactions of those around them, for example in the form of embarrassment and keeping a distance, which can also affect other people with a physical handicap.

For some soldiers sent home with serious injuries, it is not possible to continue in the military. However, for those who do continue, there is the risk that the job will be less challenging. Nonetheless, the military may be the best alternative in this situation. A returnee with injuries who remained in the service expresses it this way:

> I think the military is the best chance for me. In civilian life I don't think they would understand my wounds. And they wouldn't understand at all why I want to work again.

Serious injuries that are sustained during deployment and which result in the soldier being sent home ahead of time can create problems with feelings of guilt that they have 'let the side down'. To deal with this feeling, a few regiments have sent a wounded soldier back to his mission to make it possible for him to complete his deployment together with his comrades.

### *Psychological Reactions*

While there is a preponderance of positive reactions to deployment among the interviewed returnees, at the same time, a number of psychological problems to a difficult transition are mentioned. These may be experienced up to 2–3 months after returning home. One family member describes his experience of a soldier on home leave: 'On arrival, several hundred people were standing about. The soldiers were very serious, none smiled.'

In the first period after coming home, many soldiers are characterised by a high level of stress and increased sensitivity to sounds and smells, restlessness, lack of concentration and a more aggressive affect: 'It is hard to go from one reality to another.' After 1–3 months, most of the respondents overcome their restlessness and their stress levels drop. There are many different ways to cope, or not cope, among returnees. Some consciously choose to avoid deadlines and stress. As one returnee says: 'In fact, the trick for me has been not to book up my calendar and to force myself to relax.' Others consciously choose to work extremely hard or to isolate themselves. The last reaction pattern seems to increase the risk for further social and personal problems.

The high stress levels which typically are found shortly after returning home can be expressed in many different ways: restlessness, nervousness, insomnia, irritability and anxiety. Families and representatives from the military support groups find that many of the returnees have difficulties to return to their former everyday lives. One mother said about her son: 'It felt like he didn't hear, he didn't feel, he avoided some places, he was enormously sad and could not sleep at night.' Another example of psychological reaction is illustrated by one of the returnees: 'And so I drove for example down Gothersgade, where the other cars drove so unbelievably close to me the whole time. I couldn't stand it.' Guilt or shame about having been on a mission is seldom encountered in the interviews. This fact is confirmed by a representative from one of the military's support groups: 'There are remarkably few who suffer from guilt or shame. They are more ashamed of having thought [...] thank goodness, it wasn't me who was wounded.'

### *Positive Consequences of Deployment*

Despite the problems associated with returning home from a mission, as discussed earlier, the interviewed soldiers cite a range of positive consequences connected with their deployment. They feel that they have become more mature: 'I think I learned more in those months than I had in the past 4 years – both about myself and about people, the way they react, and so on.' The returnees also find that they have reached a greater understanding of the diverse nature of the world. The increase in maturity is also noted by the relatives of soldiers. One relative says, almost poetically: 'Boys leave, but men come back.' The returnees also find that they have developed professionally and have increased self-confidence: 'I think I have more reserves under stress because I know how I coped with stressful situations down there.' Finally, the returnees in the interviews attach great importance to the fact that they have experienced a comradeship which for some has developed into unbreakable friendships.

### *Relatives – A Special Factor*

The relatives of the deployed soldiers include a much wider circle of people than just close family members. Here, we focus on the closest relatives.

The feelings and concerns of close relatives can have a range of effects, partly on their own health and partly on their family relationships and on their work.

The reactions differ. Some relatives may take sick leave due to stress, talk with psychologists, or be prone to insomnia and unease. Relatives who take things as they come, may cope better. Although they are fed up and worried at the same time, some decide to support the deployed soldier. Others find it more difficult to support the deployed, especially if they find it hard to accept the soldier's choice to leave on a mission in the first place. The mothers in the study are among those who express their worry most clearly. The interviews show that it is particularly hard on the mothers to prepare for a deployment. But, as said by one of the interviewees: 'Mothers always think that boys don't become responsible until they reach 35, but they are held responsible when they reach 18 and can decide for themselves.' The relatives' fears do not necessarily cease when the soldier returns home. As discussed earlier, returnees are often so affected psychologically by being on a mission that in the first period at home they can seem like a different person. In the first months, returnees can be irritable and more aggressive than before deployment. For the relatives who take care of a soldier who has been wounded on the mission, the worries continue, with a greater focus on the future health and possible long-term psychological effects. A final aspect is the worry the relative has about a returnee who wants to go on another mission. Some react dramatically to the desire to leave, as referred to by a returnee: 'She (my girlfriend) said she would lock me in the cellar if I wanted to go.' Others promise to back up the soldiers, despite the anxiety and worry that comes with a new deployment.

### *Summary*

Many of the soldiers and their relatives experience a change in the returning soldiers. Coming home, and losing contact with one's 'military family', gives rise to a series of problems in connection with the soldiers' re-integration into everyday Danish life. In particular, two aspects appear to have a great influence on the soldiers' post-deployment experience: to be held 'accountable' by the family and the lack of recognition in the media.

A growing number of Danish soldiers come home from a deployment with physical injuries. This group has a particularly difficult time adjusting to life with a handicap. Some of the deployed experience psychological problems of different kinds as a result of their deployment, especially stress, restlessness, anxiety and aggression. These effects appear to apply to most of the homecoming soldiers in the first period of time after deployment, after which in most cases, the symptoms disappear. All of the deployed mention that despite psychological or physical problems, deployment has had a positive effect on their personal development.

## Part 2. Returning Home: The System and Challenges

The first part of this chapter focused on the consequences of a deployment. These consequences lead to their own different demands on and requests to support and rehabilitation programmes. The military, the military's support groups and the public authorities in general provide these programmes. There are also a raft of non-governmental institutions, support groups, unions and organisations standing by to help the returnee with the problems they face. In the following, we provide a description of this system – the available support programmes – and an analysis of the challenges that the military and the public authorities face when dealing with returnees.

## Description of the System – Status in 2010

### *Before Deployment – Selection and Preparation*

The two central questions here are, first, how the military ensures that the individuals who are interested in being deployed are in fact eligible to participate in an international mission. Second, there is the question of how the military creates an awareness of the risks connected with deployment on an international mission.

The military does not carry out a formal psychological screening of the soldiers who volunteer to a deployment. As an alternative, informal screening is done throughout the process until a possible deployment. An ongoing examination of the soldier's physical state is also a part of the informal screening, which does not follow a strict procedure. The military also encourages the soldiers, during this preparation period, to write a sort of 'testament' together with their relatives, so that both parties have an idea of the risks connected with a mission. This testament also gives those who are thinking about being deployed the opportunity to raise the question of risk with their families. The Danish Armed Forces have had positive experiences with this practice, which is not implemented in other countries.

### *During Deployment – Defusing, Debriefing and Army Chaplain*

The programmes available during deployment depend on the nature of the actions and experiences that took place during a mission. The programmes comprise the following:

- defusing with the soldier's primary group;
- debriefing with a psychologist; and
- possibility to talk things over with the Army chaplain.

*Defusing:* The purpose of defusing is to give the soldiers the chance to talk about situations that have made a strong and deep impression on them. The situation or action is talked through so that any future insecurities or frustrations during action are raised by the soldier with the leader of the group. The interviews do not indicate any single attitude towards defusing.

*Debriefing with a psychologist:* In connection with violent operations, and always in connection with a death on a mission, a psychologist comes to the camp to carry out a psychological debriefing and discussions. The interviews reveal that representatives from the military's support organisations were sceptical about this type of debriefing taking place in the area where the mission is located, partly because any diagnosis of psychological reactions cannot be made immediately after an action. Some studies have also shown that debriefing of this kind does not protect against later psychological problems (Roberto, Hyams, & Wessely, 2005).

In contrast to this scepticism, the soldiers in the interviews are positive about the psychological debriefing, which as stated by a representative from the military's supporting group, can also be perceived as 'personal care in some way'.

*Talking to the Army chaplain:* The interviews show that the Army chaplain plays an important role during a mission. A soldier describes him as follows: 'He is a psychologist, a chaplain, a friend and a social worker.' Another soldier says:

> After a patrol one can just go over to him and say one needs to talk [...] He is like a neutral person one can go to when one is tired of the others.

## *After Deployment – Psychological Effects and Physical Injuries*

Different support programmes have appeared to deal with the problems and challenges soldiers encounter when they return home. These support programmes apply both to direct challenges in the form of physical injuries and psychological problems and to the transition to civilian life for those not continuing in the military.

The support programmes available to the returnees can be divided into four areas:

(1) the military's procedures in connection with winding down and acclimatisation after a deployment;
(2) support programmes to the individuals who experience psychological reactions after they return home;
(3) support programmes to soldiers with physical injuries; and
(4) support programmes to the relatives.

### Psychological Problems

In the immediate period after returning home, soldiers encounter a range of support programmes at the same time that they are going through various obligatory activities. These latter include a health check and a talk with a psychologist from the Institute for Military Psychology (IMP) for those returning from a 'hard' mission. The obligatory talks for some returnees include an offer of permanent support from the military's psychologists both for the veterans – soldiers who have been on at least one mission, regardless of their age and their current soldiers' military status – and for their relatives. The interviewees were positive about this offer. After the obligatory talk with the returnees from 'hard' missions, it is up to the returnee to contact the IMP if he wants to take advantage of any of the other support programmes. Although some find it completely natural to seek psychological help, for others it may take a lot of time before they are ready to do it. The last reaction is described by a returnee:

> One has to admit to oneself that one is not so strong, and not a hero. One can't carry everything on one's shoulders. Once in a while, one also has to ask for help.

All returnees undergo a doctor's examination at the Military Health Service (*Forsvarets Sundhedstjeneste* (FSU)). Only the soldiers with injuries are further examined. A part of the purpose of the health check is to discover whether the returnees have work-related injuries eligible for financial compensation.

**Reunion Arrangements and Questionnaires**

Three months after a veteran's return, the military holds a reunion. After seven months, this reunion is repeated for those from 'hard' missions. On these occasions, the various support groups provide information about the support programmes available to veterans. Six months after returning home, all veterans are sent a questionnaire by the IMP, the purpose of which is to uncover any need for professional psychological help. The questionnaire includes a box-item that can be ticked if a returnee wants to contact a psychologist from the IMP. IMP uses the filled out questionnaires to conduct a 'screening', in which the respondents are divided up into high- and low-risk groups. On the basis of the answers, help and support are offered to the veterans considered to need them, just as IMP contacts the veterans – regardless of their risk group – who have wished to be contacted by a psychologist. The response rate is about 70%, so it is possible that among the 30% who did not answer the questionnaire some veterans have such severe problems that they could neither fill out the questionnaire nor avail themselves of the standing offer of psychological support. Of course, the group of non-respondents may also include veterans who do not have problems and simply neglected to fill out the questionnaire, but it is not possible to determine the proportion of each group. Chapter 8 investigates further this issue by combining answers to this questionnaire and administrative records that cover the entire deployed population.

**Re-integration – 'Battlemind–Homemind' Project**

In 2008, the problems some veterans experienced when they returned to civilian life inspired a single regiment, the Life Guards, to carry out a trial, in which instead of having a week to wind down, veterans were offered a three-month extension in the military. The project was called 'Battlemind–Homemind'(see Jonasen, 2009). The main aim of the project was to support the veterans' re-adjustment and to improve the transition to civilian life for the HRU soldiers who left the military. A representative from the military's support group described 'battlemind' as a situation where veterans walk around as if they were in enemy territory [...] and often react strongly if they are frightened [...]' One of the central aims of the project was to '[...] return an automatic, impulsive reaction to a level where one maybe thinks before reacting, which is more normal here at home where there is no need for impulsive reaction'. Both officers and privates describe 'Battlemind–Homemind' as a good project, especially compared with previous one-week winding down procedures for HRU soldiers not continuing in the military. Especially for this latter group, veteran homes were established in various parts of the country where previously deployed soldiers and their relatives can meet up in informal surroundings and where there is the chance to be presented with physical challenges in order to bring stress levels down.

**Focus on Permanent Physical Injuries**

In this section, we review the situation of, and support programmes to, those veterans with permanent physical injuries sustained during a mission. In 2009, the military established a rehabilitation unit with the purpose of supporting veterans with permanent injuries in making the best possible transition to normal life. Before this unit was set up, veterans with injuries were offered a contract by the military with employment until the age of 60. With the increase in the number of returnees with permanent injuries, this offer has become less appropriate for both the veterans and the military.

The rehabilitation unit consists of a contact officer, who co-ordinates a team consisting of a doctor on call, a social worker, and a training and job advisor from the Military Personnel Service (*Forsvarets Personeltjeneste* (FPT)). The team assists the soldier in seeking support from the local authorities and in planning their future, including getting jobs. The primary purpose of this unit is to assist in the various phases during the veteran's transition to a normal life. The rehabilitation unit maintains contact with the veterans until they find an ordinary job or are receiving support from the local authorities. The relatives can also get help from the rehabilitation unit. Social workers encourage the relatives to concentrate on their relationship with the wounded soldier, and leave it to the rehabilitation unit to organise contact with the local authorities, medication, prostheses, etc. As a social worker said to the relatives: 'So you can be a family and argue, and be angry and happy and everything else, just like other families.' The aim is to enable relatives to 'concentrate on being relatives' and leave it to the rehabilitation team to sort out controversies with municipal authorities.

**External Support**

With the increased number of deployed soldiers from 1992 to 2009, the number of external support groups has also drastically increased. Generally, the interviewees were satisfied with the increase in these external support groups. The external support groups approach the problems from different angles. The organisations for military personnel are among those that are the most active. To these are added a network of relatives and veteran organisations, together with a number of foundations and organisations with a tradition of social work among serving and retired soldiers.

**Possibilities for Compensation**

Under certain conditions, veterans with permanent injuries are eligible for compensation. In contrast to normal insurance practice, an injury is often not reported until returning home from a mission. All deployed personnel groups are covered by a special Compensation and Reimbursement (*Erstatnings- og Godtgoerelsesordning*) system that is fairly complex in that it distinguishes between injuries that are the result of accidents and work-related injuries. The border between the two has shifted since 1992 and now a greater number of injuries are regarded as accidents.

Psychological damage such as post-traumatic stress disorder (PTSD) is recognised as an accident if it is acute, for example, if a soldier has been in a life-threatening situation during a patrol or under heavy fire. If PTSD appears later, it is reported as a work-related injury conditional on the presence of several other symptoms and on the first symptoms appearing at most six months after returning home. Since 2013, symptoms that appear more than six months after returning home may also be considered. In cases where a soldier dies during a mission, the wife/husband or partner receives compensation from the Workers' Compensation Insurance system (*Arbejdsskadeforsikringen*). If the soldier was unmarried and childless, parents whose son or daughter has died received compensation from the special Compensation and Reimbursement system previously mentioned.

**Support Programmes to Relatives**

In the interviews, there is a positive response from all groups of respondents considering support programmes to the relatives. These support programmes fall under following main headings:

- information and events organised by the military before deployment;
- events and family/friends groups during deployment;
- possibility to contact the military psychologists and social workers during and after deployment; and
- military contact officer.

On the whole, the relatives of soldiers are satisfied with the military support programmes. These programmes are also important to the military, because acceptance and support from the relatives play such an important role in the appropriate conduct of a mission by influencing whether a soldier actually chooses to go out on a mission and how he/she functions during the mission. In 2001, the Military Privates and Corporals Union (*Haerens Konstabel- og Korporal Forening* (HKKF)) set up a family network. The network consists of volunteers who have experience dealing with the relatives of soldiers. The network provides the opportunity to communicate with the relatives of other soldiers by mail or telephone. An initiative springing from the network has been the formation of volunteer groups of wives or girlfriends, and mothers of the deployed soldiers.

The military psychologists are also available to the relatives while the soldiers are deployed and after, as is the military contact officer, who can be reached any time of the day or night, before, during and after deployment.

Military social workers can also be contacted by relatives and soldiers. The social workers play a special role during a deployment, when serious problems in the family may mean that the soldier will have to be sent home in the middle of a mission. In this case, the social worker has an important task, and his/her good advice can improve the family situation and thereby preventing having to send a soldier home before their deployment is finished.

### *Challenges – Gaps in the System*

We have described and analysed the deployment conditions for soldiers and other personnel who were deployed from 1992 to 2009. We also discuss how to improve the post-deployment support programmes offered to the deployed. The main problems we encounter is the following:

- The military support programmes do not include a formal proactive search procedure. The veterans with serious psychological problems risk not receiving the relevant support programmes.
- Information is not shared between different military institutions.
- The increased number of returnees with physical injuries and psychological problems constitute a group of citizens/patients with new requirements.

The first area of problems indicates a need for a better proactive search procedure. Over the years both attitudes towards the deployed and support programmes have drastically improved. The first group of deployed soldiers from the first Balkan missions point out that in the 1990s, when one returned home, it was almost taboo to seek psychological support. As an example, returnees in that period who wanted psychological help had to stand up in front of the ranks, with the obvious result that soldiers who needed help typically did not seek it. Since then, a very positive change has occurred in this area, not the least because of an acceptance at leadership level. This change is described in an interview: 'There is a completely different openness about all this. The bosses also see a psychologist and tell you when they go. So it immediately becomes much more legitimate.' This change in attitude is of course an advantage for later returnees, but some of the veterans from the Balkan missions may not have received the appropriate help.

The study indicates problems with the fact that many of the support programmes are only available if the soldiers themselves take the initiative. Although the situation creates problems, changing it also involves a difficult balancing act between, as far as possible, not failing those who need help and not infringing on their personal integrity. A possible way forward, as stated by an interviewee, is that officers and non-commissioned officers take the initiative to develop informal methods to reach the veterans with psychological problems who have not requested help. An example of such an informal – and unorthodox – method is for an officer to 'order' one of his soldiers to talk with a psychologist. Another example is that after a company's return home, the officer makes an informal list of the company's soldiers, with a (subjective) evaluation of their potential risk of having or developing psychological problems. Soldiers who are placed in the highest risk category are then contacted by the officer on a regular basis by telephone. This procedure also applies to those who have left military service.

It is a difficult balancing act, weighing how appropriate help should be given in a situation in which the veteran should in principle initiate this, while knowing that many of those with severe psychological problems tend to isolate themselves. Any approach to this group carries the risk of depriving them of control and can also be problematic in terms of the law. In the interviews, most consider that they have received the information they need about health care support programmes. For example, one respondent said: 'I feel that we are well cared for. If we need to talk with a psychologist, all we have to do is ring.'

Participation in the interviews was voluntary, which undoubtedly means there is a certain over-representation of psychologically robust veterans in the interview group. One way to increase the knowledge about the situation of those who first 'fall through the net' in the treatment system involves the use of administrative records, which form the basis of the health profile presented in Chapter 8.

Another problem area, also in terms of the legal rights, is that the military psychologists and FPT must not exchange information about individual soldiers because of professional secrecy. Again, there is a balancing act between both formal and informal aspects. Within the framework of administrative law, it is permitted to discard the right to privacy if holding back the information is judged to have fatal consequences for the deployed soldiers or others.

### Veterans with Health Problems – Challenges as a Patient and as a Citizen

Returning soldiers with physical injuries or psychological problems form a new patient group for the health authorities in terms of both treatment and rehabilitation. This is also true with regard to local social services and the job market, where veterans represent a group with special problems. The principle of equal treatment of all citizens thus has to be balanced against the needs of a group of people who have lived outside the country under special conditions.

For example, the study points out that veterans have been turned away from emergency psychiatric treatment departments. Another example reported in an interview concerns a soldier diagnosed with PTSD who lost his social support from the municipality because he, due to massive psychological problems, was not able to fulfil an administrative requirement to appear at or participate in active job market policy programmes.

The challenges and problems presented here form the background of the gradual implementation of a separate veteran policy (see Danish Government, 2010), which both covers a deliberate valuation of the returnees and at the same time addresses itself more consciously to a range of the problems discussed. After 1992–2009, the years examined here, a proper veterans' policy was drafted, coming into force in 2010. Some ongoing experiences with veterans' policy were evaluated in a report from the Ministry of Defence in 2013.

### *Summary*

- The above analyses have identified general problems in connection with gaps in the support programmes and procedures that are made available by the military and public authorities to the deployed and their relatives.
- The analyses emphasise that the military is not able to 'follow up' the groups of homecoming soldiers who after returning home leave the military and enter civilian life and who thereafter experience severe psychological problems. Various support programmes have been created specifically for the purpose, among other things, of psychological counselling from the military. However, these and other support programmes are based on the soldiers themselves taking the initiative, and this can carry the risk of soldiers with severe psychological problems 'falling through the net'.
- In the same way, there is a general problem concerning the support that the public authorities offer returning soldiers. The large number of soldiers deployed on international missions, introduces into the public systems a new group of citizens and patients with special needs.

Chapter 6

# Mission Experiences and Subsequent Careers – Survey-based Analyses

## Introduction

In this chapter, we use the term of veteran to both design the previous soldiers no longer employed in the military, and the soldiers deployed at least one time but still employed in the military. This chapter elucidates the current situation of these veterans from a questionnaire (survey). We can investigate some aspects of the veteran's experience that we cannot observe in the administrative records. This questionnaire provides the veterans' own evaluations of their situation today and what they experienced during deployment. The analysis is descriptive in nature and deals with the correlation between different conditions. Therefore, we cannot use this analysis to draw conclusions about causality.

The questionnaire was directed at those who were deployed between 1992 and 2009. From lists from the Danish Armed Forces (DAF), we choose a population of veterans as a simple random sample of previously deployed soldiers between 1992 and 2009. In all, 3,198 respondents from an initial sample of 4,000 answered the questionnaire. The analysis of the non-respondents shows no large non-response bias and that in terms of their military background, the respondents were representative of the soldiers who were deployed at least once during 1992–2009.

As a point of departure in the questionnaire structure, this chapter focuses on seven areas:

- the socio-demographics of the veterans, such as age, gender, upbringing and current family and living conditions;
- the manner in which the veterans joined – and later left – the military, placing particular weight on the later work careers;
- the veterans' experience of their mission and whether it had placed a severe strain on them;
- the veterans' evaluation of the direct consequences of having been on a mission and whether they were wounded or repatriated;
- the one-time deployed's statements of enriching and challenging conditions during a mission. The focus is on these one-time deployed because it can be difficult for many-time deployed to judge and remember each mission separately;

- the veterans' social relationships, health and contacts with the military's support services; and
- the veterans' smoking habits and drug use.

## Demographic Profile of the Veterans

The purpose of this section is to describe the differences between veterans and to identify possible vulnerable groups among them. We therefore divide the veterans who answered the questionnaire into different groups using specific criteria. The first division is whether veterans still are employed in the military or not (in service, not in service). The second division is about the number of deployments (one-time deployed, many-time deployed). We start by examining all those deployed, but later in the chapter, we focus on the veterans deployed only once (one-time deployed).

Among the veterans still employed in the military at the time of the study, slightly over 90% expect to be deployed again, both those who have been on only one mission and those who have been deployed more than once. The motive for focusing particularly on veterans who are no longer in the military is that they constitute a more 'invisible' group concerning the problems and challenges they encounter when they return home. A priori, we expect a large heterogeneity in this group. However, those still in service are not necessarily more homogeneous and considerable variation can also be expected in this group. The division of the respondents using these two criteria – continued service or not – and participation in one or more missions is shown in Table 6.1.

Table 6.1. Veterans by Number of Deployments and Whether They are Still in Service or Not.

| | In Service | No Longer in Service | All Veterans |
|---|---|---|---|
| One Deployment | | | |
| Number | 343 | 1,245 | 1,588 |
| Per cent | 11 | 39 | 50 |
| More Than One Deployment | | | |
| Number | 792 | 818 | 1,610 |
| Per cent | 25 | 26 | 51 |
| Total | | | |
| Number | 1,135 | 2,063 | 3,198 |
| Per cent | 35 | 65 | 100 |

*Source*: SFI.

Table 6.2. The Deployed Soldiers' Ages According to Whether They Are Still in Service or Not, and Whether They Have Been Deployed Only Once, or More Than Once (Age).

| | In Service | | No Longer in Service | | |
|---|---|---|---|---|---|
| | **One Deployment** | **More Than One Deployment** | **One Deployment** | **More Than One Deployment** | **Total** |
| Percentiles | | | | | |
| 25 | 27 | 32 | 30 | 35 | 32 |
| 50 | 35 | 40 | 36 | 39 | 37 |
| 75 | 48 | 49 | 40 | 45 | 44 |
| Average | 37 | 40 | 36 | 42 | 39 |

*Source*: SFI.
*Note*: Total of 3,198 observations.

The population is evenly divided between veterans with one or more deployments. However, the majority (65%) are no longer in the military. Table 6.2 presents the age distribution of the veterans who answered the questionnaire according to the two criteria – whether they are still in service and whether they have been on one or more than one mission.

It is not surprising to find that the veterans who have only been on one mission are on average considerably younger than those who have been on several missions. The percentiles show that the youngest group consists of those deployed only once and who are still in service. In Table 6.3, the soldiers are categorised by age and gender. The ages are divided up into age intervals relevant to the structure of the military's employment contracts. The interval 21–34 years includes those employed on a three-year (K3) contract or on a K35 contract that runs until the age of 35. The interval 35–59 years includes career soldiers who are permanently employed or employed under a K60 contract until the age of 60, the pensionable age in the military.

Among those still in service in the youngest group, a clear majority have been deployed only once. However, among all servicemen, it is surprising that slightly over half of the 35- to 59-year-olds have only been deployed once. A part of the explanation, not shown in the table, is that about a quarter of the groups was not eligible for a new deployment. Only 5% of the respondents are women. This low percentage reflects the low, albeit increasing, share of women being deployed. When we divide up the veterans into personnel groups according to age intervals and employment status in the military, we find that the share of privates, sergeants and officers is evenly distributed for those still employed in the military, while

Table 6.3. Veterans Divided by Age and Sex, According to Whether They Are Still in Service or No Longer in Service, by Number of Deployments.

| | Still in Service | | No Longer in Service | | Total |
|---|---|---|---|---|---|
| | One Deployment | More Than One Deployment | One Deployment | More Than One Deployment | |
| 21–34 Years | 48 | 34 | 42 | 24 | 36 |
| 35–59 Years | 51 | 65 | 53 | 64 | 59 |
| 60 Years or older | 1 | 2 | 4 | 12 | 5 |
| Total | 100 | 100 | 100 | 100 | 100 |
| Male | 91 | 96 | 94 | 96 | 95 |
| Female | 9 | 4 | 6 | 4 | 5 |
| Total | 100 | 100 | 100 | 100 | 100 |

*Source*: SFI.
*Note*: Total of 3,198 observations.

there is a large over-representation of privates in the group of veterans no longer in service.

### *Family Relationships of Veterans*

The registry information on veterans' family relationships can be compared with information from the questionnaire concerning the situation after returning home. Comparisons of this kind are descriptive and cannot, without further information, be interpreted causally. Aside from age, which naturally increased from the time of deployment to answering the questionnaire, other relationships – apart from being deployed – obviously have an influence on the veterans' family situations and changes in them since before deployment. With these reservations in mind, Figure 6.1 shows the veterans' civilian status according to both the criteria.

It is obvious that the age difference must have a significant importance for the pattern shown in Figure 6.1. Regardless of whether they are still in service, the many-time deployed soldiers also have the highest share of divorces. However, it is not possible to conclude from the figure whether there is a causal correlation with the number of deployments – or whether this finding reflects the higher average age of this group.

For the veterans in the study, there is a very large variation in the length of time since their, possibly first, deployment and their status at the time they

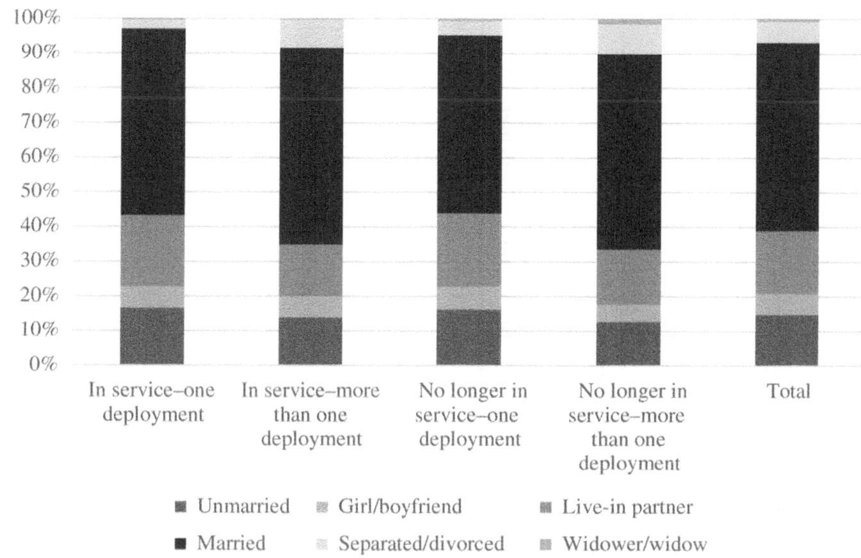


Figure 6.1. Civilian Status of Veterans According to Number of Deployments and Employment Status (%). *Source*: SFI. *Notes*: Total of 3,193 observations, five non-responses. 'Married' is defined as deployed soldiers who replied that they were married or living in a registered relationship.

answered the questionnaire. In Table 6.4, we compare civilian status one year before the deployment with the current status. The transitions shown in Table 6.4 should be interpreted with caution as there is a large variation in the time interval between the two points of time.

With this reservation in mind, Table 6.4 shows that most of the veterans who were unmarried before their first deployment are now married, and most of those who were originally married are still married. In the group who initially were divorced, three-quarters have either married again or are living with a partner. Thus, we do not find strong evidence that veterans have an especially high rate of either divorce or frequency of marriage.

When we look at the veterans who have children – and the number of children – there is also no indication that the group diverges from the general population. Figure 6.2 illustrates the share of veterans with and without children according to the two criteria 'in service' and 'no longer in service'. In the group no longer in service who have been on more than one deployment, the number of children is slightly above average. In the group still in service, the number of children is slightly below average. In both cases, the age difference probably explains a significant part of the divergence from the average. Looking only at the veterans who have children, they have on average 2.1 children, a number that is at least on a level with the rest of the population in the same age group.

Table 6.4. Veterans Divided up by Civilian Status Currently and in the Year before Deployment (%).

| **Civilian Status One Year before First Deployment** | **Current Civilian Status** | | | | | | |
|---|---|---|---|---|---|---|---|
| | **Unmarried** | **Married** | **Separated/ Divorced** | **Widower/ Widow** | **Girl/ Boyfriend** | **Live-in Partner** | **Total** |
| Widower/widow | 0 | 17 | 0 | 83 | 0 | 0 | 100 |
| Separated/divorced | 3 | 61 | 22 | 0 | 1 | 12 | 100 |
| Married | 0 | 88 | 9 | 2 | 0 | 1 | 100 |
| Unmarried | 18 | 46 | 5 | 0 | 8 | 22 | 100 |
| Total | 15 | 54 | 6 | 1 | 6 | 18 | 100 |

*Source*: SFI.
*Note*: Total of 3,110 observations, 88 non-responses.

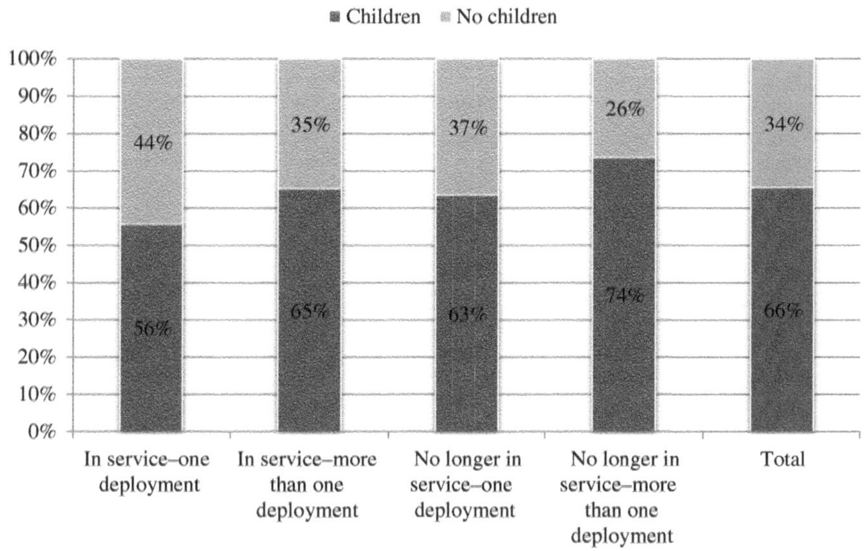


Figure 6.2. Veterans According to the Number of Children, by Employment Status and One or More Than One Deployment. *Source*: SFI.

### *Housing Conditions of Veterans*

The housing conditions of the veterans compared with the general population of comparable age are an indicator of the financial situation after returning home from one or more than one mission. Figure 6.3 illustrates the relative distribution among the veterans of owned and rented housing divided according to the two criteria. Just as in Figure 6.2, the veterans with more than one deployment stand out, regardless of whether they are still in service or not. Again, it is obvious that their higher average age explains this difference. Compared with the population as a whole, the number of veterans who are homeowners is high, indicating a relatively good financial situation.

### *Veterans' Upbringing*

In Chapter 4, we looked at how many of the deployed soldiers were brought up in families where there was only one adult. However, it was not possible to find out how many grew up in a divorced household. The reason for including this parameter is to examine the hypothesis that growing up in a divorced household can in some cases result in an increased vulnerability. In the questionnaire, we had the opportunity to obtain information about the veterans whose parents were divorced or separated before the veteran reached the age of 18. We find that it was the case for 28% of all veterans. The number of divorces while the veterans were growing up is on the same level as for the population as a whole. In relation to the two criteria we use, it is among the

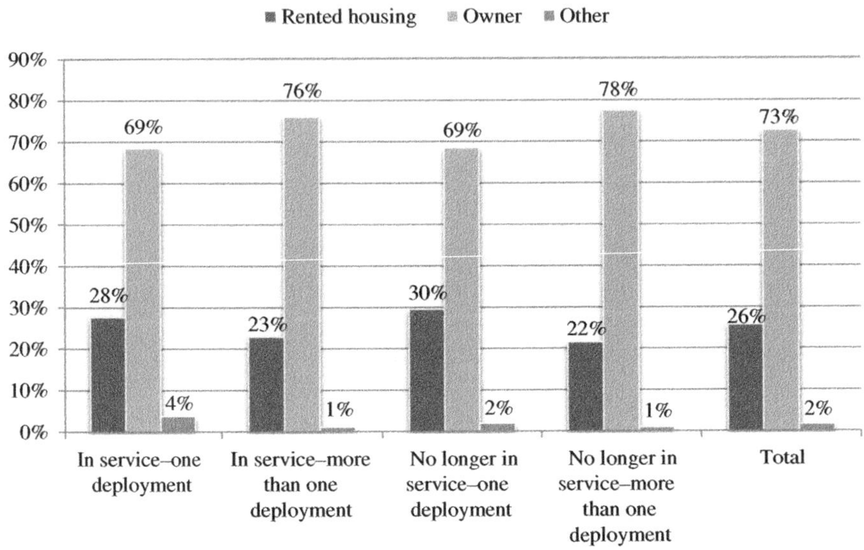


Figure 6.3. Veterans' Current Housing Situation, Proportion with Owned Property or Rented Property. Divided by Employment Status and Deployment on One or More than One Mission. *Source*: SFI. *Notes*: Total of 3,198 observations. Partly collectively owned property (*andelsbolig*) is included under Rented housing.

group of veterans who have been deployed once and are no longer in service that we find the highest number who grew up in a home where the parents were separated or divorced. The group of the most 'invisible' veterans have therefore the greatest expected risk of being vulnerable because their having grown up in a divorced household.

## The Path into and out of the Military

The focus in this section is on which veterans remain in service and which veterans leave the service for civilian life. In addition, we look at whether there are differences between veterans still in service in relation to the kind of contract they have with the military. We also look at the importance of seniority in the military and whether the veterans were originally in the group that volunteered for military service. Among the veterans no longer in service, we look partly at the causes or reasons for leaving the military and partly at how their careers in civilian life are going. In particular, we focus on the group of veterans who left the military and were under contracts that typical run until they are 35 years old. The unusual thing about this group is that they leave the military long before pensionable age but have only a limited work experience to apply for jobs in civilian life.

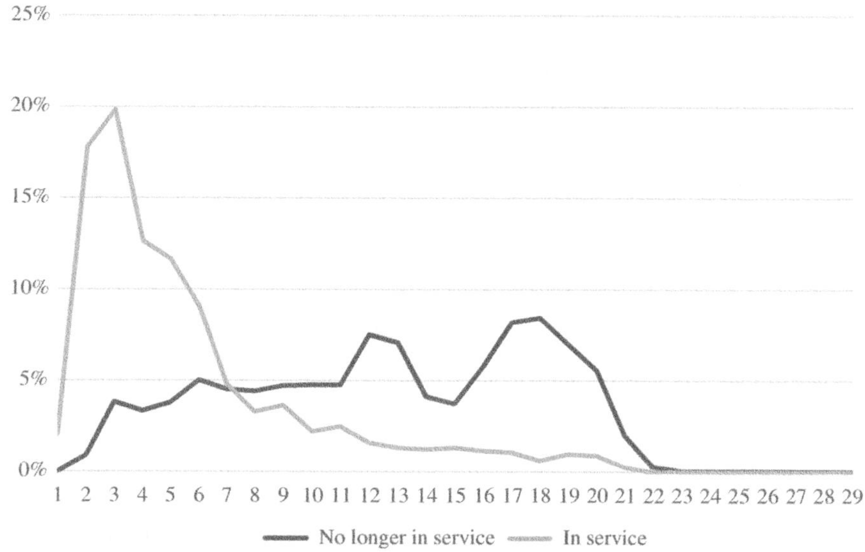


Figure 6.4. Veterans by Number of Years Since Their Last Deployment and Whether They Are Still in Service. *Source*: SFI. *Note*: Total of 3,162 observations, 36 non-responses.

***Last Deployment and Seniority in the Military***

The respondents in the questionnaire show very large differences in the time interval since their last deployment. There is a particularly large difference between those still in service and those who have left the military. In the first group, the last deployment is between a few months and up to 20 years back in time. For those no longer in service, the last deployment is from one year to more than 20 years in the past. However, most of the respondents were deployed between 1992 and 2009. In Figure 6.4, the respondents are categorised according to the number of years that have passed since their last deployment, divided into whether they are still employed by the military or not. As shown, very few of those answering the questionnaire had their last deployment more than 20 years ago.

However, it is surprising that a number of soldiers who are still employed have only been on one mission, fairly far back in time. As earlier mentioned, a part of explanation is that 12% of this group have been deemed ineligible for further deployment. In this group, there is an over-representation of privates who state that they were wounded or hurt during a deployment. We return to this group in the next section about individual experiences during a mission. Among the veterans who were considered eligible, about 90% have been deployed in the last 10 years. In the group of eligible, slightly over 20% of the veterans still in service state that their next deployment is planned to take place in the coming 3–4 years.

In relation to the types of contracts and employment conditions within the military, most of the veterans still in service are employed under a K60 contract, which runs until they reach 60 years. Most of those no longer in service were employed under other kinds of contracts, as shown in Table 6.5.

K35 is a contract that typically runs out at the age of 35; Denmark's International Brigade (DIB), an organisation that has not existed since 2005. K3/HRU is a short contract, typically for three years. It appears that the group no longer in service was predominately employed under short-term contracts, implying that, after leaving the military, they would make a career shift to civilian life.

### *Path into the Military – Volunteering for Military Service*

There are two types of voluntary entry into the Military. Conscripts who signed on voluntarily for (basic) military service under all circumstances are called *true volunteers*. Others, who draw a number on Armed Forces Day that means they are very likely to be called up, gain certain advantages by volunteering. This group is called *technical volunteers*. Figure 6.5 shows how veterans split themselves with regard to the two types of voluntary duty and with regard to not having originally signed on as a volunteer. It is important to emphasise that after HBU (basic military service), participation in HRU and signing contracts with the military is voluntary.

Of all veterans in the study, 85% were volunteers, most (59%) true volunteers, and the remaining 26% were technical volunteers. It is interesting to note that

Table 6.5. Veterans by Contract Type and Employment Status (%).

| | **K60/Permanent Personnel** | **K35** | **DIB** | **K3/HRU** | **Other Contracts** | **Total** |
|---|---|---|---|---|---|---|
| Seniority of Those in Service | | | | | | |
| 2–3 Years | 8 | 60 | 0 | 16 | 16 | 100 |
| 4–17 Years | 36 | 50 | 2 | 2 | 10 | 100 |
| ≥18 Years | 90 | 0 | 1 | 2 | 8 | 100 |
| Total | 64 | 23 | 1 | 2 | 9 | 100 |
| Seniority of Those No Longer in Service | | | | | | |
| ≤1 Year | 1 | 19 | 39 | 36 | 13 | 100 |
| 2–3 Years | 3 | 34 | 36 | 25 | 7 | 100 |
| 4–17 Years | 13 | 43 | 29 | 8 | 6 | 100 |
| ≥18 Years | 69 | 9 | 5 | 6 | 12 | 100 |
| Total | 15 | 33 | 30 | 17 | 8 | 100 |

*Source*: SFI.
*Notes*: Total of 2,001 observations, 62 non-responses. 'Seniority' describes how many years the soldier has been in the Military.

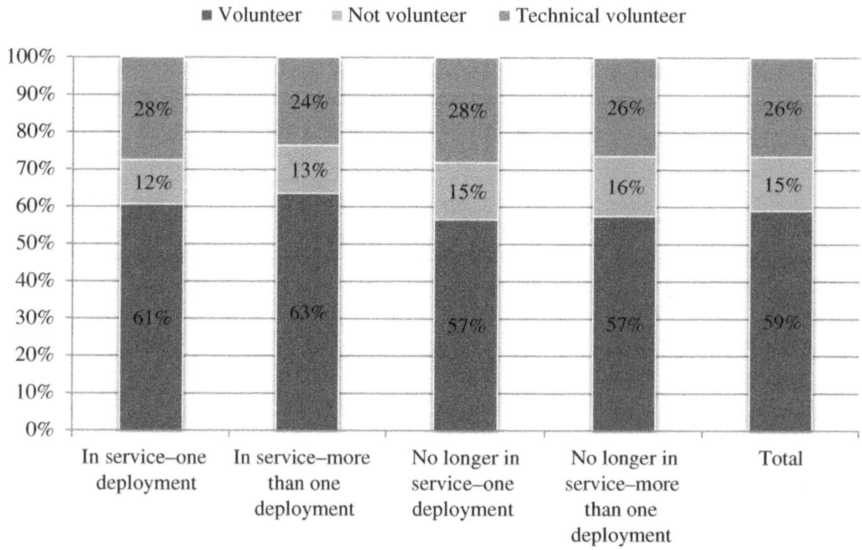


Figure 6.5. Veterans Classified by Volunteer Status on Entry into the Military, by Employment Status and One or More Than One Deployment. *Source*: SFI. *Note*: Total of 3,184 observations, 14 non-responses.

15% of the veterans were originally not volunteers – neither true nor technical – but nonetheless chose a career in the military with at least one deployment. It is not surprising that a greater number of the soldiers still in service originally signed up as true volunteers. A special characteristic of those who did not volunteer originally is their educational background. At the time they entered the military, 37% were skilled workers, as opposed to 26% of all veterans. The decision to stay in the military, despite originally not volunteering, can therefore be attributed to either a change in preferences, or economic motivation in conjunction with a downturn in the economy. In connection with seniority in the military, a substantial part of the original non-volunteers continued in service for a relatively long time.

### *Veterans' Educational Level at Entry to the Military – and Currently*

The questionnaire makes it possible to compare information about the veterans' education at the time they entered the military with their education at the time of the questionnaire. Again, when we consider changes in educational level, accounting for the large variation in time elapsed between entry into the military and the current situation is important. Table 6.6 shows the educational level at entry and the current situation divided into six educational categories and further classified into those in service and those no longer in service.

Overall, the educational level rose for both those in service and those no longer in service. In some cases, the changes are similar for the two groups,

Table 6.6. Educational Status of Veterans at the Time of Entry into the Military and at the Time of the Questionnaire, Divided into Those in Service and Those No Longer in Service (%).

| | **In Service** | | **No Longer in Service** | | **Total** | |
|---|---|---|---|---|---|---|
| | **At Entry** | **Currently** | **At Entry** | **Currently** | **At Entry** | **Currently** |
| Basic compulsory education (age, 7–15) | 24 | 19 | 26 | 14 | 25 | 15 |
| Secondary/high school (age, 16–18) | 42 | 35 | 35 | 17 | 38 | 23 |
| Vocational training | 22 | 24 | 28 | 32 | 26 | 29 |
| Short further education (1–2 years at university) | 4 | 6 | 3 | 9 | 3 | 8 |
| University degree (BA/BSc) | 5 | 9 | 5 | 18 | 5 | 15 |
| Postgraduate (MA/MSc, PhD) | 3 | 8 | 2 | 10 | 2 | 10 |
| Total | 100 | 100 | 100 | 100 | 100 | 100 |

*Source*: SFI.
*Note*: Total of 3,196 observations, two non-responses.

whereas others clearly reflect changes related to whether the veterans are still in service or not. Looking at both basic and secondary education, there is a significant fall in the numbers of veterans no longer in service with only this education. This fall may indicate that some of those who apply for the military with only a secondary education do not necessarily intend to have a military career, but to a greater degree have taken a gap year (a sabbatical) between two educational levels (see Vincent Lyk-Jensen & Glad, 2018). There is a much greater rise in the number with a graduate degree (BA/BSc) among those no longer in service, which may reflect difficulties in combining such an education with military employment. Therefore, it is interesting that the levels and the increase in numbers with a postgraduate education are the same for those still in service and those not. Finally, as regards vocational training and a short university education, there are only minor differences between the two groups of veterans. When comparing the educational level of all the veterans with the general population, it appears that, regardless of age, a larger share of veterans has taken a further education, that is above secondary (not shown).

Veterans who were employed under a K35 contract are in this connection of particular interest. Most of this group have more education than when they entered the military. The greatest increase is among those with a university degree, rising from 5% to 22%. This increase may have occurred partly after the veterans left the military and may indicate that some used the opportunity to take a complete or partial civilian education while in service. The right to a civilian education is granted after 33 months of service. When seniority is achieved, one earns the right to one week of civilian education for every further month in service. At the time of the questionnaire, 25% of those on a K35 contract were either taking or had finished a civilian education. Among the former employed veterans on a K35 contract, 17% had taken a civilian education, whereas 27% had earned the right to it but had not yet taken advantage of it. Granted right to a civilian education ends either at the end of the contract or when one signs a long-term contract or begins officer training.

### *Reasons for Leaving the Military*

The reasons veterans leave the military are presented in Figure 6.6 for soldiers with one or more deployments. The two equally large dominant groups are those veterans who do not wish to continue in service when their contract expires and those who quit. The first group mainly encompasses veterans who have been deployed only once, whereas the second group is equally divided among those with one and those with more than one deployment. It appears

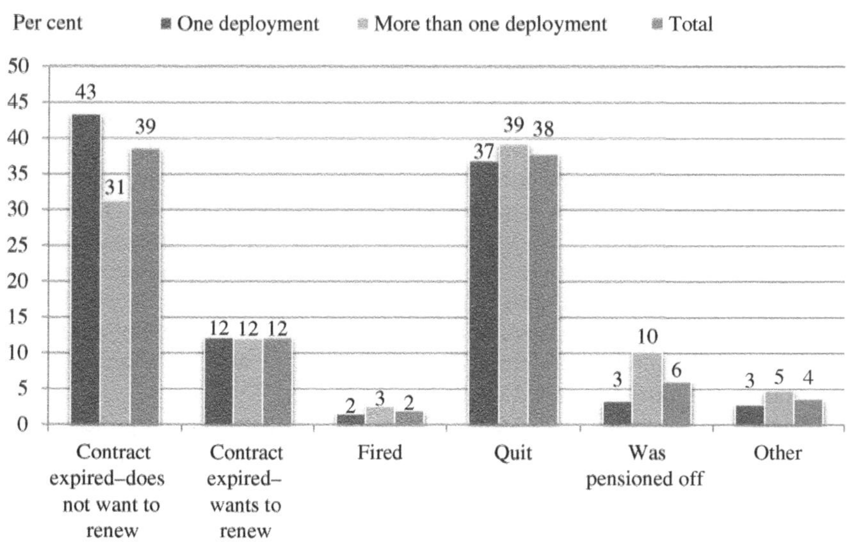


Figure 6.6. Background for Leaving the Military of Veterans No Longer in Service, by One or More Than One Deployment. *Source*: SFI. *Notes*: Total of 2,061 observations, two non-responses. Among 'Other' are included those who stated that their contract had finished but they did not know whether they wanted to continue in the military.

that 12% of those who have left the military did so at the end of their contract, but at the same time, they state that they would have preferred to have continued in the military. Among these, 39% had been on several deployments.

As expected, the reasons for leaving the military vary among the different personnel groups. The expiry of a contract together with a desire not to continue is prevalent among privates. Among sergeants and officers, the predominant reason is that they quit. The differences in age distribution among the personnel groups means that for the officers, the pension is the dominant reason for leaving the military. It is not clear which factors lie behind the relatively large group who indicated that they left when their contract expired but would have liked to continue. This reason is more prevalent among women veterans. However, this difference should be viewed taking into account that the absolute number of women who participated in the study was very low.

### Work after the Military

The veterans' jobs after leaving the military vary as expected with age, personnel group and the period that has elapsed since they left the military. The largest group of jobs are office workers, 35–40% of the veterans, and show no particular variation between the various personnel groups. Jobs as skilled workers are most widespread among veterans who were on a K35 or shorter contract. Positions in management, in the professions or as self-employed workers are taken by 10% of veterans, with an expected share of 14% of the former officers. It is interesting that unemployment among the veterans was only 5% in a society experiencing a financial crisis. However, unemployment was higher (10%) among veterans who only had a basic or secondary school education when they left the military.

Considering that some of the veterans were affected physically or mentally while on deployment, it is also important to look at the proportion who were receiving a disability pension after leaving the military. The share of veterans receiving a disability pension is surprisingly low compared with the share in the general male population, 1.2% vs 6.5%, respectively. Of the veterans on a disability pension, 20% stated that they were wounded while on a mission, some of these during combat. We cannot reach a definite conclusion about whether the low incidence of disability pensions among veterans is a result of their self-selection and screening before entry into the military or whether a smaller share of pensioned veterans responded to the questionnaire.

Regarding the veterans' age, positions in top management, liberal professions or as self-employed are of course concentrated in the age group 35–59 years. Among those who are office workers, the share of jobs with leadership responsibilities is almost double among the 35- to 59-year-olds than among 21- to 34-year-olds. In contrast, the share of those in education is larger among the 21- to 34-year-olds but is only 2% in the 35- to 59-year-old group, who includes veterans who were employed under a K35 contract and therefore only started civilian life after the age of 35.

One last relevant aspect in connection with work after the military is the period that has elapsed between leaving the military or the latest mission and the time of the questionnaire. The patterns we found are shown in Table 6.7.

Table 6.7. Main Occupations for Veterans Who Have Left the Service by the Number of Years Since Their Last Deployment (%).

| | 1–5 Years | 6–10 Years | 11–15 Years | ≥16 Years | Total |
|---|---|---|---|---|---|
| Top management | 1 | 1 | 2 | 2 | 2 |
| Liberal professions | 2 | 3 | 3 | 3 | 3 |
| Self-employed | 2 | 4 | 6 | 6 | 5 |
| Unskilled worker | 10 | 7 | 8 | 11 | 9 |
| Skilled worker | 14 | 23 | 22 | 19 | 20 |
| White-collar worker without leadership responsibilities | 17 | 21 | 26 | 22 | 22 |
| White-collar worker with leadership responsibilities | 6 | 13 | 17 | 20 | 15 |
| Unemployed or not in the labour force | 5 | 6 | 5 | 5 | 5 |
| Pension or early retirement | 5 | 5 | 4 | 5 | 5 |
| In education | 30 | 9 | 3 | 2 | 8 |
| Other | 8 | 6 | 5 | 5 | 6 |
| Total | 100 | 100 | 100 | 100 | 100 |

*Source*: SFI.

After 11–15 years, there is no further increase in the numbers of those working in top management, the liberal professions or as self-employed. Table 6.7 also reflects presumed cohort and age differences as regards education. The proportion of those working as unskilled labour is greatest among those who have just left the military and among those who left the military longer ago. The proportion working as skilled workers and office workers rises with the length of time since they were in service. Finally, we find no association between the length of time since leaving the military and the share of either the unemployed or those on disability pension (see Humensky, Jordan, Stroupe, & Hynes, 2013; Rutledge, Sanzenbacher, & Crawford, 2016; Schulker, 2017, for US veterans' experiences in entering the civil labour market).

## Experiences during a Mission

The purpose of this section is to describe missions using two different approaches. Both approaches are based on the survey data, providing the opportunity to include several topics that cannot be described or analysed from registry data in Statistics Denmark or by the military registers.

The first approach describes missions in terms of several objective factors – the number of missions a veteran has been deployed on over a certain period and the characteristics of the missions, including whether it was an individual or a team deployment. There is also information about the type of mission (PK or PE), the destination country and the duration of the mission. We also consider the circumstances in which veterans have been outside of the camp compared to those when his/her duties were primarily inside the camp. Finally, we investigate whether there is a tradition of deployment in the veteran's family.

The second approach focuses on subjective experiences during missions, where a central part of the questionnaire consists of 14 statements about the characteristics of the missions broken down into equal numbers of enriching or positive statements and challenging or negative statements. The respondents rated these on a scale from 1 (disagree) to 10 (agree).

### *The Missions – Objective Factors*

The 3,198 veterans who answered the questionnaire are again divided into those who have been deployed only once and those with more than one deployment. For the latter, it is the most recent deployment that is described here. In all, 75% of the responses concern deployments to the former Yugoslavia, 10% to Iraq and 12% to Afghanistan. This distribution reflects the fact that the study is aimed at those who have been deployed since 1992. The division according to the number of years since deployment – either one or the latest – is shown in Table 6.8. It appears that, on average, the latest mission is more recent for soldiers deployed more than once, whereas for those deployed only once, the mission for more than half of the veterans was more than 10 years prior to the survey.

Table 6.8. Veterans Deployed Once or More Than Once by Number of Years Since Deployment (%).

| | **Once** | **Several Times** |
|---|---|---|
| No. of Years since Deployment | | |
| 1–2 | 9 | 25 |
| 3–5 | 17 | 22 |
| 6–9 | 17 | 17 |
| 10–14 | 23 | 18 |
| 15–19 | 33 | 15 |
| ≥20 | 1 | 2 |
| Total | 100 | 100 |

*Source*: SFI.

Among the veterans still employed in the military, 55% have been in Afghanistan, 26% in Iraq and 15% in the former Yugoslavia. Most of the veterans still in service were thus last on peace-enforcing missions, whereas more of the veterans who are no longer in service were on PK missions in the former Yugoslavia.

The veterans are divided by year of deployment as shown in Figure 6.7. It is evident that a considerable share of the veterans deployed only once were on missions in the 1990s, primarily to the former Yugoslavia. A strong increase after 2005 occurs as a result of Parliament's decision to increase involvement in Afghanistan.

For some of the soldiers, called 'mission bums', taking part in a large number of international missions can become a lifestyle. It is possible from the questionnaire to investigate the occurrence of very frequent deployments. We find that 8% of veterans have been deployed five to nine times, and 1% have been deployed more than 10 times. Thus, 4–5% of the many-time deployed veterans can be characterised as 'mission bums', that is, 2–2.5% at most of all veterans in the study. Brænder (2016) suggests a possible explanation to this phenomenon. In fact, soldiers become 'adrenalin junkies', as their tolerance towards excitement is 'pushed upward' by being exposed to danger. His study is based on an interview survey of two companies of Danish soldiers deployed to Helmand in Afghanistan in 2011. The study also finds that 'excitement motivation' is higher for young men exposed to combat.

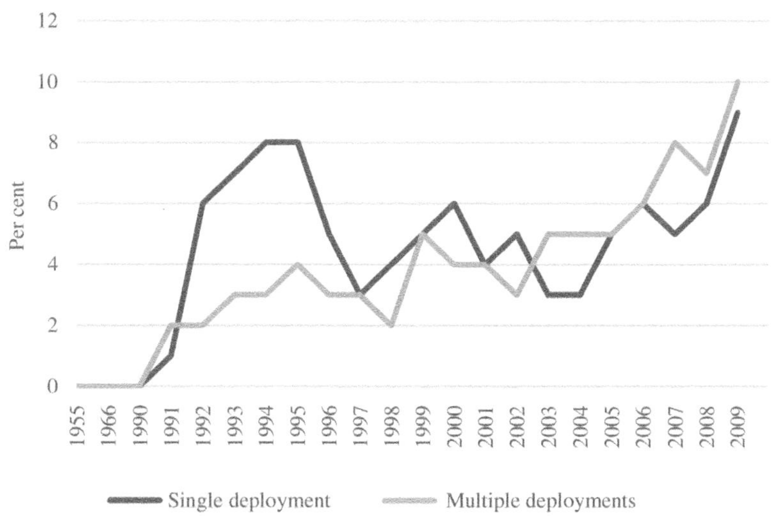


Figure 6.7. Veterans Sent on Single or Multiple Deployments by Year of Deployment. *Source*: SFI. *Notes*: Total of 1,573 observations, 15 non-responses for single deployments, 1,603 observations and seven non-responses for multiple deployments.

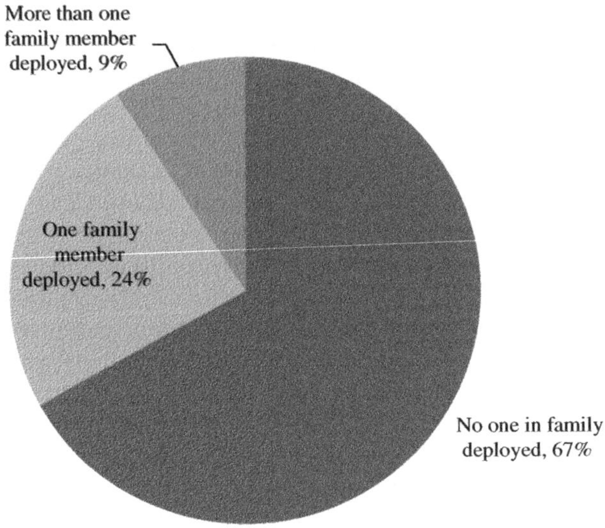


Figure 6.8. Veterans Categorised by Per cent of Family Members Deployed Previously. *Source*: SFI. *Note*: Total of 3,189 observations and nine non-responses.

### *Is There a Family Tradition of Being Deployed?*

There is a hypothesis that there is a greater share of veterans who have had one or more family members deployed compared with the general population. The veterans are categorised using this criterion in Figure 6.8.

We find some evidence for family tradition, as 33% of veterans have had one or more family members who have been deployed. There is only a small difference in the number of veterans who have deployed family members when divided up by personnel group and single or multiple deployments.

### *Duties during Deployment*

Apart from categorising the veterans according to the number of missions and their service status, one can divide them up according to whether the deployment was as part of a team or as an individual. Another division is based on whether the veterans had leadership responsibilities or not. For both these criteria, veterans deployed several times and those with a longer seniority in military were to a greater extent sent on individual deployments and had leadership duties during their deployments.

Table 6.9 presents an overview of how the veterans deployed only once are categorised in a number of work areas.

A third of veterans were in combat troops, and the rest were spread over a number of other work areas. One would expect that the duties of a combat trooper were related to a greater risk of challenging experiences. However, this

Table 6.9. Veterans with Single Deployments by Type of Work.

| | Per cent | Total Number |
|---|---|---|
| Administration | 7 | 110 |
| Logistics | 17 | 272 |
| Operations | 15 | 243 |
| Sanitation | 7 | 111 |
| Manoeuvres | 3 | 52 |
| Military police | 2 | 25 |
| Combat troops | 34 | 544 |
| Other | 15 | 231 |
| Total | 100 | 1,588 |

*Source*: SFI.

hypothesis does not exclude deployed soldiers with other duties also having such experiences, although combat troops are better trained and geared to deal with such experiences. Most combat soldiers are privates. The sergeant group is divided more evenly between the work areas, but there is a greater representation of officers in Operations and Logistics. The many-time deployed could choose more than one work area in the questionnaire: Combat troops, followed by Logistics and Operations, are the most frequently named.

The veterans were also asked how often their duties carried them outside the camp. Among the one-time deployed, 84% said they left the camp every day or several times a week. As expected, 75% of combat troops left the camp every day. In the group of privates, 66% left the camp every day.

### *Combat Conditions*

On a PK mission, the sense of powerlessness in a specific situation can cause psychological problems which may be harder to uncover than reactions to combat situations in peace-enforcing missions. Combat situations are defined as an exchange of fighting between two sides and not, for example, a rocket attack on a camp. All deployed veterans were asked whether they had been in combat situations as defined above, which was the case for 48% of them. There is a very great difference between destination countries and missions. Among those deployed only once, 65% of the combat troops in the former Yugoslavia had never been in a combat situation, whereas this finding applied to only 4% in Afghanistan. Combat situations can result in physical as well as psychological damage but, conversely, one could imagine that hard-trained combat soldiers who do not go into combat, risk frustration and boredom during a deployment. We discuss this point and other considerations in the next section.

### Missions – Subjective Factors

Based on a review of the literature and on questions asked by the Institute of Military Psychology (Institute for Militaer Psykologi, IMP), we formulated 14 statements which the veterans in the survey rated on a scale from 1 (disagree) to 10 (fully agree). Half of these statements were enriching or positive and the other half were challenging/stressful or negative. Only one-time deployed veterans were asked to indicate their agreement with these statements, as it might be problematic for many-time deployed to compare missions. These questions gave us the chance to differentiate between types of missions and different groups of veterans. In the latter, there was the opportunity to differentiate those still in service and those no longer employed by the Military, as well as different personnel groups and the destination countries of the missions.

## Subjective Experiences of One-time Deployment – Enriching or Challenging

As earlier mentioned, only the one-time deployed were asked to rate the 14 different statements about possible characteristics of a mission they had participated in. One-time deployed are characterised by the fact that a large share of them were on a team deployment to the former Yugoslavia, were privates and were in many cases no longer employed by the military. In addition, 6% of the one-time deployed were repatriated during the mission, and 9% were women. This share of women is almost double that among all veterans, where they represent 5%.

Enriching experiences during deployment were concretised by seven of the statements dealing, among other things, with how much the veterans had experienced a good comradeship with the others, had gained greater self-confidence and had had experiences that could be used in civilian life. In a similar fashion, difficulties or challenges were concretised by seven statements dealing, among other things with how lonely the veterans felt on the mission, if they missed their families, and if they feared for their lives and health. All 14 statements are presented in Table 6.10. We found predominately that the veterans generally agree with the statements about enrichment and were generally in disagreement with the statements about the difficulties/challenges. In other words, overall the veterans were positive in their subjective evaluation of participation in a mission.

### Enriching, Positive Statements

In this section, we focus on the seven statements concerning the enriching experiences of having participated in a mission. In Table 6.11, we show for these seven statements the average evaluation and the distribution of answers for different quartiles. In the table, the statements are listed from the highest to the lowest scoring statements.

Table 6.10. Statements about Experiences of the One-time Deployed during the Mission.

| No. | Statements about Experiences during the Mission |
|---|---|
| 1 | You received a good military training |
| 2 | You experienced good comradeship |
| 3 | You had experiences that could be used in civilian life |
| 4 | You learned something about other countries and/or other people |
| 5 | You learned to deal with difficult situations |
| 6 | You have greater self-confidence |
| 7 | You think that it was a demanding time for your partner, family or parents |
| 8 | You missed your family, your children or your friends very much |
| 9 | You experienced poor leadership |
| 10 | You were bored a good deal of the time |
| 11 | You thought the level of risk was stressful |
| 12 | You feared for your life and health |
| 13 | You are proud to have done international service |
| 14 | You felt very lonely or alone |

*Source*: SFI.
*Note*: Statements 1–6 and 13 express enriching experiences during the mission, and statements 7–12 and 14 challenging experiences during the mission.

**Comradeship**

The experience of a good comradeship is the highest rated statement. Comradeship is typically valued very high in the military. Moreover, these results are also in line with those from the qualitative study of Chapter 5, which indicated that comradeship is very important for the soldiers' psychological state and effectiveness during deployment. Two personnel groups had a score that was marginally, but significantly, below average – the group of repatriated and the officer group. For officers, the fact that 33% of this group were sent on individual deployments could explain this result.

**Pride, Handling Difficult Situations and Confidence**

The veterans gave the second highest rating to the statement that they are proud to have done international service. This result supports the overall assessment that there is a predominance of positive experiences, and that the military has been able to convey to the soldiers that the work they are doing is important and a priority for the State. The ability to handle difficult situations is also deemed highly enriching, whereas the lowest rated statement was that the soldier

Table 6.11. One-time Deployed Veterans' Rating of Enriching Statements.

| No. | Statements 1–6 and 13 | Average Rating | First Quartile | Median | Third Quartile | Standard Deviation | N |
|---|---|---|---|---|---|---|---|
| 2 | You experienced good comradeship | 8.94 | 8 | 9 | 10 | 1.45 | 1,586 |
| 13 | You are proud to have done international service | 8.60 | 8 | 9 | 10 | 1.89 | 1,585 |
| 5 | You have learned to deal with difficult situations | 8.08 | 7 | 8 | 10 | 1.74 | 1,582 |
| 1 | You received a good military training | 7.98 | 7 | 8 | 9 | 1.88 | 1,568 |
| 3 | You had experiences that could be used in civilian life | 7.72 | 7 | 8 | 10 | 2.13 | 1,576 |
| 4 | You have learned something about other countries and/or other people | 7.71 | 7 | 8 | 10 | 2.09 | 1,588 |
| 6 | You have greater self-confidence | 7.32 | 6 | 8 | 9 | 2.17 | 1,584 |

*Source*: SFI.

had gained confidence. Veterans of Afghanistan generally express greater pride and to a higher degree an increase in confidence.

**Veterans in the Former Yugoslavia – Enriching Statements**

Veterans who were deployed in the former Yugoslavia after 2000 generally felt more enriched than those deployed before 2000. The missions to the Balkans changed character from the 1990s to the 2000s. In the 1990s, they were marked by more turmoil than in later years, while at the same time, the PK missions carried the risk of feeling powerless and being frustrated at not being able to intervene in certain situations. Veterans deployed during the 1990s indicate to a relatively greater extent that they have become better at dealing with difficult situations, whereas those deployed later feel that they have received better military training and experienced a better comradeship.

**Individual Deployment**

Only 146 people in the survey had been on an individual deployment. Generally, these soldiers rated the statements concerning enrichment lower than did those who had been on team deployments. An exception is the statement that one has learned about other countries and people – soldiers deployed individually rated this significantly higher than did the soldiers in team deployments. One obvious explanation for this is that this type of deployment often involves co-operation with the destination country and with soldiers from other countries.

**Veterans Still in Service and Those No Longer in the Military**

For a number of the statements, there are significant differences in the assessment of veterans in service and those no longer in service. In Table 6.12, an asterisk indicates a statistically significant difference between those in service and those no longer in service. Apart from the statement about having learned about other countries and people, the assessment is higher for those no longer in service. The largest difference for the other statements concerns the statement that the soldier was proud to have done international service. Veterans no longer in service also experienced comradeship as significantly more positive, possibly because they were more frequently deployed as a team and were mostly former privates.

Table 6.12. Average Assessment of Enrichment Statements by Veterans in Service and Those no Longer in Service.

| No. | Statement | In Service | No Longer in Service | *t*-Test |
|---|---|---|---|---|
| 1 | You received a good military training | 7.9 | 8 | |
| 2 | You experienced good comradeship | 8.8 | 9 | ** |
| 3 | You had experiences that could be used in civilian life | 7.5 | 7.8 | ** |
| 4 | You have learned something about other countries and/or other people | 8.1 | 7.6 | ** |
| 5 | You have learned to deal with difficult situations | 8 | 8.1 | |
| 6 | You have greater self-confidence | 7.3 | 7.3 | |
| 13 | You are proud to have done an international service | 8.3 | 8.7 | ** |

*Source*: SFI.

*Notes*: Total of 343 observations for veterans still in service and 1,241 for those no longer in service. Significance levels: $***p < 0.01$; $** p < 0.05$; $* p < 0.10$.

**Positive Experiences in Relation to Civilian Life**

Table 6.11 shows a large spread around the mean in the rating of this statement (large standard deviation), while Table 6.12 indicates that the average is significantly higher for those no longer in service, who have actually tested the statement in practice. Because of the considerable spread in the answer for this statement, it is important to look at which groups of veterans give this statement a high or low rating. We find that when looking at the personnel groups, the officers on average rate this statement significantly higher compared with the other groups. In relation to the destination countries, the veterans who have been deployed on peace-enforcing missions to Iraq and Afghanistan give this statement the highest rating. As expected, veterans in the age group 21–34 years, also give this statement a significantly higher rating compared with the 35- to 59-year-old veterans. When we look at the assessment in terms of the time that has elapsed since deployment, the differences are small, but the assessment is significantly higher for groups who completed their mission more than 20 years ago. Finally, the assessment was significantly lower among the veterans who were repatriated during deployment. Veterans with self-assessed physical injuries and psychological damage do not rate the statement significantly differently compared with the entire group of veterans. In those with permanent physical injuries, when we distinguish between those in service and those no longer in service, the former has an amazingly high average rating. As they are still employed by the military, and therefore presumably have limited experience of civilian life, it is difficult to determine the reason for this very high rating.

### *Challenging, Negative Statements*

We now look at the assessment of statements that contain challenging factors in relation to deployment. Table 6.13 shows the average values and the distribution of responses through different quartiles, In Table 6.13, the statements that veterans disagree with the most are placed at the top of the table. The table shows that the veterans generally did not feel that international missions were difficult. However, Table 6.13 also shows large spread around the mean – large standard deviation. We will examine which groups depart the most from the average statements.

**Families, Partners and Friends**

We find the greater consensus with respect to the statement that deployment was a demanding period for a partner and family, and at the same time, the veteran him/herself missed them. Similar findings emerged from the qualitative part of the study, reported in Chapter 5. If we look at the large group of veterans from the former Yugoslavia, we find that in general those who were deployed in the 1990s, during which there was a predominance of peace-keeping missions, reported that the deployments were more demanding for family and friends and that they also experienced the risk level as more stressful and they feared more for their lives and health.

Table 6.13. One-time Deployed Veterans' Rating of Stressful and Negative Statements Statements.

| No. | Statements 7–12 and 14 | Average Rating | First Quartile | Median | Third Quartile | Standard Deviation | *N* | |
|---|---|---|---|---|---|---|---|---|
| 14 | You felt very lonely or alone | 2.3 | 1 | 2 | 3 | 1.9 | 1,588 | Disagree |
| 12 | You feared for your life and health | 3.4 | 1 | 3 | 5 | 2.6 | 1,586 | |
| 10 | You were bored a good deal of the time | 3.8 | 1 | 3 | 6 | 2.6 | 1,585 | |
| 11 | You thought the level of risk was stressful | 3.8 | 2 | 3 | 5 | 2.5 | 1,584 | |
| 9 | You experienced poor leadership | 5.2 | 3 | 5 | 8 | 2.9 | 1,584 | Agree |
| 8 | You missed your family, your children or your friends very much | 6.3 | 5 | 7 | 8 | 2.4 | 1,581 | |
| 7 | You think that it was a demanding time for your partner, family or parents | 7.5 | 6 | 8 | 10 | 2.5 | 1,581 | |

*Source*: SFI.

**Individual Deployments**

Those sent out on individual deployments have a greater tendency to agree with the negative statements. In particular, these veterans felt lonely and bored for a large part of their deployment.

**Service Status**

Comparing those in service and no longer in service, a number of significant differences emerge. Veterans in service missed their family and friends, whereas those no longer in service were to a greater degree bored much of the time, thought that the risk level was stressful, and feared for their lives and health. However, it should be emphasised that we are looking here at the differences in valuation between two groups. Generally, there is only a modest agreement about the challenging, negative statements. The significant differences between the two groups probably reflect in some cases differences in age and family situation.

**Leadership during Deployment**

Table 6.13 shows a large spread around the mean for the statement of having experienced poor leadership during a mission, while the average consensus is relatively high. In Chapter 5 – the qualitative part of the study, we found that returning soldiers pointed to the important role that leadership played in the well-being of the deployed soldiers. From the survey, it is not possible to further identify elements in the leadership that veterans found less satisfactory. However, we can investigate how the assessment of leadership varies between different groups.

Among personnel groups, the officers agree significantly more with the statement of poor leadership. Broken down by gender, women are significantly more dissatisfied. Divided up by destination country, the veterans who were on peace-enforcing missions in Iraq and Afghanistan are in greatest agreement with the statement that they experienced poor leadership. In contrast, there are no significant differences between the assessment given by those in service and that no longer in service. Veterans aged 60 and over and those deployed for 10–14 years ago differ significantly in that they agreed less with the statement. Finally, veterans with self-assessed psychological damage agree significantly more that they experienced poor leadership.

**The Repatriated and Wounded**

To assess the consensus in the various enriching and stressful statements, we also examine the veterans who were sent home before the end of a mission (repatriated) and two groups of wounded, those wounded in combat and those with injuries occurring in other circumstances. Here, a clear picture emerges, where those wounded in combat to a predominant degree are in greater agreement concerning both the enriching and the challenging statements. Not surprisingly, the repatriated veterans generally felt lonelier and not surprisingly those who were wounded in battle felt greater fear for their lives and health.

**Veterans with Several Deployments**

As mentioned earlier, the questions about enriching and challenging/stressful statements concerning deployment were only asked to those deployed on single missions. The main reason for this choice being that veterans who had been deployed several times could have had difficulties in rating several different deployments. Instead, those deployed several times were asked to give an overall assessment of their deployments, again on a scale from 1 to 10, where 10 indicates the highest level of satisfaction. As veterans in this group chose to be deployed several times that itself may indicate some degree of satisfaction. However, it is still interesting that about 90% give the deployments a score of 5 or more, with an average of just less than 8.

**Recommend Deployment to Others?**

Both veterans with one and those with more than one deployment were asked whether they would recommend international military deployment to others. Based on the answers to the questionnaire, we do not know veterans' motives for recommending or discouraging others from being deployed. We find clear differences in this statement between the two groups of veterans. Among one-time deployed, nearly 70% would recommend a deployment to others, whereas this figure is barely 50% for many-time deployed. Only about 10% in both groups would not recommend others to seek deployment, whereas 40% of many-times deployed and 20% of those sent on single deployments are in doubt as to whether they would recommend others to go. Divided by personnel groups, the officers in both groups would most recommend seeking a deployment.

### *Summary*

This section has clarified some aspects of veterans' mission experiences that registry data could not cover. In all, 75% of one-time deployed soldiers' experience is from the former Yugoslavia, while many-time deployed soldiers' experience more frequently refers to the ISAF mission. In other words, many-time deployed soldiers refer to missions within the last five years, whereas missions that one-time deployed were sent on are spread more widely and go further back to the 1990s.

At most, 2% of all veterans fall into the category 'mission bums', that is, those having been sent on more than five missions within 15 years; this group represents 4.5% of the many times deployed. 'Mission bums' is an existing phenomenon, but far from a common pattern, among veterans.

Of the veterans, 33% have a family member who has been deployed, and therefore, we can, in some extent, talk about a family pattern within the military in Denmark.

## Wounded, Repatriated and Self-assessed Problems

In this section, we examine more closely groups of veterans that may encounter problems when they are returning home. These groups are the repatriated and the group of wounded in general. Finally, the section covers answers from the veterans who consider themselves to have sustained physical injury and/or psychological damage during deployment. In Chapter 8, we will further investigate these self-assessments and compare them with the health profile collected from registry data.

### *The Repatriated*

In all, 211 veterans in the survey were repatriated during a mission. The repatriated do not differ from the rest of the veterans, when they are divided up by age, gender and service status (in service, no longer in service). We only find a difference when we split them by number of deployments, with those deployed several times being repatriated more often. But as many-time deployed obviously run a higher risk of being exposed to an event or circumstance that results in being repatriated, this difference is not surprising. The reasons for the 211 repatriations are given in Figure 6.9, which shows that health problems and social reasons are the two dominant reasons, whereas being wounded is the reason behind barely 10% of the repatriations.

### *Wounded Soldiers*

Among the veterans taking part in the survey, 87 were wounded in combat and 300 hurt or damaged for reasons other than fighting, while 23 soldiers sustained both types of damage. The risk of being wounded in battle is clearly higher for 21- to 34-year-olds, for those still in service and for the many-time deployed. In other words, the risk was highest for the most recent, peace-enforcing missions to Iraq and Afghanistan. The wounded and repatriated are the groups at highest

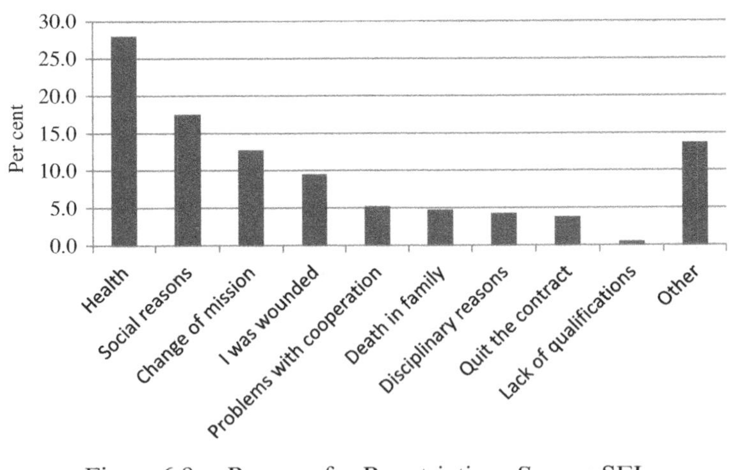


Figure 6.9. Reasons for Repatriation. *Source*: SFI.

risk of having problems after returning home. In the following, we examine the veterans' self-assessment of physical and psychological damage.

### *Self-assessed Psychological and Physical Problems*

In all, 6% of the veterans stated that they had severe psychological or physical problems and 16% that they had less severe problems; in other words, 22% consider that they have psychological or physical damage to a greater or lesser extent. Interestingly, 64% of those considering that their problems were caused by deployment were neither repatriated nor injured. We find no differences in the level of self-assessed damage between women and men, or between those still in service and those no longer in service. However, the share of self-assessed damage is significantly higher in the youngest group, among one-time deployed, and especially among those who experienced combat. Although the share who consider that they have problems caused by deployment is the same among those who are still in service and those no longer in service, in the group of those no longer in service who consider that they incurred severe psychological problems, no less than 27% are unemployed in the civilian job market or are outside the labour market, compared with the average of 3% in the group of the veterans who left the military.

Table 6.14 shows that in relation to the prevalence of self-assessed psychological problems, combat exposure may have a stronger impact, the younger the soldier is. Among the 596 veterans in the questionnaire survey who experienced combat, more than 75% assessed themselves as having no problems. At the same time, we observe an age-dependent relationship among those who report having psychological problems, especially more severe ones. As a comparison, for one-time and many-time deployed together, these percentages are 4% and 13% for more and less severe problems, respectively.

Table 6.14. One-time Deployed Who Experienced Combat, by Self-assessed Psychological Problems and Age at Deployment.

| Age at Deployment | Self-assessed Psychological Problems | | | Number of People (*N*) |
|---|---|---|---|---|
| | More Severe Problems | Less Severe Problems | No Problems | |
| Younger than 20 | 9 | 15 | 76 | 54 |
| 20–24 Years | 7 | 17 | 76 | 356 |
| 25–29 Years | 3 | 14 | 83 | 86 |
| 30–39 Years | 5 | 12 | 83 | 59 |
| ≥40 Years | 2 | 12 | 85 | 41 |
| Total | 6 | 15 | 79 | 596 |

*Source*: SFI.

When we examine the prevalence of self-assessed psychological problems by personnel group and military employment status (service, no longer in service), we find small differences, with an over-representation of privates who experience psychological problems. When we split up the veterans by whether they have been repatriated during a mission and whether they have been injured, it turns out – not surprisingly – that self-assessed problems are the most common in the group wounded in combat. A third of the veterans repatriated during the mission and wounded in actions other than combat self-assess some degree of psychological problems.

Throughout the relatively long period covered by the study, the focus on the possible psychological effects of a deployment has increased. A possible consequence of this change in attitude is that the further back in time a deployment, the greater the risk of undiagnosed and untreated psychological problems. Table 6.15 clearly shows that the share of self-assessed more severe psychological damage is considerably higher in the group deployed the furthest back in time, i.e., the first deployments to the former Yugoslavia. Self-assessed physical problems show the opposite correlation with the number of years since deployment, that is, the highest incidence being for the most recent deployment.

We now examine the relationship between self-assessed problems and the missions that veterans have participated in. Table 6.16 presents the results for the one-time deployed. Overall, the frequency of self-assessed problems is greatest among veterans who were deployed on peace-enforcing missions in Iraq and Afghanistan. However, among veterans of the Balkan missions, a relatively high share of veterans consider that they sustained psychological damage, whereas the share of physical problems is low.

Table 6.17 presents similar figures for many-time deployed divided by type of mission, for their latest mission. Overall, veterans of Afghanistan in

Table 6.15. The Share of Veterans with Self-assessed Problems by Number of Years Since Last Deployment (%).

| Years Before Last Deployment | Self-assessed Psychological Problems | | Self-assessed Physical Problems | |
|---|---|---|---|---|
| | More Severe Problems | Less Severe Problems | More Severe Problems | Less Severe Problems |
| 1–5 Years | 2 | 14 | 3 | 8 |
| 6–10 Years | 3 | 10 | 2 | 3 |
| 11–15 Years | 4 | 12 | 1 | 4 |
| ≥16 Years | 7 | 13 | 2 | 4 |
| Total | 4 | 13 | 2 | 5 |

*Source*: SFI.
*Note*: Total of 45 non-responses.

Table 6.16. One-time Deployed with Self-assessed Problems Divided by Missions (%).

| | Self-assessed Psychological Problems | | Self-assessed Physical Problems | |
|---|---|---|---|---|
| | **More Severe Problems** | **Less Severe Problems** | **More Severe Problems** | **Less Severe Problems** |
| UNPROFOR | 5 | 10 | 0 | 2 |
| IFOR | 0 | 14 | 0 | 2 |
| SFOR | 1 | 7 | 1 | 1 |
| KFOR | 1 | 8 | 0 | 3 |
| ISAF | 3 | 18 | 3 | 10 |
| Iraq | 2 | 15 | 1 | 7 |
| Other missions | 4 | 11 | 3 | 4 |
| Total | 3 | 11 | 1 | 4 |

*Source*: SFI.
*Notes*: Total of 325 observations with no mission name. There are only 56 observations for the IFOR mission.

Table 6.17. Many-time Deployed with Self-assessed Problems by Type of Mission, Based on the Most Recent Mission (%).

| | Self-assessed Psychological Problems | | Self-assessed Physical Problems | |
|---|---|---|---|---|
| | **More Severe Problems** | **Less Severe Problems** | **More Severe Problems** | **Less Severe Problems** |
| UNPROFOR | 4 | 16 | 2 | 2 |
| IFOR | 5 | 7 | 0 | 0 |
| SFOR | 3 | 13 | 2 | 3 |
| KFOR | 5 | 12 | 4 | 7 |
| ISAF | 4 | 20 | 4 | 12 |
| Iraq | 6 | 14 | 2 | 3 |
| Other missions | 4 | 15 | 4 | 5 |
| Total | 5 | 16 | 3 | 6 |

*Source*: SFI.
*Notes*: Total of 328 non-responses. There are only 42 observations for the IFOR mission.

particular state that they have numerous, mostly minor, psychological and physical problems. Like those deployed only once, there is a relatively high share of psychological problems among the veterans of early missions to the former Yugoslavia.

Taken together, the questionnaire survey shows that the risk of experiencing self-assessed psychological problems is greater if the veteran:

- has been deployed several times;
- has experienced combat situations;
- is no longer in service;
- was among the younger age groups at the time of deployment (for one-time deployed);
- was wounded or repatriated during the mission; and
- was deployed more than 15 years ago.

### *Summary*

More than 7% of the respondent veterans have been repatriated. Almost 3% of the respondent veterans were wounded in combat, and 9% injured for other reasons than combat. These veteran groups overlap, and all in all, 16% of them have either experienced a repatriation or have been injured (either in combat or not). A large share of the repatriated and wounded has been deployed more than once and the majority is no longer employed in the military.

When self-assessing the consequences of a deployment on their mental and physical health, 4% reported severe problems and 13% less severe ones. About physical injuries, 2% reported severe problems, and 5% reported less severe problems. All in all, about 21% report both physical and mental problems.

The most affected groups are veterans who have been deployed to the former Yugoslavia at the beginning of the period. As most of these veterans are no longer employed in the military, they may become 'invisible' for the system and specific attention to this group is probably needed. Another group of interest is the veterans recently deployed to missions to Iraq and Afghanistan – some of them also reported mental and physical problems.

## Social Relationships and Health

In this section, we focus on the social network after homecoming. Because of their deployments, veterans have to live for one or more periods far from their home social networks. It is therefore relevant to examine how the return from a deployment works in terms of relationships with family, friends and acquaintances. In addition, we look at the veterans' use of the support provided by the military. Finally, we use the questionnaire to examine how the veterans assess their own health. Some of the challenges discussed here are also covered in the qualitative interviews in Chapter 5.

### *Veterans and the General Population*

We chose two specific questions to assess the importance of social contacts. First, we ask how often veterans are alone even when they would prefer to be with others, thus a situation where one is not alone by choice. Second, we ask whether they never, or almost never, have anyone to talk to if they have problems. This section compares responses from male veterans with answers from the rest of the male population (SST, 2011). Table 6.18 shows the share of veterans of different age groups who are often lonely. This share among the veterans is constant until they are in their mid-50s, and then it falls by about 50%. Moreover, this share among veterans is significantly lower than that for the general male population, regardless of age.

Table 6.19 shows another measure of the social relationships for male veterans compared with the male population as a whole. Table 6.19 shows the share who never, or almost never, have someone to talk to if they have problems or need for support. Again, veterans obviously differ in comparison with the rest of the male population, for whom the share clearly increases with age. For veterans, the share at all ages is partly slightly below that for the general male population, partly increasing until 45–54 years and then declining. Unfortunately, we cannot deduce from these figures whether the group who replied in the affirmative is mainly formed by veterans from the former Yugoslavia.

### *Social Relationships – Different Groups of Veterans*

In the following, we split the answers of the veterans according to different categories. We find a larger share of those no longer in service than those in service who are not alone by choice and who are often lonely. This result applies to

Table 6.18. Male Veterans and Men in the General Population Who Often Are Alone Not by Choice.

| | **Veterans – Male, %** | **General Population – Male, %** | **Veterans, *N*** | **General Population, *N*** |
|---|---|---|---|---|
| Age | | | | |
| 25–34 Years | 2.6 | 5.1 | 897 | 7,833 |
| 35–44 Years | 2.6 | 4.4 | 1,251 | 12,898 |
| 45–54 Years | 2.6 | 5.3 | 418 | 14,997 |
| 55–64 Years | 1.0 | 4.2 | 198 | 16,887 |
| 65–74 Years | 1.3 | 4.0 | 77 | 12,722 |

*Source*: SFI. Figures for the general population come from Board of Health (2011).
*Notes*: Data for veterans and the general population were gathered using various methods. There are no observations for 75+-year-olds because of the small number of veterans in that age group.

Table 6.19. Share of Male Veterans and of Men in the General Population Indicating That They Never or Almost Never Have Someone to Talk to If They Need to.

| Age | Veterans, % | General Population, % | Veterans, *N* | General Population, *N* |
|---|---|---|---|---|
| 25–34 Years | 1.3 | 3.6 | 898 | 7,836 |
| 35–44 Years | 1.9 | 4.7 | 1,252 | 12,896 |
| 45–54 Years | 3.3 | 6.6 | 419 | 14,986 |
| 55–64 Years | 2.0 | 6.3 | 198 | 16,862 |
| 65–74 Years | 2.6 | 8 | 77 | 12,695 |

*Source*: SFI. Figures for the general population come from Danish Health Authority (2011).
*Notes*: Data for veterans and the general population were gathered using different methods. There are no observations for 75+-year-olds because there were too few of these among the veterans.

both male and female veterans, but the share of women in this category is greater.

Those in service and those no longer in service can also be divided up according to a number of other criteria, including the experiences and knowledge gained during the missions. We find a larger share of feeling often lonely among veterans who were repatriated, those wounded in battle and those who have self-assessed psychological damage.

We make similar breakdowns in relation to the question of whether one never or almost never has anyone to talk with about problems. Again, a larger share of these are no longer in service. However, when we consider age, we only find a larger share for the middle-age group of 35–59 years. By gender, the percentage is slightly higher among men regardless of service status. The share is significantly higher among repatriated no longer in service, those wounded in battle and those who have self-assessed psychological damage.

For both questions, the share who may have problems is highest among the veterans who are no longer employed by the military, thus involving a risk that any future problems may not be dealt with satisfactorily as these are more 'invisible' for the system.

### *Morbidity – Veterans and the General Population*

This section examines the answers about veterans' morbidity in the last 14 days up to the time of the interview. Specifically, it addresses the question of pain and discomfort. The questions are based on a survey conducted by the Danish Health Authority in 2011 (Sundhedsstyrelsen, 2011), which makes it possible to compare the responses of male veterans with the responses of the rest of the male population. Table 6.20

Table 6.20. Male Veterans and Men in General Who Say They Have Been Very Troubled by Pain/Discomfort Within the Last 14 Days.

| | **Veterans, %** | **General Population, %** | **Veterans, *N*** | **General Population, *N*** |
|---|---|---|---|---|
| Age | | | | |
| 25–34 Years | 27.1 | 26.2 | 898 | 7,867 |
| 35–44 Years | 28.6 | 28.2 | 1,250 | 12,971 |
| 45–54 Years | 24.6 | 32.6 | 419 | 15,097 |
| 55–64 Years | 17.7 | 32.7 | 198 | 17,030 |
| 65–74 Years | 19.5 | 29.5 | 77 | 12,927 |

*Source*: SFI.
*Note*: The Table lists pain/discomfort in connection with pain in shoulder/neck, back/loins, arm/hand/leg, etc.

shows the share of them who are very troubled by pain and/or discomfort according to age. The share of men up to their mid-40s is similar among veterans and men in general. For men 45 years and older, the share is significantly greater among men in general than for veterans, in whom the share decreases with age.

### *Morbidity – Groups of Veterans*

When we look at veterans categorised by different criteria: our measure of morbidity, as previously defined, is significantly higher among those no longer in service. By age, the share is pretty much the same until a drop occurs for veterans over 60 years old. By gender, bearing in mind that the number of female veterans is low, no less than 45% of the female veterans no longer in service have been very troubled by pain/discomfort in the past 14 days.

The trend towards a higher share among those no longer in service is again found when they are viewed in terms of what they have experienced during the mission. For example, the most significant difference is for those wounded in battle.

### *Use of Support Services*

The veterans are increasingly met with offers from a number of support services, provided both by the military and by outside organisations. The veterans were asked in the survey whether they had used any of these support services. The result is shown in Figure 6.10 divided up into each support service for all veterans and for the four subgroups (repatriated during a mission, wounded in combat or in other circumstances, veterans with self-assessed psychological damage). Among veterans wounded in combat, just over 60% have had contact with Military psychologists and just over 30% have been in contact with the Office of Industrial Injury and

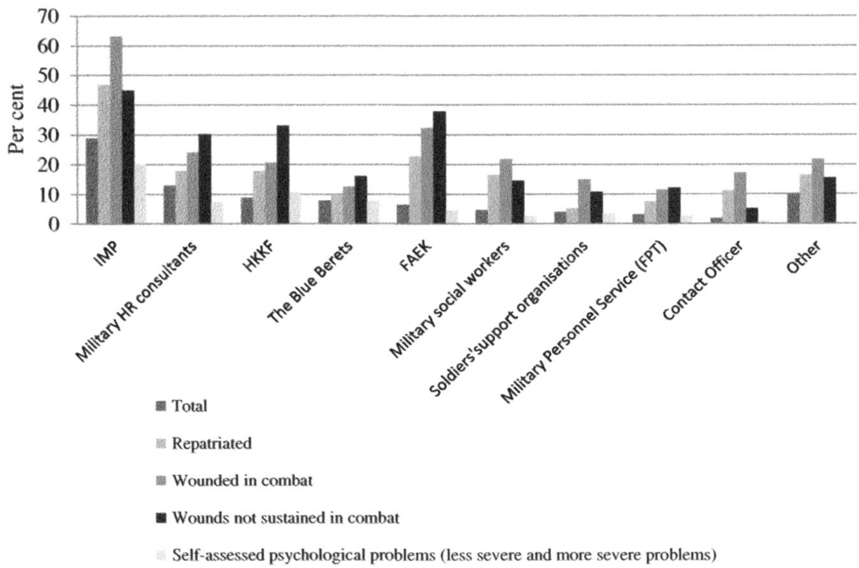


Figure 6.10. Share of Veterans Who Have Dealt with Various Support Services, Categorised as Repatriated and Wounded, and Those with Self-assessed Damage. *Source*: SFI. *Notes*: Total of 3,198 observations, 211 repatriated. Wounded in combat, $N$ = 87. Wounds not sustained in combat, $N$ = 300. Self-assessed damage, $N$ = 526.

Compensation for the Military (*Forsvarets Arbejdsskade og Erstatningskontor* (FAEK)). A smaller number have used one or more of the other support organisations, especially Military HR consultants (*Udstikkerne*) and the Military Privates and Corporals Union (*Haerens Konstabel og Korporalforbund* (HKKF)).

Slightly less than half of the veterans have not been in contact with any of the support services listed in Figure 6.10. Contact with most of the support services, not surprisingly, decreases with time since the last deployment. The only exception is the veteran organisation The Blue Berets, established back in 1968. In general, veterans who have used these support services are satisfied. However, veterans are less satisfied with FAEK, which is probably related to the fact that one does not always get the desired compensation.

### *Summary*

This section has discussed veterans' social relationships, morbidity and support organisations. We find that fewer veterans than men in the general population are alone by choice. This result is strengthened by the fact that more veterans have someone to talk to. However, the social relationships are weaker among those repatriated, wounded or with self-assessed psychological problems. In the younger age group, the prevalence of health problems is similar in veterans and the general population. One could have expected that this level would have been lower among veterans because of the military physical health requirements, but this was in fact not the case. Use of the military support systems is generally higher among those in service, repatriated or wounded, as well as veterans with self-assessed psychological problems. One veteran out of two have not used any of the support systems on offer.

## Veterans' Smoking Habits and Drug and Alcohol Consumption

Generally, there is no agreement in the literature concerning the effect of deployment on smoking habits, alcohol consumption and drug use. Thomsen et al. (2010) analysed the consumption of alcohol and cannabis among the soldiers in a particular team, Team 7, sent to Afghanistan in 2009. (for the US and alcohol use, see the study by Jacobson et al., 2008; and Teachman, Anderson, & Tedrow, 2015). The authors of that study found a stable alcohol consumption before and after deployment, with about 5% of the soldiers with an alcohol consumption above the high-risk limit established by the Danish Health Authority (*Sundhedsstyrelsen*). They also find that the share who smokes cannabis rose from 4% before to 6.6% after deployment. The data presented in this chapter provide the opportunity to describe the consumption of a much larger group. However, we cannot provide any information on consumption before deployment. In principle, during a deployment, there is a zero-tolerance policy regarding the use of drugs and alcohol.

In this part of the study, we use the questions from a population study made by the Danish Health Authority (2011). Using the same questions provides us with an ideal opportunity to compare the veterans' response with the population in general. Just as for the Danish Health Authority (2011)'s study, veteran consumption is self-reported and therefore there is a risk of bias due to intentional or unintentional under-reporting. Based on available studies in this area, we find no consensus as to how alcohol consumption is affected by a deployment. In the following, we first look at the results for alcohol from the present questionnaire study.

### *Alcohol Consumption – Veterans and the Rest of the Population*

As the vast majority of veterans are men, we here focus on male veterans and their alcohol consumption compared with the male population in general. Alcohol consumption is assessed in terms of the risk limits set by the Danish Health Authority. For men the high-risk limit is 21 units a week, while seven units is considered as the low-risk limit. Table 6.21 shows the share, by age, of male veterans and the male population in general, which exceeds these two limits. We find that in general, alcohol consumption by veterans is considerably below that of the population as whole. In relation to the percentage above the high-risk threshold, while the low share among

Table 6.21. Share of Male Veterans and Men in the General Population Who Admit Exceeding the Danish Health Authority's Recommended Low and High Alcohol Limits.

| Age | Over Low-risk Limit | | Over High-risk Limit | | Total Number of Men | |
|---|---|---|---|---|---|---|
| | Veterans | General Population | Veterans | General Population | Veterans | General Population |
| 25–34 Years | 12 | 21 | 3 | 10 | 878 | 7,742 |
| 35–44 Years | 8 | 15 | 3 | 7 | 1,223 | 12,773 |
| 45–54 Years | 12 | 23 | 3 | 13 | 403 | 14,818 |
| 55–64 Years | 12 | 29 | 3 | 16 | 197 | 16,600 |
| 65–74 Years | 24 | 29 | 4 | 16 | 75 | 12,359 |

*Source*: SFI. Figures for the general population are from the Danish Health Authority (2011).
*Notes*: Data for veterans and the population in general are from two different studies using different data collection methods. There are no data for 75+-year-olds because of the low number of observations for veterans.

veterans is constant by age, it increases with age for the general population. However, we cannot conclude whether these findings reveal a regular habit because of deployment, or whether men with relatively low alcohol consumption are more likely to join the military and be deployed.

We also compared the veterans with the general population, looking at the prevalence of heavy consumption of alcohol over a short period of time, 'binge-drinking'. We define 'binge-drinking' as the consumption of more than five drinks on the same occasion. We have figures for the incidence of this kind of binge-drinking at least once a month. Table 6.22 shows a completely different picture from Table 6.21. Recreational drinking of this type is clearly more common among veterans. For veterans, the alcohol consumption is lower but more concentrated than for the male population in general.

### *Alcohol Consumption – Groups of Veterans*

When we examine the veterans in terms of age, gender, employment status in the military and number of deployments, we find no significant differences in the share exceeding the Danish Health Authority's upper limits. Concerning 'binge-drinking', the tendency clearly falls with age and is considerably less for women than for men.

When we look at alcohol consumption for different groups of veterans, for example wounded, repatriated or exposed to combat, we find very small differences both in the share that consume more than the high-risk limit and the share who drink heavily recreationally at least once a month. Only two groups are relatively high up in relation to the high-risk limit – veterans still in

Table 6.22. Male Veterans and Men in General Who Drink More Than Five Drinks on the Same Occasion at Least once a Month.

| Age | More than Five Drinks on the Same Occasion – at Least Monthly | | Total Number of Men | |
|---|---|---|---|---|
| | Veterans | General Population | Veterans | General Population |
| 25–34 Years | 58 | 51 | 878 | 7,821 |
| 35–44 Years | 44 | 37 | 1,223 | 12,883 |
| 45–54 Years | 43 | 38 | 403 | 14,954 |
| 55–64 Years | 31 | 32 | 197 | 16,818 |
| 65–74 Years | 27 | 21 | 75 | 12,653 |

*Source*: SFI. Figures for the general population are from the Danish Health Authority (2011).

service, but who were not considered eligible for deployment and veterans no longer in service with self-assessed psychological problems.

### *Smoking – Veterans and the Rest of the Population*

As for alcohol consumption, there is no consensus in the literature regarding whether participation in a mission has any effect on soldiers' smoking habits. Based on the survey, we can determine the levels of smoking at the time of the interview, but we lack data on smoking habits before compared with after the mission. Table 6.23 compares the share of the daily smoker between veterans and the general male population. We only find a notable difference for the 25- to 34-year-olds, with a significantly larger share of veterans than of men in the general population who are daily smokers. This group also corresponds with those with the most recent deployment.

### *Smoking – Groups of Veterans*

When we split up the veterans by age, gender, employment status in the military and the number of deployments, we find no significant differences in the share of daily smokers. When breaking down by specific groups of soldiers such as repatriated wounded or exposed to combat for example, we find some variations in the share of daily smokers, but none of the differences is significant.

### *Cannabis and Other Illicit Drugs – Veterans and the Rest of the Population*

As previously mentioned, Thomsen et al. (2010) examined cannabis consumption among soldiers before and after a mission using data that cover only a single team deployed to Afghanistan. Here, we have the opportunity

Table 6.23. Share by Age of Male Veterans and Men in General Who Are Daily Smokers.

| Age | Daily Smokers | | Total Number of Men | |
|---|---|---|---|---|
| | **Veterans – Male (%)** | **General Male Population (%)** | **Veterans – Male** | **General Male Population** |
| 25–34 Years | 29 | 20 | 878 | 7,770 |
| 35–44 Years | 26 | 23 | 1,223 | 12,829 |
| 45–54 Years | 26 | 27 | 403 | 14,917 |
| 55–64 Years | 23 | 27 | 197 | 16,812 |
| 65–74 Years | 21 | 22 | 75 | 12,728 |

*Source*: SFI. Figures for the general population from Danish Health Authority (2011).
*Notes*: Data for veterans and the general population come from two different studies using different data collection methods. There are no observations for 75+-year-olds because there were too few observations in this group among veterans.

Table 6.24. Per cent of Male Veterans and of Men in General Consuming Cannabis Within the Last Year, by Age (%).

| **Used Cannabis within the Last Year** | | |
|---|---|---|
| **Age** | **Veterans – Male** | **General Population – Male** |
| 25–29 Years | 9 | 14 |
| 30–34 Years | 8 | 10 |
| 35–39 Years | 4 | 6 |
| 40–44 Years | 2 | 4 |

*Source*: SFI. For the general population Danish Health Authority (2010): Narcotics Situation in Denmark 2010 (*Narkosituation i Danmark 2010*), Centre for Prevention.

to compare consumption among a much larger number of veterans with consumption in the rest of the male population. However, we cannot observe the change in the consumption of cannabis from before to after a deployment. As shown in Table 6.24, the share of veterans who have used cannabis within the past year is significantly lower among veterans than among the population as a whole. For both groups, we find that the share who consumed cannabis within the past year falls sharply with age, the cut-off here being 44 years.

### *Cannabis and Other Illicit Drugs – Groups of Veterans*

For the group of veterans as a separate group, we have the opportunity to look at the following:

- the share who have ever smoked cannabis;
- the share who have smoked cannabis in the last year; and
- the share who have used other illicit drugs than cannabis.

At some point in their lives, 56% of the veterans smoked cannabis but only 5.1% report having done so in the past year. Regarding illicit drugs other than cannabis, 18.7% of veterans had tried them at some point in their lives, but only 2% in the past year. We also found that the share of those consuming cannabis or other illicit drugs declines sharply with age, is higher among men than among women and is higher among those no longer employed by the military than among those employed by the military (who are mostly older). However, we found no differences in relation to the number of deployments.

We also found only small differences when we split the veterans up according to the various groups (repatriated, wounded, etc.). For example, the highest share consuming cannabis within the last year is among veterans with self-assessed psychological damage (8.7%), and the highest share of consumption of other illicit drugs within the last year is among those wounded in combat (5.7%).

### *Summary*

In this section, we compare the use of alcohol and drugs in veterans and in the general population. While, we could compare veterans' use of drugs and smoking habits with the population in general, we could not establish any changes before and after deployment, as the questionnaire only provides information on the situation after deployment.

The general finding is that although the veterans' weekly alcohol intake is lower than the general population's, they are more subject to binge-drinking. There are more daily smokers among the male veterans in the younger age group compared with the general population, but the distribution is more equal in the older groups.

A greater share of the Danish general population (25- to 44-year-olds) has used cannabis in the past year, compared with the male veterans. However, the reverse tendency is seen for other illegal substances, with a markedly greater number of the veterans under 45 years using illegal substances other than cannabis. About 56% of the veterans responding to the questionnaire had used cannabis at some time, about 5% in the past year. About 19% of the veterans had used other illegal substances, about 2% in the past year.

Chapter 7

# Homecoming Soldiers: A 'before-and-after' Analysis of Motivations, Financial Situation and Criminality

## Introduction

The purpose of this chapter is to examine the motivations of Danish soldiers before and after deployment, as well as to investigate the consequences of the deployment for the soldiers' finances and criminal behaviour.

- Soldiers' motivations change after a deployment. Before they are sent out, they place more of an emphasis on ideological reasons and the desire to help others. When the soldiers come home, they are more centred on themselves, for example, on their earnings and personal development.
- The deployed have lower overall debt and more disposable income than comparable control groups.
- There is less criminality among the deployed than among the control group, considering both criminality as a whole (with the exception of traffic offences) and the proportion of violent crimes.

We first examine what motivates soldiers before and after deployment. Then, we investigate (any) changes in their financial situation and (any) criminal behaviour and compare these results with those of a control group that has not been deployed. The three themes – motivation, finances and criminality – cover a wide selection of possible changes in the soldiers' status, changes that may result directly from their deployment. Motivation is an important element that can reveal both who the deployed are and why they choose to be sent on an international military mission. Moreover, the analysis can provide insight into how motivation changes when a soldier is sent on a single mission, as opposed to several missions. The motivational analysis leads to a broader understanding of what it meant to be deployed in 2011 and how far soldiers' expectations were met when they returned home.

Analysis of the soldiers' financial situation, including debt, sheds further light on these points. First, we look at the role that financial incentives play before deployment (i.e. money as motivation). Second, we look at the level of debt (both before and after deployment) as an indicator of how the soldiers manage their deployment in financial terms. The analysis of debt largely reveals whether the veterans have a longer-run perspective on their lives.

The effect of deployment on a soldiers' criminality has been the subject of much discussion in both Denmark and other countries. We therefore check for any indications that deployment has an effect on criminality among Danish soldiers.

The motivations underlying deployment were investigated with a questionnaire survey covering the period before and after deployment for two teams of soldiers: between February and August 2011, a team of peace-enforcers (PE) was sent to Afghanistan (ISAF[1]) and a team of peacekeepers (PK) was sent to Lebanon (UNIFIL 4[2]). In all, there were 447 respondents. The pre- and post-deployment surveys investigate whether changes occurred in soldiers' motivations before and after deployment and whether these differences were related to different military situations (e.g. number of deployments, types of mission, personnel group) to socio-economic characteristics of the deployed (age, gender, education, etc.), or both.

The data on the financial situation and criminality are based on administrative records from the military (about 26,000 deployed between 1992 and 2009) and from Statistics Denmark.

## Motivations of Soldiers – A before-and-after Analysis

- Soldiers' motivations before and after deployment were explored with data generated by the questionnaire survey (see Chapter 3 for greater detail of the data and methodology of the questionnaire). An investigation of motivation is important for eliciting the attitudes of the deployed and learning their reason(s) for choosing deployment to an international military mission. The analysis provides an important opportunity for studying how motivations may change from before deployment to when the soldiers return home. The primary conclusion, by chapter's end, is that their motivation almost always changes.

We now outline some of the questions related to the motivation analysis:

- Do any differences exist in the soldiers' motivations before and after deployment? If so, what are they?
- Do any differences exist in before-and-after motivation for soldiers deployed under contracts of various lengths and with different perspectives in terms of their commitment to the military?

[1]International Security Assistance Force (2002–2014), team 11.
[2]United Nations Interim Force in Lebanon (initiated in 1978 and increased in 2006), team 4.

- Does any difference exist between the motivations of those deployed to different types of mission?
- Do the motivations of men and women differ?
- Does motivation among privates, sergeants, and officers differ?

### *Two Different Missions – ISAF 11 and UNIFIL 4*

The data are based on the answers of 447 respondents to the questionnaire survey about motivation before and after deployment. Two groups of soldiers were deployed in the spring of 2011 on two specific missions: ISAF 11 to Afghanistan and UNIFIL 4 to Lebanon. The difference between the missions was that ISAF 11 was a PE mission, with the risk of engagement in fighting, whereas UNIFIL 4 was a PK mission, with little risk of engagement. Most of the respondents (80%) were sent on the PE mission (ISAF 11), and a third of the 447 respondents were on their first deployment. Figure 7.1 gives an overview of the soldiers and missions.

Most of the respondents (95%) are men between the ages of 18 and 29 years, over half live with a partner, their average age is relatively low, and only a quarter of them have children. Their education level reflects their relatively low average age – two-thirds have only had a basic or a youth education (ninth grade or high school). As for military characteristics, 73% are privates, and 80% have less than 10 years of seniority in the military. Personnel who are permanently employed or have a contract up to the age of 60 make up 28% of the respondents, and 37% have one or more family member who has been on deployment. As to the question of whether a soldier would either certainly or perhaps seek a new deployment, 77% answered in the affirmative. One of the biggest differences between PE (ISAF 11) and PK (UNIFIL 4) is that a significantly greater proportion of those on the Afghanistan PE mission were on a relatively short (i.e. three-year) contract (K3).

### *Soldiers' Motivations before Compared with after Deployment*

The theme of this section is the motivations that we can derive from the answers to the questionnaire in relation to the hypotheses we have presented in the

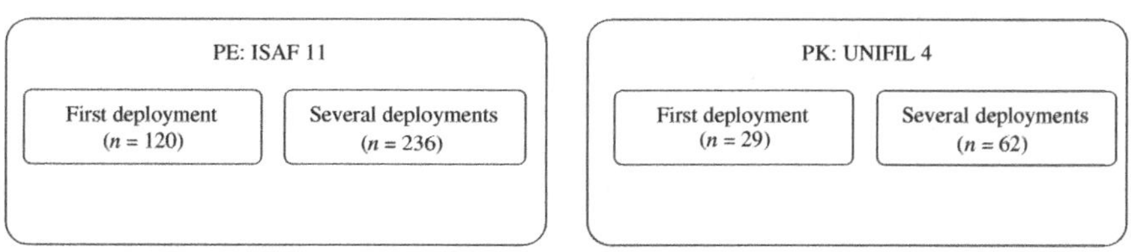


Figure 7.1. Overview of the Soldiers on ISAF 11 (PE) and UNIFIL 4 (PK) Missions and Number of Deployments Includes All Previously Deployed Soldiers Who Answered Questions about Their Motivations before and after Deployment ($n = 447$).

introduction of this chapter. In a series of descriptive sections, we first examine the differences in motivation before and after deployment and then motivation in relation to the different missions. Another important factor is the distinction between other-oriented and self-oriented motivations. The last descriptive section examines the differences in motivation between women and men and among privates, sergeants and officers.

After these descriptive sections, we continue with a multiple correspondence analysis (MCA). This statistical method is well suited for analysing and illustrating the connection between a series of categorical variables. For these types of variables, this method is analogous to factor analysis in dealing with quantitative variables.

**From Other-oriented to Self-oriented Factors – Explanation of Motivation before and after Deployment**

We asked the returning soldiers to evaluate 12 possible motivational factors, grouped in the following four general categories:

(1) self-oriented gain;
(2) dignity;
(3) other-oriented gain; and
(4) fidelity.

Table 7.1 shows the average ratings on a scale from one to 10 for the 12 possible motivational factors, before and after deployment, and gives the standard deviations around the average.

Before deployment, 'work with people whom I respect' and 'experience comradeship during deployment' received the highest ratings. Slightly below them is 'have a challenging job'. The more idealistic motivations, in relation to both the individual and the military community, are rated highly.

After deployment, the average ratings decrease. The more idealistic motivations are still valued highly but at a lower level. The only factor remaining above average is 'earn good money'. This increase, however, is not very large.

We also have data on how motivational factors before and after deployment are assessed by both first-timers and soldiers who have been on several deployments. Generally, many-time deployed soldiers give the motivational factors lower ratings. In the before-and-after rankings, the rating of the two factors in the category 'other-oriented gain' drop for both the one-time and the many-time deployed. Again, the rating of 'earn good money' increases after deployment in both groups. After deployment, the highest rated factor for first-time deployed soldiers is 'have a once-in-a-lifetime experience'. Overall, we find a change from more ideal other-oriented motivations to more self-oriented motivations ones.

**Different Missions – Different Motivations**

This section examines differences in motivational factors between the PE mission ISAF 11 and the PK mission UNIFIL 4. We distinguish between one-time and

Table 7.1. Soldiers' Average Rating of 12 Areas of Motivation before and after Deployment.

| | **Before Deployment** | | **After Deployment** | |
|---|---|---|---|---|
| | **Average** | **Standard Deviation** | **Average** | **Standard Deviation** |
| Self-oriented Gain | 8.1 | 1.7 | 7.2 | 2.0 |
| Have a challenging job | 5.8 | 2.6 | 6.1 | 2.5 |
| Earn good money | 7.9 | 2.1 | 7.2 | 2.4 |
| Practise my military training | | | | |
| Dignity | 7.9 | 1.7 | 7.3 | 1.9 |
| Have a job with responsibilities | 8.5 | 1.5 | 7.8 | 1.8 |
| Work with people whom I respect | 7.9 | 2.1 | 7.1 | 2.4 |
| Have a once-in-a-lifetime experience | 6.4 | 2.5 | 5.7 | 2.5 |
| Be part of an elite team | | | | |
| Other-oriented Gain | 7.2 | 2.3 | 5.9 | 2.5 |
| Make a positive difference for people needing help in the mission area | 5.4 | 2.4 | 4.2 | 2.3 |
| Build democracy in the mission area | | | | |
| Fidelity | 6.7 | 2.3 | 5.8 | 2.5 |
| Do something for my country | 6.7 | 2.7 | 4.9 | 2.7 |
| Prevent a terrorist attack in Denmark | 8.2 | 1.8 | 7.7 | 2.0 |
| Experience comradeship during deployment | 8.1 | 1.7 | 7.2 | 2.0 |

*Source*: SFI.

many-time deployments, focusing on the average ratings before and after deployment. The average values and standard deviations for the two missions appear in Tables 7.2 and 7.3.

Across the various factors, 'work with people whom I respect' is rated the highest. At the other end of the scale, 'build democracy in the mission area' is rated the lowest. That 'make a positive difference for people needing help in the mission area' consistently received more weight than the 'build democracy' argument may reflect a realistic attitude. When we compare the first-timers

Table 7.2. Average Assessment of the Motivational Factors for Deployed Soldiers on ISAF 11 (PE) by Mission Experience and the Responses before and after Deployment.

| | First Deployment | | | | Several Deployments | | | |
|---|---|---|---|---|---|---|---|---|
| | Before Deployment | | After Deployment | | Before Deployment | | After Deployment | |
| | Average | Standard Deviation | Average | Standard Deviation | Average | Standard Deviation | Average | Standard Deviation |
| Self-oriented Gain | | | | | | | | |
| Have a challenging job | 8.3 | 1.5 | 7.8 | 1.7 | 8.2 | 1.6 | 7.3 | 2.1 |
| Earn good money | 4.7 | 2.5 | 5.4 | 2.6 | 5.7 | 2.4 | 6.0 | 2.3 |
| Practise my military training | 8.3 | 2.0 | 8.1 | 1.9 | 8.0 | 2.1 | 7.3 | 2.2 |
| Dignity | | | | | | | | |
| Have a job with responsibilities | 7.9 | 1.7 | 7.7 | 1.6 | 7.9 | 1.7 | 7.4 | 1.9 |
| Work with people whom I respect | 8.8 | 1.5 | 8.0 | 1.8 | 8.4 | 1.5 | 7.9 | 1.8 |
| Have a once-in-a-lifetime experience | 8.8 | 1.5 | 8.5 | 1.6 | 7.4 | 2.3 | 6.4 | 2.5 |
| Be part of an elite team | 7.3 | 2.3 | 6.4 | 2.5 | 6.4 | 2.4 | 5.7 | 2.4 |
| Other-oriented gain | | | | | | | | |
| Make a positive difference for people needing help in the mission area | 7.5 | 2.1 | 6.2 | 2.4 | 7.1 | 2.3 | 5.8 | 2.5 |
| Build democracy in the mission area | 6.0 | 2.2 | 4.6 | 2.3 | 5.4 | 2.4 | 4.3 | 2.3 |
| Fidelity | | | | | | | | |
| Do something for my country | 6.8 | 2.5 | 6.3 | 2.5 | 6.8 | 2.2 | 5.8 | 2.5 |
| Prevent a terrorist attack in Denmark | 7.3 | 2.5 | 5.6 | 2.8 | 6.8 | 2.6 | 5.0 | 2.6 |
| Experience comradeship during deployment | 8.7 | 1.6 | 7.9 | 1.9 | 8.0 | 2.0 | 7.7 | 2.0 |

*Source*: SFI.

Table 7.3. Average Ratings of the Motivations for Deployment on UNIFIL 4 (PK), by Mission Experience and Responses before and after Deployment.

| | First Deployment | | | | Several Deployments | | | |
|---|---|---|---|---|---|---|---|---|
| | Before Deployment | | After Deployment | | Before Deployment | | After Deployment | |
| | Average | SD | Average | SD | Average | SD | Average | SD |
| Self-oriented Gain | | | | | | | | |
| Have a challenging job | 8.1 | 1.4 | 5.9 | 2.0 | 7.3 | 2.0 | 6.4 | 1.9 |
| Earn good money | 6.8 | 2.3 | 6.8 | 2.6 | 7.3 | 2.5 | 7.5 | 2.1 |
| Practise my military training | 7.4 | 2.3 | 5.4 | 2.7 | 7.0 | 2.2 | 5.6 | 2.6 |
| Dignity | | | | | | | | |
| Have a job with responsibilities | 7.8 | 1.4 | 6.6 | 2.0 | 7.7 | 1.6 | 6.6 | 2.0 |
| Work with people whom I respect | 8.3 | 1.7 | 7.1 | 2.2 | 8.3 | 1.7 | 7.4 | 2.0 |
| Have a once-in-a-lifetime experience | 8.2 | 2.2 | 7.1 | 2.3 | 8.1 | 1.8 | 7.1 | 2.1 |
| Be part of an elite team | 4.9 | 2.5 | 3.8 | 2.4 | 5.5 | 2.3 | 4.9 | 2.5 |
| Other-oriented Gain | | | | | | | | |
| Make a positive difference for people needing help in the mission area | 7.3 | 2.3 | 5.4 | 2.8 | 7.1 | 2.4 | 5.8 | 2.2 |
| Build democracy in the mission area | 4.9 | 2.7 | 2.7 | 1.8 | 4.9 | 2.5 | 3.6 | 2.1 |
| Fidelity | | | | | | | | |
| Do something for my country | 6.2 | 2.6 | 4.7 | 2.5 | 6.6 | 2.1 | 5.5 | 2.4 |
| Prevent a terrorist attack in Denmark | 5.9 | 2.8 | 2.9 | 2.0 | 5.8 | 2.5 | 3.9 | 2.7 |
| Experience comradeship during deployment | 8.2 | 1.6 | 7.4 | 2.0 | 8.2 | 1.6 | 7.7 | 1.8 |

*Source*: SFI.
*Note*: SD, standard deviation.

and the many-time deployed, we see that on average the many-time deployed on PE (ISAF 11) rate the 12 factors significantly lower than the first-timers do. For the PK mission (UNIFIL 4), we find the opposite, a presumable reflection of the soldiers' positive experience of that mission in comparison with previous ones.

Another relatively clear difference between the missions, both before and after deployment and between first-time and many-time deployed soldiers, is the rating of 'earn good money', which was consistently lower for the PE mission (ISAF 11). Similarly, the factors 'practise my military training' and 'be part of an elite team' are rated more highly by soldiers deployed on PE mission (ISAF 11) than by those deployed on PK mission (UNIFIL 4).

**Deployed Women Soldiers Want to be Challenged and to Make a Difference**

The women who choose deployment generally rated the motivational factors more positively. However, as only 25 of the 447 respondents were women, the differences we find should be interpreted with caution. Both women and men agree on the highest rated factor, 'work with people whom I respect', both before and after deployment. The women assess the three factors 'make a positive difference for people in the mission area needing help', 'experience comradeship during deployment' and 'have a challenging job' more highly than men.

**Privates Are Motivated by Comradeship Officers, by Responsibility and Challenge**

For the three personnel groups – privates, sergeants and officers, we generally find a tendency for the rank and file, the privates, to rate the factors more positively than the sergeants or officers. That these last two groups that are inherently more experienced both in the military and in terms of deployment may explain part of this difference.

The highest rated factor among privates is 'work with people whom I respect' for sergeants and officers, 'have a challenging job' and 'have a job with responsibility'. For these last two factors, the privates' ratings are significantly lower. Other factors generally rated significantly lower by the officers are 'have a once-in-a-lifetime experience', 'make a positive difference for people in the mission area needing help', 'build democracy in the mission area' 'be part of an elite team' and 'experience companionship during deployment'.

### *Multiple Correspondence Analysis*

The data we use in this chapter contain a large number of covariates and an assessment of 12 motivational factors. Therefore, to clarify the relationships between several variables simultaneously, this section uses MCA. The basic idea is to exploit the strong correlation between the individual background factors and the different motivational factors. From the different socio-demographic variables, we construct a coordinate system that allows us to position the various groups of subjects, according to their respective characteristics in relation to one another.

We now turn to individual background factors ('structuring variables') and the motivational factors ('supplementary variables'). The two types of variables in the analysis appear in Box 7.1. For inclusion in the analysis, all the variables must be categorical. The categories that apply to the structuring variables also appear in Box 7.1. For the supplementary variables, we have constructed a dichotomous transformation, setting the lowest half of the responses to 'no' (not important) and the highest to 'yes' (important).

A significant part of the interpretation of the MCA model consists of linking the two groups of variables to the axes of the coordinate system (see Le Roux & Rouanet, 2010). In Table 7.4, the background factors (structuring variables) are

**Box 7.1. Overview of Structuring and Supplementary Variables Used in the Multiple Correspondence Analysis.**

*Structuring variables*

Gender: male/female
Age: 18–24, 25–29, 30–44, >44 years
Personnel group: Private/sergeant/officer
In couple relationship/not in couple relationship
Children/no children
Mission: ISAF 11(PE)/UNIFIL 4(PK)
Contract: Permanent (K60)/up to 35 years (K35)/three-years contract (K3)
Education: Basic, youth education/technical/further education
Leadership/non-leadership
Seniority <6 years/8–10 years/>10 years

*Supplementary variables*

Have a challenging job (Yes/No)
Have a job with responsibilities (Yes/No)
Work with people whom I respect (Yes/No)
Do something for my country (Yes/No)
Make a positive difference for people in the mission area needing help (Yes/No)
Have a once-in-a-lifetime experience (Yes/No)
Prevent a terrorist attack in Denmark (Yes/No)
Build democracy in the mission area (Yes/No)
Be part of an elite team (Yes/No)
Experience comradeship during deployment (Yes/No)
Earn good money (Yes/No)
Practise my military training (Yes/No)

*Source*: SFI.

Table 7.4. Overview of the Social Background Variables (the Structuring Variables) and Which Axes They Contribute to in the Multiple Correspondence Analysis.

| | **Contribute to *x*-axis (Life Experience)** | **Contribute to *y*-axis (Military Experience)** | **Contribute to Both Axes** |
|---|---|---|---|
| Gender | | | X |
| Age | X | | |
| Relationship | X | | |
| Children | X | | |
| Rank | | X | |
| Mission | | X | |
| Number of deployments | | X | |
| Contract | X | | |
| Education | | X | |
| Leadership | | X | |
| Seniority | X | | |

*Source*: SFI.

assigned to one of the axes according to which they contribute to the most. We call the x-axis 'life experiences' because the largest contribution to this axis comes from variables connected with age and life history. We call the y-axis 'military experience' because the individual variables connected to military life contribute the most to this axis. Only one variable, gender, contributes to both.

In Table 7.5, we assign the motivational variables (structuring variables) to one of the two axes according to the MCA model. The motivational variables fall mainly into four categories. We assign the category 'self-oriented gain' to military experience on the *y*-axis. We assign the other categories – 'dignity', 'other-oriented gain' and 'fidelity' – to the *x*-axis (life experience). The one exception is 'have a job with responsibilities', which is related to the *y*-axis. Finally, a single factor, 'do something for my country', is assigned to both axes.

The distribution of outcomes for background factors (the structuring variables) appears in Table 7.6, in which the MCA model divides respondents into four distinct groups, according to whether their commitment or affiliation to the military is a fixed or indefinite term contract and whether they are one-time or many-time deployed.

**Self-oriented Motivation**

In this subsection, we examine how the self-oriented motivational factors are ranked in the MCA model. The results appear in Table 7.7 according to the

Table 7.5. Summary of Motivational Variables (Supplementary Variables) and the Axes They Contribute to in the Multiple Correspondence Analysis.

| | **Assigned to *x*-axis (Life Experience)** | **Linked to *y*-axis (Military Experience)** | **Contribute to Both Axes** |
|---|---|---|---|
| Self-oriented Gain | | | |
| Have a challenging job | | X | |
| Earn good money | | X | |
| Practise my military training | | X | |
| Worth | | | |
| Have a job with responsibilities | | X | |
| Work with people whom I respect | X | | |
| Have a once-in-a-lifetime experience | X | | |
| Be part of an elite team | X | | |
| Other-oriented Gain | | | |
| Make a positive difference for people in the mission area needing help | X | | |
| Build democracy in the mission area | X | | |
| Fidelity | | | |
| Do something for my country | | | X |
| Prevent a terrorist attack in Denmark | X | | |
| Experience comradeship during deployment | X | | |

*Source*: SFI.

grouping in Table 7.6. The majority of self-oriented motivations are linked to the *y*-axis (military experience). According to the structure of the model, the 'diagonal quadrants' are the opposite of one another relative to the importance of motivational factors. For example, the northeast quadrant comprises sergeants and officers who primarily view job content as important, whereas the loosely affiliated, many-time deployed in the southwest quadrant do not regard those job characteristics as important instead considering 'work with people

Table 7.6. Summary of Results Shown by Outcome of the Structuring Variables and Which Quadrants They Are Placed in by the Multiple Correspondence Analysis.

| **Northwest Quadrant: One-time Deployed, Loosely Affiliated** | **Northeast Quadrant: Strong Affiliation** |
|---|---|
| Children, no | Further education |
| Not in a couple relationship | Officer |
| 18–24 Years | Sergeant |
| 25–29 Years | Leadership responsibilities |
| First Deployment | 6–10 Years' seniority |
| Youth Education | Male |
| K3 | |
| ISAF 11 (PE) | |
| <6 Years' Seniority | |
| **Southwest Quadrant: Loosely Affiliated** | **Southeast Quadrant: Many-time Deployed, Firm Affiliation** |
| Basic Education | 30–44 Years |
| Private | >44 Years |
| No Leadership Responsibilities | UNIFIL 4 (PK) |
| K35 | Vocational training |
| Female | Children, yes |
| | Several deployments |
| | In a couple relationship |
| | Permanent service contract/K60 |
| | > 10 Years' seniority |

*Source*: SFI.

whom I respect', 'be part of an elite team' and 'have a once-in-a-lifetime experience' important.

**Motivations Concerning Others**

Table 7.8 shows the same distribution of outcomes for other-oriented motivational factors. Again, we find a striking difference in the outcome of the motivational factors between the group of officers and sergeants in the northeast corner and the loosely affiliated, many-time deployed in the southwest corner (in Table 7.5, all other-oriented motivational factors relate to the *x*-axis, life experience).

Table 7.7. Summary of Results Shown by the Outcome of Supplementary Variables Describing Self-oriented Motivations and the Quadrants They Belong to in the Multiple Correspondence Analysis.

| **Northwest Quadrant: One-time Deployed, Loosely Affiliated** | | **Northeast Quadrant: Strong Affiliation** | |
|---|---|---|---|
| Practise my military training | Yes | Have a challenging job | Yes |
| Earn good money | No | Have a job with responsibilities | Yes |
| | | Have a once-in-a lifetime experience | No |
| | | Work with people whom I respect | No |
| | | Be part of an elite team | No |
| **Southwest Quadrant: Loosely Affiliated** | | **Southeast Quadrant: Many-time Deployed, Strong Affiliation** | |
| Have a challenging job | No | Practise my military training | No |
| Have a job with responsibilities | No | Earn good money | Yes |
| Have a once-in-a lifetime experience | Yes | | |
| Work with people whom I respect | Yes | | |
| Be part of an elite team | Yes | | |

*Source*: SFI.

**Relevance of Results from MCA**

The analyses in this subsection primarily show great variation in the motivation of the deployed soldiers, both before and after having been on a mission. This variation covers a wide range, from primarily career-oriented, more professional groups driven mainly by more idealistic objectives connected with a mission, to relatively young, experience-seeking soldiers.

For the military, analyses of this type are relevant both because they reflect a great latitude of staff policy in the recruitment and management of the deployed and because the analyses provide an instrument that can help us to obtain greater clarity about the needs of veterans when they return home. In contrast, the next section uses a considerably larger database on the financial situation of the deployed.

### *Summary*

The analysis is based on a questionnaire survey carried out in 447 soldiers deployed on ISAF 11 and UNIFIL 4 in the spring of 2011. The Afghanistan mission (ISAF 11) was a peacekeeping mission, and the Lebanon mission

Table 7.8. Summary of Results Shown by the Result of Supplementary Variables Describing the Motivations Directed towards Others and the Quadrants They Belong to in the Multiple Correspondence Analysis.

| **Northwest Quadrant: One-time Deployed, Loosely Affiliated** | | **Northeast Quadrant: Strong Affiliation** | |
|---|---|---|---|
| Build democracy in the mission area | Yes | Make a positive difference for people in the mission area needing help | No |
| | | Prevent a terrorist attack in Denmark | No |
| | | Do something for my country | No |
| | | Experience comradeship during deployment | |
| **Southwest Quadrant: Loosely Affiliated** | | **Southeast Quadrant: Many-time Deployed, Strong Affiliation** | |
| Make a positive difference for people in the mission area needing help | Yes | Build democracy in the mission area | No |
| Prevent a terrorist attack in Denmark | Yes | | |
| Do something for my country | Yes | | |
| Experience comradeship during deployment | Yes | | |

*Source*: SFI.

(UNIFIL 4) a peace-enforcing one. We have investigated the motivation of soldiers using a typology that divides our 12 motivational factors into four different categories: self-oriented gain, dignity, other-oriented gain and fidelity.

The analysis shows that:

- Soldiers' motivations are more idealistic before deployment than after.
- First-timers are generally more positive in their evaluation of motivation than the many-time deployed. Both before and after deployment, the experienced soldiers are more positive than first-timers about 'to earn good money'.
- Women place more weight on making a difference for people who need their help in the mission area, and they also want to have a challenging job.
- The higher the rank, the lower the rating of motivations: the privates particularly differ from the other groups because 'experience comradeship during

deployment' is important for them, whereas the officers generally rate 'to have a challenging job' as important.

## Soldiers' Financial Situation before and after Deployment

An analysis of the soldiers' financial situation, including debts, sheds light on whether economic incentives play a role before deployment. The level of debt (before and after) provides a good indicator of how the deployed are faring in general, because debt is a measurable factor reflecting the extent to which veterans are forward looking and have control over an important part of their lives.

A poor economic situation may have an impact on how the soldiers fare after deployment. Financial difficulties, which may be a consequence of a deployment, may also compound any after-effects of a deployment. Thus, debt may indicate problems in everyday life. In addition, acquiring debts at a relatively young age creates a burden that may influence the veterans' later lives.

Debt also reflects a person's discounting factor. That is the way they assess the future and their planning and savings behaviour. While an increase in debt may reflect an investment in the future (e.g. buying a home), it can also be an expression of over-consumption of non-durable goods and a stronger preference for living in the present, in the form of high consumption 'now' rather than saving and investing for the future. Debt levels vary throughout an individual's life, also in relation to whether that individual plans his or her life. Debt is normally low for young people and increases with age, before finally falling again. The US military has various programmes for teaching and advising soldiers about their personal finances. One such programme has been evaluated by Bell, Gorin, and Hogarth (2009), who used a questionnaire to study the saving habits of American soldiers. Their survey showed that almost half of the soldiers responding to the questionnaire had a very short planning horizon of less than one year.

This section investigates how the debts of the deployed develop before and after deployment, as well as the extent to which the soldiers make a long-term investment in the form of buying a home. We also examine the differences between one and several deployments. To investigate changes in debt from before to after deployment, we use the year before the first deployment as our starting point. We study selected groups of deployed to follow the progression of their debt, then compare that progression with a control group (men deemed eligible for military service, but not deployed).

### *Financial Situation – Variables in the Analysis*

This section presents a picture of the deployed soldiers' financial situation by focusing on the following factors:

- disposable income (the amount that the soldier has available in a particular year);
- bank debt;
- savings (money in bank deposits at year end); and
- home ownership status.

**Population**

As the relevant variables are available only from 1997 to 2009 for those who were deployed for the first time in 1999, we examined the two years before deployment and the two years after, that is, those deployed in 1999–2007. We also examined another subset of this group, those we can follow two years before and five years after the first deployment in the 1999–2004. In addition, this population is limited, as only those in the population registers in all those years were included. We find only a slight difference between the two groups in terms of socio-demographic and military background variables.

**One-time and Many-time Deployed**

We are able to follow this population for a number of years and further divide it into one-time and many-time deployed soldiers. We do so because the two groups differ on a number of background variables, and we can therefore expect them to differ in terms of their financial situation.

### *Financial Situation of Soldiers before and after Deployment*

We first present a descriptive analysis of the trends in home ownership, disposable income and debt, defined as bank loans minus deposits in the period before and after the deployment of the selected groups. Developments in these variables are shown annually from two years before and up to five years after deployment. All figures are converted to 2000 price.

**Disposable Income during Deployment – An Economic Incentive?**

The wages that deployed soldiers receive are determined by a collective agreement. During deployment, soldiers receive (in addition to wages) a taxable 'UN additional compensation' for extra work and inconvenience, as well as a tax-free allowance as compensation for additional expenses during deployment. Thus, soldiers' disposable income during deployment is significantly higher than what most of them earned the year before deployment.

This important change in disposable income makes relevant asking whether the financial aspect is an essential incentive in choosing deployment. While Winslow (1999) concludes for Canadian soldiers in Kosovo that the financial incentives were very important, we find earlier in this chapter that making money was not a major motivational factor for the Danish soldiers. Admittedly, among motivation factors, earning money was rated slightly higher after returning home but still less highly than most of the other factors.

**Disposable Income among the Deployed**

The pre- and post-deployment distribution of disposable income, broken up in intervals, is shown in Table 7.9 for the large groups of deployed, who were followed up for two years after they return home. As the population is dominated by relatively young soldiers, incomes rose significantly from two years to one year before deployment. However, that deployment results in a very sharp rise in disposable income is very clear. The year before deployment, 17% had a

Table 7.9. Distribution of Disposable Annual Income among the Deployed, Spread over the Periods before, during and after Deployment. Deployment Period 1999–2007. 2000 Price (Percentages).

| Disposable Income, in DKK | Two Years before | One Year before | Year of Deployment | One Year after | Two Years after |
|---|---|---|---|---|---|
| 1–100,000 | 45 | 27 | 2 | 6 | 9 |
| 100,001–200,000 | 43 | 55 | 60 | 46 | 41 |
| 200,001–300,000 | 10 | 15 | 34 | 39 | 38 |
| Over 300,000 | 2 | 2 | 5 | 8 | 12 |
| Total | 100 | 100 | 100 | 100 | 100 |

*Source*: SFI.
*Note*: Total of 11,118 annual observations.

disposable income above 200,000 DKK. In the year of deployment, this share rose to 39%. While the increase continued, it was significantly slower after returning home. We find the same profile when we look at the small subset that we can follow up for five years after they return home. The increase continues after year two, but at roughly the same rate as from year one to year two after the return, that is, reflecting a predominately age-related increase.

When we distinguish between the one-time and many-time deployed, the median income for many-time deployed soldiers rises by about 15% up to two years after returning home, whereas for the one-time deployed, it remains largely unchanged. This finding is likely an age effect, as many of the one-time deployed soldiers begin or return to education and have a relatively low income after returning home.

**Debt among the Deployed**

An important element of the soldiers' financial position is net bank debt, measured as loans minus deposits. A *negative* debt therefore indicates that the individual has deposits greater than or equal to their loans, whereas someone with a *positive* debt has deposits lower than the loans. Figure 7.2 breaks up this net debt by amount interval for two years before to five years after deployment. In the two years before deployment, about 40% of the deployed had larger deposits than loans. The proportion rises to just over 50% in the year of deployment, then drops to 30%. Similarly, two years before deployment, another group consisting of about 40% of the deployed soldiers had net debts of less than 100,000 DKK. The profile for this group is 'analogous', in the sense that the share with a net debt of less than 100,000 DKK falls to 30% at the same time that the proportion of those with a positive net debt status in the banks increases to just above 50%. For both groups, this finding is the result of the significant increase in income during deployment. After returning home, a general life-cycle-specific increase occurs in the proportion of these with a net debt of more than 100,000 DKK.

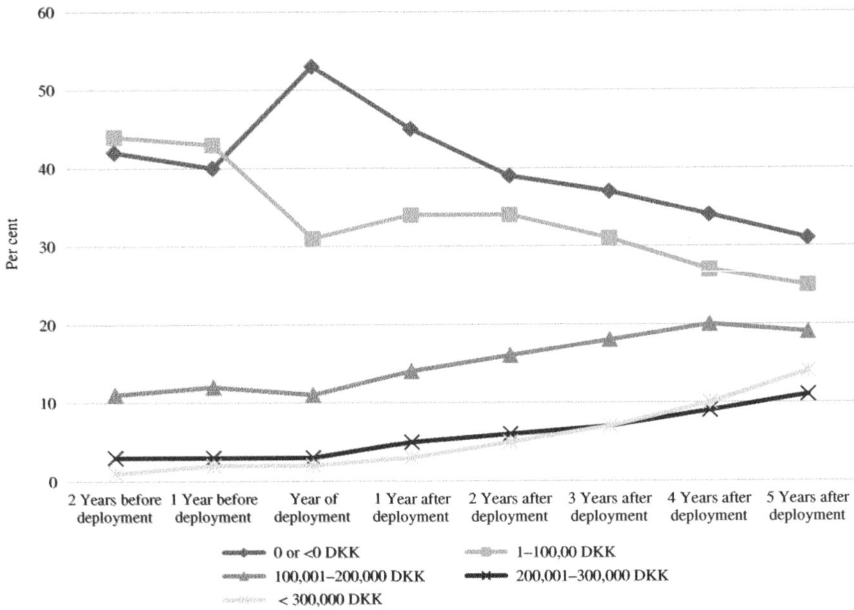


Figure 7.2. Yearly Net Debt, by Amount Interval, from Two Years before to Five Years after Deployment. Deployed between 1999 and 2004. 2000 Price. *Source*: SFI. *Note*: Total of 6,914 observations.

An alternative picture of the net debt profile is shown in Figure 7.3. The median value of net debt from two years before to five years after deployment is shown for four age intervals. The figure shows an expected decrease for all groups in the deployment year, most markedly for the 18- to 24-year-olds, who change from having nothing in the bank to having net deposits.

Finally, we compare the profile of the median of the debt for soldiers deployed once and several times from two years before to two years after deployment. We find a significantly stronger increase in debt after returning home for those deployed several times. The large differences that we find in a number of financial variables between one and several deployments form the background for distinguishing between the two groups in the following regression analyses.

**Disposable Income, Debt and Home Ownership among the Deployed**

Buying a house or a flat is an obvious possible explanation for the changes in soldiers' bank debt, as up to 20% of a house purchase can be financed by a bank loan. Therefore, we have also looked at how the proportion who own their home changes from two years before to up to five years after deployment. About 20% own their own home two years before deployment. This proportion increases to 25% in the deployment year and thereafter by approximately five percentage points for each year after returning home, so that 47% own their homes five years after the

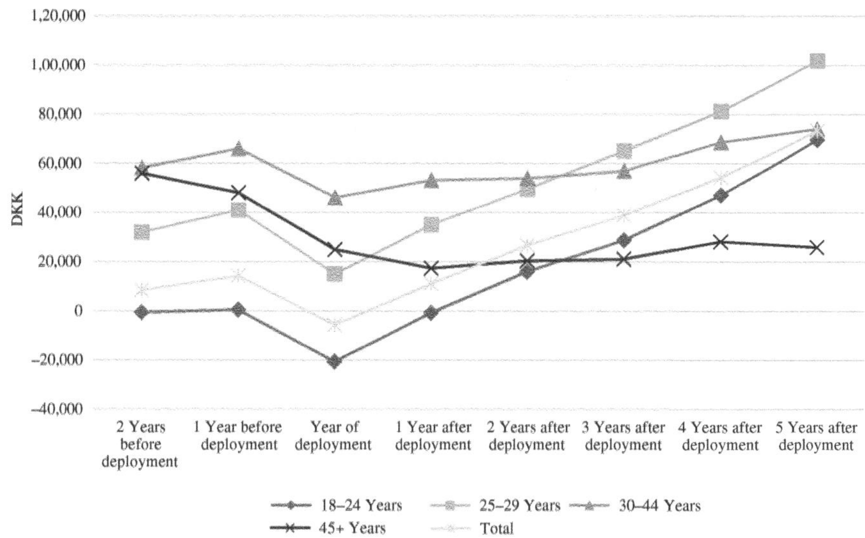


Figure 7.3. Median Values for Net Debt by Age Group for Each Year from Two Years before to Five Years after Deployment. Deployed between 1999 and 2004. 2000 Price. *Source*: SFI. *Note*: Total of 6,914 observations.

deployment. Across the socio-economic backgrounds and military characteristics, the differences in housing ownership five years after they return are primarily linked to age differences between the various categories of soldiers. To better link the development of debt to the many background factors, we look in the next section at results from regression analyses of debt before and after deployment.

### *Before-and-after Analysis of Debt among the Deployed*

This section presents the results of the following equation explaining the change in the soldiers' debts from before to after deployment:

$$\Delta Y_i = Y_{i,\text{after}} - Y_{i,\text{before}} = \beta_0 + \beta_1 X_i + u_i$$

where $Y_i$ is the debt of a person, respectively, before and after deployment, $X_i$ is a vector of background variables that are assumed to have an impact on the change in debt, and $u_i$ is an error term, which is assumed to be 0 on average. 'Before' and 'after' refer to two years before and either two or five years after returning home, depending on the time frame we use. Background variables summarised by $X_i$ refer to the year before deployment.

The results of the equation, partly for all the deployed in 1999–2007 and partly for the subset formed by those deployed only once, appear in Table 7.10. The significance of each background factor is determined with respect to a reference category.

Table 7.10. Analysis of Debt. Before and after the Regression Analysis for All Deployed and One-time Deployed, 1999–2007.

| Explanatory Variables | Deployed 1999–2007 (Two Years before to Two Years after) | | One-time Deployed 1999–2007 (Two Years before to Two Years after) | |
|---|---|---|---|---|
| | **Coefficient** | **Standard Error** | **Coefficient** | **Standard Error** |
| 18–24 Years old | −7.060* | 4.046 | −2.191 | 6.315 |
| ≥45 Years old | −24.248*** | 8.153 | −20.971* | 12.616 |
| Male | 13.069** | 6.608 | 10.048 | 10.584 |
| Married, cohabiting | 25.374*** | 7.381 | 36.838*** | 11.642 |
| Of immigrant descent | −14.715 | 10.970 | −45.492*** | 17.245 |
| With child living at home | 5.999 | 6.637 | 6.004 | 10.250 |
| Education (low) | −2.656 | 3.259 | −5.459 | 4.813 |
| Education (high) | −10.416* | 5.910 | −14.724 | 9.488 |
| In out-of-home care as a child | 18.440*** | 6.951 | 19.848* | 10.937 |
| Grew up in single-parent family | 11.032*** | 3.970 | 8.448 | 6.732 |
| Unemployed one year before deployment | −33.528 | 21.943 | −33.948 | 42.933 |
| Homeowner | −23.996*** | 5.591 | −41.497*** | 8.080 |
| One-time deployed | 22.703*** | 3.213 | | |
| Deployment year – 2000 | −6.692* | 3.648 | −8.966* | 5.157 |
| Deployment year – 2001 | −2.789 | 4.600 | −116.000 | 8.119 |
| Deployment year – 2002 | 12.007** | 4.845 | 9.775 | 9.384 |
| Deployment year – 2003 | 10.084 | 6.141 | 15.722* | 9.034 |
| Deployment year – 2004 | 258.000 | 6.541 | 3.663 | 9.986 |
| Deployment year – 2005 | 26.440*** | 7.479 | 32.384*** | 11.191 |
| Deployment year – 2006 | 27.695*** | 6.866 | 26.484** | 10.639 |
| Deployment year – 2007 | 15.443* | 8.342 | 31.185** | 13.290 |
| Iraq | 18.604** | 7.510 | 20.324* | 11.484 |
| ISAF | 2.657 | 8.258 | 5.715 | 14.271 |
| KFOR | 4.761 | 5.780 | 9.908 | 8.956 |
| SFOR | 10.591* | 5.980 | 17.059* | 9.517 |

Table 7.10. (*Continued*)

| **Explanatory Variables** | **Deployed 1999–2007 (Two Years before to Two Years after)** | | **One-time Deployed 1999–2007 (Two Years before to Two Years after)** | |
|---|---|---|---|---|
| | **Coefficient** | **Standard Error** | **Coefficient** | **Standard Error** |
| Private | −862.000 | 4.360 | −3.339 | 5.492 |
| Sergeant | 1.299 | 5.299 | 9.808 | 7.628 |
| Officer | −4.210 | 8.231 | −1.818 | 11.895 |
| Other personnel | 8.426 | 15.517 | 30.058 | 23.866 |
| Constant | −21.326** | 9.193 | −1.651 | 13.612 |
| $R^2$ | | 0.018 | | 0.022 |
| Total | | 11,118 | | 4,747 |

*Source*: SFI.
*Notes*: ***$p < 0.001$; ** $p < 0.005$; * $p < 0.1$. Robust standard error. Dependent variables Net $\text{debt}_{\text{After 2}} - \text{Net debt}_{\text{Before 2}}$

In the regression with all the deployed, all these reference categories correspond to a many-time deployed, single Danish woman, 25–44 years old with a medium length education (1–2 years of university), who grew up with both parents, who did not own her home one year before deployment, who was deployed in 1999 on other missions and whose employment rank in the military is unknown. On average, this individual's net debt falls by 21,300 DKK from before to after deployment.

Table 7.10 shows the estimated coefficients for background factors and their degree of significance. The significant coefficients predominantly have the expected signs (+/–). Net debt falls for the youngest and oldest groups, consistent with the life-cycle theory, as well as for those who were homeowners before deployment. The debt rises for men, for those married or cohabiting, for soldiers who were in out-of-home care for all or part of their childhood or who grew up in a single-parent family and for the one-time deployed. The last group, as mentioned earlier, likely includes some individuals who are beginning or returning to education, with a consequent reduction in income and increase in loans. To determine whether soldiers' disposable income in the deployment year had an influence on the change in debt, we carried out an additional regression analysis, but found no influence.

### *Differences in Debt between the Deployed and the Control Group*

The deployed clearly do not represent a random sample of the population. To assess trends in debt among those deployed, we must compare them with a control group from the approximately 300,000 people declared eligible for military service on Armed Forces Day in 1994–2010. We compare the 1975–1982 birth cohorts, as all the relevant variables are available for these age groups. A further requirement for comparison was that both the deployed and the control groups in the analysis were individuals observed for all 13 years, the period for which data on debt are available (1997–2007).

To examine the before-and-after differences between the deployed and the control group, we used a difference-in-differences method (described in detail in Chapter 3). This method allowed us to assess a possible effect, for example of a treatment (deployment) by comparing the change in the appropriate amount of the net debt of the deployed with the performance of the control group. The control group is comparable to the deployed group in all areas except that they have not been deployed. If the estimation includes relevant background factors, any significant difference between the deployed and the control group relative to changes in debt can be attributed to having been deployed.

We use the following equation to assess whether statistically significant differences occur in the change of net debt between the deployed and the control groups:

$$\text{Debt}_{\text{it}} = \beta_0 + \beta_1 \text{Deployed}_i + \beta_2 \text{after}_t + \beta_3 (\text{Deployed}_i \times \text{after}_t) + \beta_4 X_{i.} + u_{it}$$

where $\text{Debt}_{i,t}$ is the debt of person $i$ in year $t$, $\beta_0$ is a constant, $\text{Deployed}_i$ is set to 1 if the observation is from the deployed group and 0 if not, $\text{after}_t$ is set to 1 if the observation is from the period after the deployment year and 0 if not, $X_i$ contains individual background factors and $u_{i,t}$ is the error term. The parameter of interest is $\beta_3$. If it is significant and positive, then the deployed increase their debt relative to the control group, but if it is significant and negative, then the deployed reduce their net debt.

We chose to look at deployment year 2002, in which a relatively high number of the cohorts in this analysis were between ages 20 and 27 years. Table 7.11 presents the socio-demographic background variables for the 979 deployed and the 124,330 controls.

We are primarily interested in the coefficient $\beta_3$ of the interaction between the variables *deployed* and *after* in the equation. Table 7.5 shows the results in terms of $\beta_3$ for four different specifications of the estimated model. Models 1a and 1b are estimated for both homeowners and non-homeowners one year before deployment. In model 1a, the before-and-after focus is on the two years before and two years after deployment. While models 2a and 2b are analogous, they are estimated only for non-homeowners in 2001. All the parameters are significant and negative that is deployment leads to less debt than for the control group, both two years and five years after returning home (Table 7.12).

### *Summary*

We analysed the financial situation of the deployed by focusing on net debt. The level of debt (both before and after) is a good indicator of how the deployed

Table 7.11. Socio-demographic Background Variables for Cohorts Born in 1975–1982, Shown Separately for Those Deployed for the First Time in 2002 and for the Control Group. The Variables Refer to the Status in 2001.

| | **Deployed** | | **Control Group** | |
|---|---|---|---|---|
| | **Total** | **Per cent** | **Total** | **Per cent** |
| Born in 1975 | 54 | 6 | 9,904 | 8 |
| Born in 1976 | 69 | 7 | 16,740 | 13 |
| Born in 1977 | 80 | 8 | 17,536 | 14 |
| Born in 1978 | 93 | 9 | 17,280 | 14 |
| Born in 1979 | 205 | 21 | 16,705 | 13 |
| Born in 1980 | 235 | 24 | 16,215 | 13 |
| Born in 1981 | 180 | 18 | 15,067 | 12 |
| Born in 1982 | 63 | 6 | 14,883 | 12 |
| Male | 925 | 94 | 123,200 | 99 |
| Married, cohabiting | 9 | 1 | 2,362 | 2 |
| Of immigrant descent | 9 | 1 | 4,376 | 4 |
| With child living at home | 9 | 1 | 3,684 | 3 |
| Education (low) | 504 | 51 | 54,413 | 44 |
| Education (medium) | 458 | 47 | 66,467 | 53 |
| Education (high) | 17 | 2 | 3,450 | 3 |
| In out-of-home care as a child | 49 | 5 | 4,914 | 4 |
| Grew up in single-parent family | 204 | 21 | 21,448 | 17 |
| Homeowner | 59 | 6 | 15,929 | 13 |
| Unemployed one year before deployment | 3 | 0 | 1,162 | 1 |
| Total | 979 | 100 | 124,330 | 100 |

*Source*: SFI.

manage life in general. The analysis of the soldiers' debt before and after deployment covers bank debt, including consumption loans held by financial institutions, regardless of whether the deployed are homeowners. Data are available starting in 1997. Findings are as follows:

- The descriptive analysis does not indicate a large amount of debt before the first deployment, a finding agreeing with the fact that this factor was not the most important in the motivation analysis. A comparison of the deployed (born 1975–1982) with a control group of the same age likewise does not show that the financial situation of the deployed is worse than that of the control group.

Table 7.12. Effect of Deployment on Debt. Results from the Difference-in-difference Regressions.

| | Model 1a | Model 1b | Model 2a | Model 2b |
|---|---|---|---|---|
| Deployed after deployment, coefficient | −26.116*** | −21.818*** | −33.344*** | −32.291*** |
| Deployed after deployment, standard deviation | 3.229 | 4.058 | 3.580 | 4.651 |
| No. of observations | 501,236 | 877,163 | 259,276 | 453,733 |
| Two years before, two years after | X | | X | |
| Two years before, five years after | | X | | X |
| All (both homeowners and non-homeowners) | X | X | | |
| Non-homeowners | | | X | X |

*Source*: SFI.
*Notes*: ***$p < 0.00$; ** $p < 0.005$; *$p < 0.01$. Robust standard error. The regressions are calculated with a fixed effect for individuals.

- Those deployed in 1999–2007 and 1999–2004 did not have serious financial problems when they returned home, respectively, two and five years after their first deployment.
- When we compare soldiers before and after deployment, the net debt (bank debt minus deposits) varies according to socio-economic characteristics, year of deployment and type of mission.
- Income during the year of deployment has no impact on debt either before or after deployment. Thus, during deployment, soldiers do not use their wages to pay off debt.
- When we compare those deployed in 1975–1982 with the control group, the deployed have both a lower net debt and a higher disposable income.

## Criminality among Soldiers – Before and after Deployment

No previous research has studied soldiers' pre-enlistment criminality in detail that we do. Moreover, the literature shows no consensus on whether deployment increases or decreases subsequent crimes. To investigate whether deployment has an influence on criminality after soldiers return home, we use access to administrative records on crime both before and after the soldiers' deployment. Given that those deployed on international military missions do not represent a random sample of the population and that both self-selection and military screening take place before a soldier can be deployed, we handle this selection problem by comparing criminality among soldiers before and after deployment with a relevant control group.

This section focuses on four main questions:

(1) How widespread is criminality among soldiers before and after deployment?
(2) What is the level of criminality of the deployed relative to a control group?
(3) Do deployed soldiers commit more violent crimes than those in the control group?
(4) What effect does deployment have on soldiers who have not previously committed crimes?

While in Chapter 4, we briefly examined juvenile criminality among the deployed, the focus in this section is on the impact of military deployment on soldier's criminality over time.

### *Measuring Criminality*

We use criminal convictions in the civil courts as a measure of whether an individual has committed a crime (excluding traffic offences). In the analyses, we use a dummy variable with the outcome set to 1 or 0 to indicate whether or not an individual has committed a crime in a given period and another variable giving the total number of convictions.

### *Population*

Our purpose is to investigate crime both before and after the first deployment. To do so, we examine criminality in a population of first-timers two years before and two years after their deployment and a subset of this population two years before and up to five years after returning home: 21,266 and 16,996 observations, respectively. In addition, we divide the soldiers into the one-time and the many-time deployed (the latter may have fewer years after deployment to commit crime).

### *Description of Criminality among Deployed Soldiers*

#### Overall Criminality

In relation to deployment, the observations fall into four possible outcomes:

(1) Crimes were committed both before and after the first deployment.
(2) Crimes were committed only before the first deployment.
(3) Crimes were committed only after the first deployment.
(4) No crimes were committed either before or after the first deployment.

In the large group that we followed two years before and two years after deployment, 94.5% had no criminal convictions either before or after deployment. The opposite outcome, crimes committed both before and after deployment, occurs only in 0.5% of that group, whereas those with convictions only before deployment occur in 2.9% and those with convictions only after returning home occur in 2.1%. In the subset of the population that we followed up to five years after returning home, the share that received convictions only after returning home is 4.5%, due to the longer follow-up period.

Figure 7.4 shows the annual profiles of the share of criminals for the one-time and many-time deployed, divided according to the length of the observation period after returning home. We then compare the profile of the deployed with a relevant control group.

**Violent Crime**

We treat violent crime separately. Using the same criteria we used for convictions in general, we find very few incidences of violent crime. For example, among the 21,026 soldiers followed up from two years before to two years after returning home, fewer than five were convicted of violent crimes either before or after deployment. Only 1% received a conviction for violent crime in the group that we followed up two years before to two years after deployment, and only 1.5% in the subpopulation that we followed up for five years after returning home.

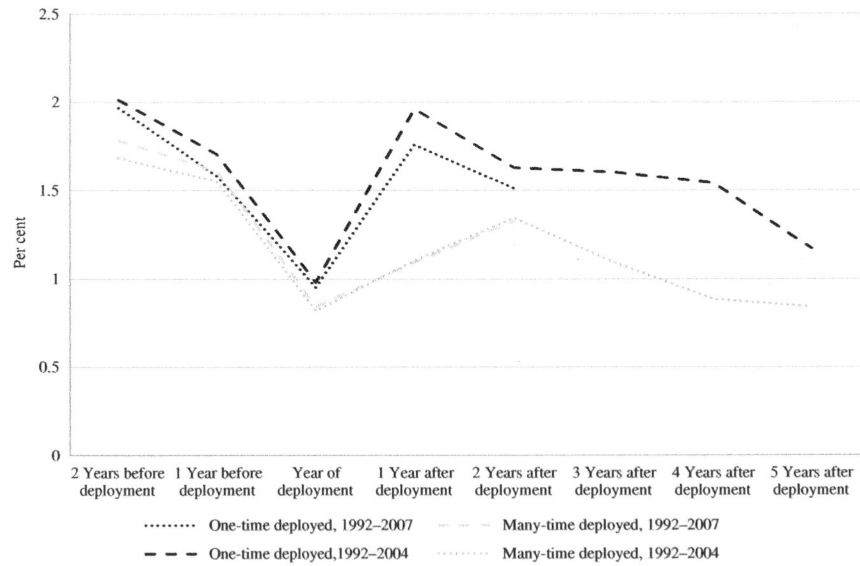


Figure 7.4. Share of One-time and Many-time Deployed Soldiers Who Committed Crimes in the Years before, during and after the Year of Deployment. *Source*: SFI.

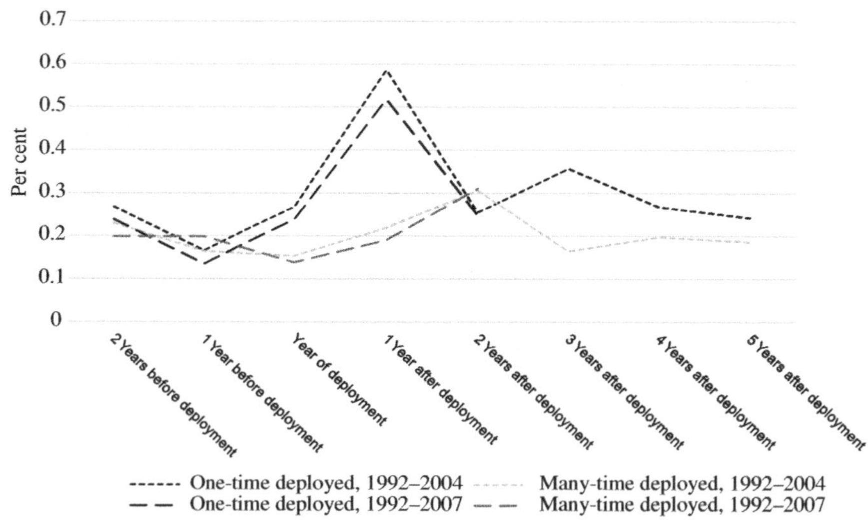


Figure 7.5. The Share of One-time and Many-time Deployed Soldiers Who Committed Violent Crimes in the Years before during and after the Year of Deployment. *Source*: SFI.

Figure 7.5 shows the same profiles as Figure 7.4, but now only for violent crime. For those sent on only one mission, the profile is significantly different, with a sharp increase the year after deployment and a higher share of those committing crime from year two onwards than before deployment. However, Figure 7.5 also shows that the crime rate is very low. Moreover, as those sent on only one mission are on average younger, some of the difference between them and the many-time deployed is probably due to an increase in violent crime with age.

When we compare the profiles of the one-time deployed in Figure 7.5 with those for total crime in Figure 7.4, we find an increase in the relative share of violent crime from before to after deployment. This finding is likely the result of the military screening procedures and approval requirements before deployment, most of which are very stringent in terms of violent crime.

### *What Explains Criminality after Deployment?*

The likelihood of an individual's committing a crime is related to many factors. We focus on whether factors associated with deployment have an independent impact on criminality. We thus conduct a logistic regression analysis of the probability of a deployed soldier committing a crime during a fixed period of time after returning home. We use a wide range of background factors as possible explanatory variables. The results appear in Table 7.13 for all first-timers in 1992–2007 and for a subset consisting of those who were deployed only once.

Table 7.13. Logistic Regression of the Likelihood of Committing a Crime for up to Two Years after the First Deployment for All Deployments and for One-mission Only Deployments in 1992–2007.

| Explanatory Variables | Deployed 1999–2007 (Two Years before to Two Years after) | | One-time Deployed 1999–2007 (Two Years before to Two Years after) | |
|---|---|---|---|---|
| | Coefficient | Standard Error | Coefficient | Standard Error |
| Criminality up to two years before deployment | 1.572*** | 0.124 | 1.423*** | 0.181 |
| 18–24 Years old | 0.325*** | 0.123 | 0.499*** | 0.178 |
| ≥45 Years old | −0.987** | 0.468 | −1.902* | 0.985 |
| Not single | 0.126 | 0.248 | 0.028 | 0.376 |
| Of immigrant descent | 0.682** | 0.316 | 1.241*** | 0.424 |
| With child living at home | −0.365* | 0.103 | −0.238 | 0.383 |
| Education (low) | 0.586*** | 0.324 | 0.546*** | 0.140 |
| Education (high) | −0.739** | 0.400 | −1.140* | 0.644 |
| In out-of-home care as a child | 0.439*** | 0.156 | 0.660*** | 0.209 |
| Grew up in single-parent family | 0.132 | 0.106 | 0.233 | 0.146 |
| Unemployed one year before deployment | 0.506** | 0.243 | 0.724** | 0.311 |
| One-time deployed | 0.263*** | 0.091 | – | – |
| Deployment year – 1997 | −0.975** | 0.460 | −0.652 | 0.676 |
| Deployment year – 2007 | −0.927* | 0.492 | −0.947 | 0.726 |
| IFOR | 0.456 | 0.851 | 0.391 | 1.058 |
| Iraq | 0.476 | 0.314 | 0.239 | 0.430 |
| ISAF | 0.303 | 0.342 | 0.465 | 0.515 |
| KFOR | 0.442* | 0.268 | 0.210 | 0.345 |
| SFOR | 0.208 | 0.275 | 0.071 | 0.368 |
| UNPROFOR | −0.240 | 0.288 | 0.204 | 0.477 |
| Private | −0.264 | 0.175 | −0.203 | 0.252 |
| Sergeant | −0.588** | 0.246 | −0.545 | 0.372 |
| Officer | −0.589 | 0.409 | −0.158 | 0.615 |
| Other personnel | −0.986 | 1.058 | – | – |

Table 7.13. (*Continued*)

| Explanatory Variables | Deployed 1999–2007 (Two Years before to Two Years after) | | One-time Deployed 1999–2007 (Two Years before to Two Years after) | |
|---|---|---|---|---|
| | Coefficient | Standard Error | Coefficient | Standard Error |
| Constant | −4.010*** | 0.350 | −4.140*** | 0.535 |
| Model log likelihood | – | −2,344.285 | – | −1,162.03 |
| Total number of soldiers | – | 20,314 | – | 9,146 |

*Source*: SFI.
*Notes*: ***$p < 0.001$; ** $p < 0.005$; * $p < 0.1$. Dependent variables are criminality 1–2 years after the first deployment (Yes/No).

Both regressions examine the probability of committing a crime in the first two years after returning home.

The probability is significantly higher if the deployed soldier has one or more of the following characteristics:

- 18–24 years old;
- of immigrant descent;
- no children;
- lower level of education;
- in out-of-home care for all or part of childhood;
- unemployed the year before deployment; and
- had a criminal record before deployment.

Criminality itself before deployment is an important significant factor, as also shown in the literature, for example Bouffard (2003) and Yager (1976). Using a relevant control group, we now investigate this important factor.

In relation to military characteristics, a one-time deployment is associated with a significantly higher probability of a subsequent conviction. One explanation for this finding, as mentioned earlier, is that we observe the many-time deployed for fewer years after the last deployment. Military rank and the different missions are not correlated with the risk of subsequent criminality.

A corresponding logistic regression was performed for violent crime alone. Considerably, fewer background factors contributed significantly to the explanations for such criminality:

- criminal record before deployment;
- 18–24 years old;

- lower level of education; and
- only one deployment.

For the military variables, we find a significantly higher probability of committing a crime among those deployed to Iraq and Afghanistan (both PE). However, as the descriptive overview shows, our reference point is very low levels of violent crime. Thus far, we have looked only at criminality among deployed soldiers as a single group. We now look first at a relevant control group and compare the criminality in this group with that of the population as a whole. Then, we compare those deployed with the control group. Finally, we analyse the change in criminality from before to after deployment in a difference-in-differences regression analysis, again using the control group.

### *Criminality in the Control Group Compared with That in the Population as a Whole*

The control group comprised individuals of the same age as the deployed, who on Armed Forces Day were declared eligible for military service but were never deployed. Criminality in the control group was lower than the average for the same group in the population, calculated among 20- to 29-year-old men. The lower level in the control group applies to both property and violent crimes. For this group, we find that property crimes fell from 2005 to 2007, whereas violent crimes remained at a constant, lower level. The control group that we compare with the deployed group is thus less criminal than the same-age population as a whole.

### *Differences in Criminality between the Deployed and the Control Group*

We compare convictions for the 1975–1982 birth cohorts for the control group and for all deployed, divided into those deployed once and several times in 1997–2009. Figure 7.6 clearly shows that throughout the period, the deployed had lower crime rates than the control group, who, as we have seen, had lower crime rates than the population as a whole. Moreover, the crime rate drops significantly from 2004 onwards for both the control and the deployed groups. As expected, we find higher conviction rate among the one-time deployed than the many-time deployed. Compared with UK studies (see Treadwell, 2010), which show a very high level of veterans in the UK within the criminal justice system, the Danish results provide an interesting contrast.

American analyses (see Noonan & Mumola, 2007) find indications that violent crimes are more likely to be committed by returning veterans than non-veterans. In 2004, 57% of all imprisoned veterans in the US had been convicted of a violent crime, compared to only 47% of inmates who were not veterans.

Figure 7.7 shows the Danish situation with regard to violent crime. Again, throughout the entire period, we see a lower incidence of violent crime among the deployed than among the control group. For both the deployed and the control groups, the incidence of violent crime falls in the first five years after 2000.

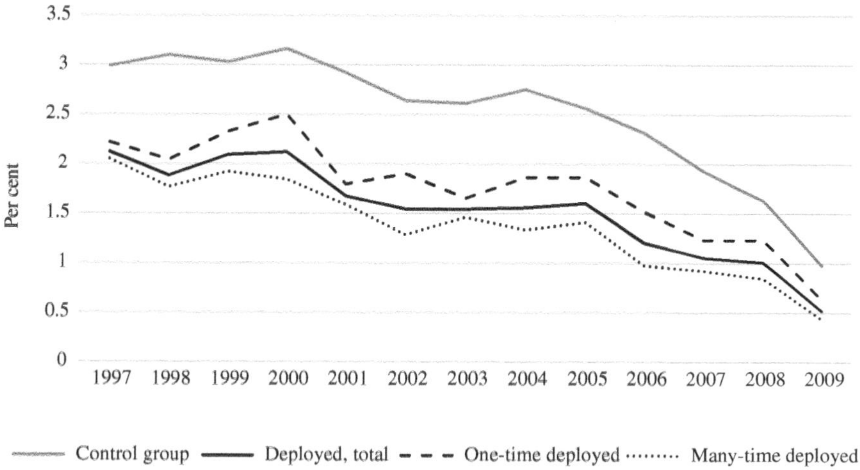


Figure 7.6. Annual Share of Those Committing a Crime among the Control and the Deployed Group, Divided into the One-time and the Many-time Deployed. *Source*: SFI. *Note*: The figure contains numbers for birth years 1975–1982.

As the numbers are very small, there is large variation around the downward trend for the one-time deployed. Most violent crime among the deployed is, in Danish legal terms, 'simple assault' (i.e. assault without the use of weapons and without the victim's suffering serious body harm).

### *Differences before and after the Year of Deployment*

We now focus on whether deployment itself changes the level of criminality from before to after deployment. We carried out a difference-in-differences regression for the deployed and the control groups, using data for the two years before deployment and up to five years after returning home. The analysis is for the 1975–1982 birth cohorts for all those deployed in 2002. We assessed the effect on crime using the sign and the significance of the parameter of interest $\beta_3$, deployed × after, in the model. If the sign is positive, the deployed soldiers committed more crimes after 2002, the year of deployment, than those in the control group. Conversely, a negative sign indicates that the deployed committed fewer crimes after deployment than those in the control group. In either case, the coefficient has to be significant to yield an effect. The result for this key parameter appears in Table 7.14 for different specifications of the model.

Models 1a and 1b are estimated from two years before to two years after (model 1a) or five years after deployment (model 1b). The coefficient of (deployed × after) is insignificant in all specifications. In other words, among the deployed, we find no significant difference in criminality before and after deployment from criminality in the control group.

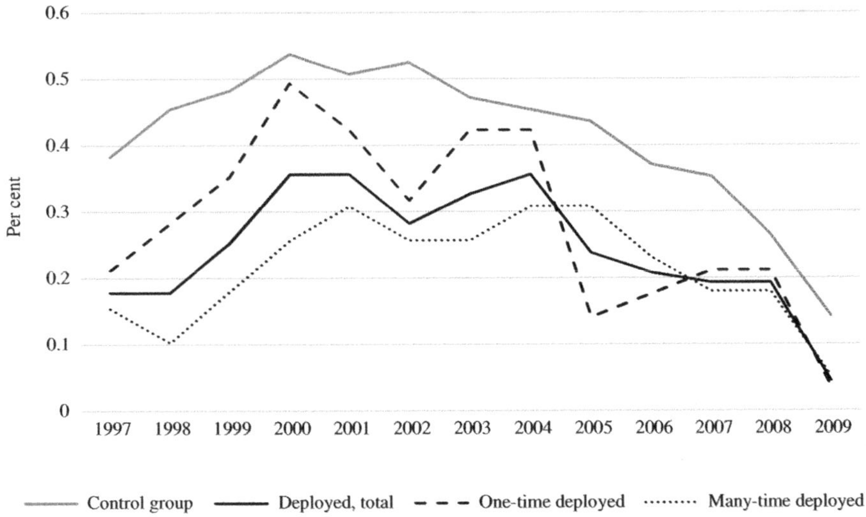


Figure 7.7. Annual Share of Those Committing Violent Crimes among the Control and the Deployed Group Separately. The Deployed are Divided into the One-time and the Many-time Deployed. *Source*: SFI. *Notes*: $n = 127{,}101$ for controls and 6,737 for all deployed (2,838 one-time and 3,899 many-time deployed). The deployed were sent on a mission at least once during 1992–2007. Any crimes committed by the deployed or control group were counted per year. Only the changes from 1997 onwards are plotted, as the youngest (birth year, 1982) were 15 years old in 1997 and therefore above the Danish legal age of criminal responsibility.

In models 2a and 2b, we examine only the group with no criminal convictions before deployment. The coefficient is significant and negative meaning that criminality among this group of deployed is lower than among the control group, measured both two years and five years after the soldiers return home. While this result is both significant and meaningful in comparison with studies in other countries, it should be viewed with caution, as we analysed only a single group of deployed soldiers in 2002 born between 1976 and 1982.

We then did the same analysis specifically for violent crimes. We found no significant results and therefore cannot demonstrate any difference between the deployed and the control group for this particular type of crime.

### *Summary*

An ongoing discussion in the scientific community and the media is to whether war deployment leads to greater criminality among the soldiers when they return home. Until now, the debate has been based on studies mostly from the USA and the UK. Those studies, however, made no systematic analysis of criminality among formerly deployed soldiers.

Table 7.14. Effect of Deployment on Criminality. Results from the Difference-in-differences Regression.

| | Model 1a | Model 2a | Model 1b | Model 2b |
|---|---|---|---|---|
| Deployed × after | | | | |
| Coefficient | −0.005 | −0.012*** | −0.002 | −0.009*** |
| Standard deviation | 0.004 | 0.003 | 0.004 | 0.002 |
| No. of observations | 526,576 | 518,894 | 921,508 | 913,826 |
| From two years before to two years after | x | x | | |
| From two years before to five years after | | | x | x |
| All crimes | x | | x | |
| No criminality before | | x | | x |

*Source*: SFI.
*Note*: ***$p < 0.001$; ** $p < 0.005$; * $p < 0.1$. Robust standard error. Fixed effects.

We have registered data on the criminal past of the soldiers before deployment. This information allows us to investigate whether an actual change in criminal behaviour occurred after deployment or whether the ensuing criminality is simply a continuation of earlier tendencies. Our analysis shows that the deployed are less criminal in general and do not commit more violent crimes than do those in a relevant control group. Using an analytical model, we studied the effects of deployment for a subsample of the deployed (first-timers in 2002 and born in 1975–1982). Therefore, our results do not necessarily apply to the entire group of deployed soldiers.

Concerning criminality overall (i.e. all types of crime except for traffic offences), we find among the deployed:

- 8% of the first-time deployed in 1992–2004 committed some act of criminality in the two years before and up to five years after deployment.
- The share of soldiers who committed criminal offences falls until the year of deployment, after which it increases again for the one-time deployed. In contrast, the many-time deployed show a more moderate increase after the year of deployment.
- The probability of a soldier's committing a crime after deployment rises if the deployed had committed a crime previously, was younger (18–24 years old), had no children living at home, had a short education, was of immigrant descent, had been in out-of-home care, had been unemployed in the year before deployment or grew up in a single-parent family.

To evaluate whether the deployed had become more or less criminal, we need to compare this group with a control group. For the control group, we used individuals who were declared eligible for military service on Armed Forces Day, but never deployed. For both groups, we considered only the birth cohort 1975–1982, and we follow the two groups over the same period. The level of criminality among the deployed is below that among the control group.

- When we restrict our analysis to violent crimes, about 1.7% of the first-time deployed in 1992–2004 had committed a violent crime in the period two years before, to up to five years after deployment.
- The share of violent criminals is lower among deployed than in the control group.
- Using the year 2002 as the cut-off point for before and after deployment, we find no significant results for violent crimes and therefore no evidence that deployment increases or decreases the tendency to commit them.

Chapter 8

# Soldiers on International Missions – Mental Health Profile before and after Deployment

## Introduction

In this chapter, we provide an analysis of the health profile before and after deployment for the about 26,000 soldiers who were deployed between 1992 and 2009. We investigate psychological health in terms of psychiatric diagnoses, purchase of mental health medication and number of contacts with the psychiatric health care system. We also include a brief examination of the work-related accidents reported to ASK (National Board of Injury and Compensation). Finally, we analyse mortality among those who have been deployed.

In the analyses, we compare those deployed with a control group made up of men who were deemed eligible for military service on Armed Forces Day (previous session). We also focus on the difference between the groups of deployed soldiers, such as personnel groups or those with different mission experience.

## Psychiatric Diagnoses and Contacts with the Psychiatric Health System

In the related literature on veterans' mental health, the methods used are often based on self-evaluation. This approach can be problematic, because of recall bias (Wessely et al., 2003) and also because the questionnaire survey itself has certain limitations, such as the lack of a control group (Bache, 1998) or dropout of respondents (non-response bias). Rona, Jones, French, and Wessely (2004) show that military personnel with potentially serious mental illness had a lower response rate than the rest of the population considered. Moreover, Hoge et al. (2004) show that soldiers at risk of mental health problems may not self-report these symptoms, because they fear for their career.

There is no consensus about the relationship between deployment and the frequency of mental health symptoms and the variation in the percentage of mental problems across studies is large. Larson, Highfill-McRoy, and Booth-Kewley (2008) found that post-traumatic stress disorder (PTSD) diagnosis is higher for the US marines exposed to combat and Hoge, Auhterlonie, and Milliken (2006) showed that deployment to combat areas in Iraq (which was the most dangerous battlefield for American soldiers on that time) was associated with higher use of mental health services after the end of the deployment, compared with other deployed groups. In contrast, Engelhard et al. (2007) reported no significant differences in the frequency of PTSD for deployed Dutch UN peacekeeping units, compared to unit which not has been deployed yet.

In Chapter 6, we showed that 17% of the respondents stated that they had various psychological problems as a result of their deployment (4% to a greater extent, 13% to a lesser extent). In this chapter, we can examine how widespread registered psychological problems are after returning home among the deployed based on observations of individuals' choices and actions as gathered from administrative records. We use different proxies for psychological problems collected from registers. Specifically, in this section, we investigate how many veterans have been registered with a psychiatric diagnosis, as well as how many have been in contact with the psychiatric health system (from the Danish Psychiatric Central register), or purchase mental health-related medication (from the Danish Register of Medical Product Statistics). Our analysis period is 1995–2010. As the decision to refer to the health system may be connected to a feeling of giving up and, for some, being stigmatised, it can take a long time before those previously deployed feel ready to do so. Our results will therefore be seen as a minimum estimate of how many of these veterans actually experience psychological problems.

### *Psychiatric Diagnoses*

We studied the occurrence of mental illness among people who have been in contact with the relevant treatment facilities and who have received a psychiatric diagnosis listed in the registers, we had access to. In International Classification of Diseases (ICD-10), psychiatric diagnoses are presented in a hierarchy depending on severity, from F00-09 to F90-99. The higher up in the hierarchy, the lower the severity grad of the illness. Like Hageman et al. (2008), we made an exception in the cases of the diagnoses F10–19, mental and behavioural disturbances due to psychoactive substance abuse and placed these at the bottom of the hierarchy, that is, secondary to other diagnoses.

Box 8.1 shows the diagnoses groups and some specific diagnostics we include in the analysis. In the top part, we have placed a number of specific mental diseases that were found to be relevant to the analyses of veterans' psychological state after a deployment.

### *Psychiatric Diagnoses among the Deployed between 1995 and 2010*

Among the approximately 26,000 deployed between 1992 and 2009, 1,410 were registered with at least one psychiatric diagnosis in 1995–2010. The great majority, 1,108 soldiers, were diagnosed after their first deployment, and 302 before their first deployment. Among these, 48 received a psychiatric diagnosis both before and after the deployment.

First, we examine the profiles of the veterans recorded in the psychiatric registry. We present two descriptive tables to show how veterans with a psychiatric diagnosis differ from veterans without psychiatric diagnosis in relation to a number of socio-demographic background factors and their military characteristics. After the introductory descriptive overview, we present results from a multiple

**Box 8.1. Psychiatric Diagnoses.**

*We have selected some specific psychiatric diagnoses that are relevant in the analysis of soldiers' psychological state after a deployment:*

Post-traumatic brain syndrome (F07.2)[a]

Schizophrenia (F20)

Major depressive disorder, single episode (F32)

Recurrent depressive disorder (F33)

Reaction to severe stress and adjustment disorders (F43), including Post-traumatic stress disorder (F43.1)

Enduring personality changes, not attributable to brain damage and disease (F62.0)

*In the analysis, we use the following categories:*

Organic, including symptomatic, mental disorders (F00–09)

Mental and behavioural disorders due to psychoactive substance use (F10–19)

Schizophrenia (F20)

Schizotypal mental suffering, psychoses, etc. (F21–29)

Mood (affective) disorders (F30–39)

Nervous and stress-related conditions (F40–49)

Behavioural syndromes associated with physiological disturbances and physical factors (F50–59)

Disorders of adult personality and behaviour (F60–69)

Other diagnoses – F diagnoses

Other diagnoses such as Z diagnoses

*Notes:* [a]The Iraq war introduced a new military medical condition: Mild-traumatic brain injury (MTBI). The diagnosis is somatic, but in reality, it is the same as post-traumatic brain injury (ICD-10, F07.2), formerly known as the post-concussion syndrome.

*Source*: SFI.

regression analysis, which included all the variables which we consider to affect the probability of receiving a psychiatric diagnosis after deployment. Table 8.1 shows how the two groups of veterans differ with regard to socio-demographic background factors. The descriptive statistics for each group of characteristics in the table indicate that the risk of being diagnosed was higher for the deployed who were 18–24 years old, women, with an ethnic background other than Danish, single, with no children and with a low educational background.

In Table 8.2, we look at the differences between veterans with and without a diagnosis in relation to their military background. The most important differences appear to be a higher risk of receiving a diagnosis in veterans who were in former Yugoslavia and in those repatriated between 2005 and 2009, primarily from missions to Afghanistan and Iraq. Table 8.2 shows a lower risk among sergeants and officers deployed to Kosovo or on single (not group) deployments to Iraq.

Table 8.1. Deployed Soldiers by Socio-demographic Characteristics One Year before First Deployment. Deployed Registered with or without Psychiatric Diagnoses in 1995–2010 (%).

| Categories | Deployed 1992–2009 | | Total |
|---|---|---|---|
| | Without Psychiatric Diagnoses in 1995–2010 | With Psychiatric Diagnoses in 1995–2010 | |
| *Gender* | | | |
| Male** | 95 | 94 | 95 |
| Female** | 5 | 6 | 5 |
| Total | 100 | 100 | 100 |
| *Age group*[a] | | | |
| 18–24 Years** | 56 | 58 | 56 |
| 25–29 Years | 19 | 21 | 19 |
| 30–44 Years | 18 | 16 | 18 |
| ≥45 Years*** | 7 | 5 | 7 |
| Total | 100 | 100 | 100 |
| *Ethnicity* | | | |
| Danish* | 98 | 97 | 98 |
| Not Danish* | 2 | 3 | 2 |
| Total | 100 | 100 | 100 |
| *Civilian status** | | | |
| Not in a couple relationship*** | 84 | 88 | 84 |
| In a couple relationship*** | 15 | 11 | 15 |
| No information | 1 | 1 | 1 |
| Total | 100 | 100 | 100 |
| *Children living at home* | | | |
| No*** | 90 | 93 | 91 |
| Yes*** | 10 | 7 | 9 |
| Total | 100 | 100 | 100 |
| *Education* | | | |
| Basic education*** | 44 | 59 | 45 |
| Youth education*** | 21 | 14 | 20 |
| Vocational training** | 20 | 17 | 20 |

Table 8.1. (*Continued*)

| Categories | Deployed 1992–2009 | | Total |
|---|---|---|---|
| | Without Psychiatric Diagnoses in 1995–2010 | With Psychiatric Diagnoses in 1995–2010 | |
| Further education*** | 14 | 8 | 13 |
| Not available** | 1 | 2 | 1 |
| Total | 100 | 100 | 100 |
| *Other variables* | | | |
| Unemployed year before deployment*** | 2 | 3 | 2 |
| Raised in out-of-home care[b]*** | 4 | 11 | 4 |
| Grew up in one-parent family*** | 17 | 24 | 17 |
| Died in 1992–2010*** | 1 | 3 | 1 |
| Total number of individuals | 24,628 | 1,410 | 26,038 |

*Source*: SFI.

*Notes*: Total of 26,036 individuals, 1,410 with a psychiatric diagnosis. Chi-square test and Fisher's exact test: $***p < 0.001$; $**p < 0.05$; $*p < 0.1$.

[a]Age at time of deployment.

[b]Raised in out-of-home care before age of 18.

## Diagnoses before and after Deployment

Table 8.3 focuses on the highest ranked diagnoses in the hierarchy for veterans before and after their first deployment. Before deployment, nervous and stress-related conditions constitute the largest group of diagnoses. After deployment, these conditions are even more prevalent and included depression.

### *Numbers of Deployed with Post-traumatic Stress Disorder (PTSD)*

In Table 8.4, we present data on the occurrence before and after the first deployment of specific psychiatric diagnoses. Surprisingly, PTSD occurs relatively more frequently before than after deployment. A possible partial explanation for this is that our deployment data are limited to the years 1992–2009 so, in principle, veterans could have been on missions before 1992, that is, their 'first' mission' in our data. In absolute numbers, 628 veterans were diagnosed with PTSD after their first deployment (see Atkinson, Guetz, & Wein, 2009; Galovski & Lyons, 2004 for PTSD among American veterans).

Table 8.2. Deployed Stratified by Military Characteristics One Year before Their First Deployment. Percentage of Deployed with and without Psychiatric Diagnoses in 1995–2010 (%).

| **Categories** | **Deployed 1992–2009** | | **Total** |
|---|---|---|---|
| | **Without Psychiatric Diagnoses in 1995–2010** | **With Psychiatric Diagnoses in 1995–2010** | |
| Personnel Group | | | |
| Private | 34 | 35 | 34 |
| Sergeant*** | 11 | 5 | 11 |
| Officer*** | 8 | 3 | 8 |
| Other | 2 | 2 | 2 |
| No information[a]*** | 45 | 55 | 45 |
| Total | 100 | 100 | 100 |
| First mission | | | |
| UNPROFOR*** | 24 | 33 | 25 |
| IFOR | 5 | 6 | 5 |
| SFOR | 17 | 16 | 17 |
| KFOR*** | 23 | 19 | 23 |
| ISAF | 10 | 10 | 10 |
| IRAQ | 8 | 7 | 8 |
| Other missions*** | 12 | 8 | 12 |
| Total | 100 | 100 | 100 |
| Overall Mission Experience | | | |
| Former Yugoslavia and Iraq and Afghanistan* | 3 | 2 | 3 |
| Former Yugoslavia and Iraq | 6 | 6 | 6 |
| Former Yugoslavia and Afghanistan** | 6 | 4 | 6 |
| Afghanistan and Iraq | 3 | 2 | 3 |
| Former Yugoslavia*** | 58 | 65 | 58 |
| Iraq** | 8 | 6 | 8 |
| Afghanistan | 11 | 11 | 11 |
| Other mission experience | 5 | 4 | 5 |
| Total | 100 | 100 | 100 |

Table 8.2. (*Continued*)

| **Categories** | **Deployed 1992–2009** | | **Total** |
|---|---|---|---|
| | **Without Psychiatric Diagnoses in 1995–2010** | **With Psychiatric Diagnoses in 1995–2010** | |
| Other Deployments | | | |
| One-time deployed* | 48 | 50 | 48 |
| Many-time deployed | 52 | 50 | 52 |
| Total | 100 | 100 | 100 |
| Other Variables | | | |
| Wounded in 1992–2009 | 0.4 | 0.5 | 0,4 |
| Repatriated in 2005–2009*** | 1 | 3 | 1 |
| Total numbers | 24,628 | 1,410 | 26,038 |

*Source*: SFI.
*Notes*: Chi-square test and Fisher's exact test. ***$p < 0.01$; **$p < 0.05$; *$p < 0.11$.
[a]We have many missing for this variable in the beginning of the period.

In addition, there is more mood affective disorders (e.g. depressive illness) (see also Table 8.3) after deployment. It would appear that a number of veterans with psychological problems as a result of a mission are known only in the primary health care sector (General Practitioner) without being referred for psychiatric treatment. There are probably also those who, for different reasons, do not want to contact the secondary health care sector (hospital) or take up offers of treatment from the military. Thus, the number of deployed with a registered psychiatric diagnosis must be an underestimate of the real extent of the problem.

### *When Were the Diagnoses Registered?*

We will now examine the time elapsed between the most recent deployment (i.e. the first or the latest) and the registration of the first psychiatric diagnosis. In the 1992–2010 period, 5% of the deployed were diagnosed with a psychiatric problem. Table 8.5 shows the differences in length of time between first deployment and first psychiatric diagnosis. It appears that 20% of those deployed only once and 22% among the many-time deployed were diagnosed with a mental illness before deployment. In addition, in the 42% of the one-time deployed who were diagnosed, the diagnosis was made six years or more after deployment. This figure is 47% for the many-time deployed.

Table 8.3. Deployed by Their Highest Ranked Psychiatric Diagnoses in 1995–2010, before and after First Deployment.

| **Diagnoses** | **Before First Deployment** | | **After First Deployment** | | **Total** | |
|---|---|---|---|---|---|---|
| | *N* | % | *N* | % | *N* | % |
| Organic, including symptomatic, mental disorders (F00–09)[a] | <5 | 1 | 21 | 2 | 23 | 2 |
| Mental and behavioural disorders due to psychoactive substance use (F10–19) | 17 | 6 | 57 | 5 | 74 | 5 |
| Schizophrenia (F20) | <5 | 0 | 36 | 3 | 36 | 2 |
| Schizotypal mental suffering, psychoses, etc. (F21–29)[b] | 11 | 4 | 44 | 4 | 55 | 4 |
| Mood (affective) disorders (F30–39) | 44 | 15 | 364 | 31 | 408 | 28 |
| Nervous and stress-related conditions (F40–49)[c] | 117 | 39 | 472 | 41 | 589 | 40 |
| Behavioural syndromes associated with physiological disturbances and physical factors (F50–59) | 13 | 4 | 34 | 3 | 47 | 3 |
| Disorders of adult personality and behaviour (F60–69)[d] | 18 | 6 | 48 | 4 | 66 | 5 |
| Other diagnoses – F diagnoses | 55 | 18 | 20 | 2 | 75 | 5 |
| Other diagnoses such as Z diagnoses | 25 | 8 | 60 | 5 | 85 | 6 |
| Totals | 302 | 100 | 1,156 | 100 | 1,458 | 100 |

*Source*: SFI.

*Notes*: Total number of individuals is greater than the population of 1,410, as the same person can be registered before and after deployment.

[a]Includes F07.2 postconcussional syndrome (commotio cerebri = concussion). The somatic diagnosis for commotio cerebri is S06.3. That diagnosis covers only commotio (acute) injury.

[b]Includes F23, acute and temporary psychosis.

[c]Includes F43.1 PTSD.

[d]Includes F62.0 personality change after catastrophic experiences.

Table 8.4. Deployed Who in 1995–2010 Were Registered with At Least One of the Psychiatric Diagnoses Shown (Diagnoses not Ranked), before and after Their First Deployment.

| | **Before First Deployment** | | **After First Deployment** | | **Total** | |
|---|---|---|---|---|---|---|
| | *N* | % | *N* | % | *N* | % |
| Postconcussional syndrome (F07.2) | <5 | 2 | 8 | 1 | 12 | 1 |
| Schizophrenia (F20) | <5 | 1 | 35 | 3 | 36 | 3 |
| Major depressive disorder, single episode (F32) | 41 | 21 | 283 | 25 | 324 | 25 |
| Recurrent depressive disorder (F33) | 15 | 8 | 128 | 11 | 143 | 11 |
| Reaction to severe stress and adjustment disorders (F43)[a] | 129 | 66 | 628 | 56 | 757 | 58 |
| Enduring personality change after catastrophic experience (F62) | <5 | 2 | 20 | 2 | 23 | 2 |
| Referred for treatment Z0461 | <5 | 1 | 16 | 1 | 18 | 1 |
| Referred for admission Z0462 | <5 | 0 | <5 | 0 | <5 | 0 |
| Totals, includes F43.1 PTSD | 195 | 100 | 1,120 | 100 | 1,315 | 100 |

*Source*: SFI.
*Note:* [a]Includes F43.1 PTSD.

As these soldiers have been on several missions, it is not surprising that in general they are diagnosed at a later date.

For the many-time deployed, we have also looked at the time interval between the most recent deployment and the first psychiatric diagnosis. Compared with the one-time deployed, as having a psychiatric diagnosis would decrease the probability of being re-deployed, there is a smaller per cent of many-time deployed (26%) first diagnosed six years or more after their latest deployment. In these descriptions and analyses, we do not have observations after 2010. Even if we had later observations, there would still be the problem of an increasing probability that such late diagnoses would not related to deployment.

Table 8.5. Deployed by Number of Years between First Deployment and First Psychiatric Diagnosis for Soldiers Deployed Once or More Than Once.

| **No. of Years between First Deployment and First Psychiatric Diagnosis** | **One-time Deployed** | | **Many-time Deployed** | | **Total** | |
|---|---|---|---|---|---|---|
| | *N* | % | *N* | % | *N* | % |
| More than 10 years before | 14 | 2 | 17 | 2 | 31 | 2 |
| 10–9 Years before | 22 | 3 | 19 | 3 | 41 | 3 |
| 8–7 Years before | 16 | 2 | 24 | 3 | 40 | 3 |
| 6–5 Years before | 26 | 4 | 23 | 3 | 49 | 3 |
| 4–3 Years before | 28 | 4 | 39 | 6 | 67 | 5 |
| 2–1 Year before | 36 | 5 | 38 | 5 | 74 | 5 |
| 0–1 Year after | 74 | 10 | 44 | 6 | 118 | 8 |
| 2–3 Years after | 105 | 15 | 86 | 12 | 191 | 14 |
| 4–5 Years after | 97 | 14 | 84 | 12 | 181 | 13 |
| 6–7 Years after | 71 | 10 | 70 | 10 | 141 | 10 |
| 8–9 Years after | 61 | 9 | 55 | 8 | 116 | 8 |
| Over nine Years after | 161 | 23 | 200 | 29 | 361 | 26 |
| Total | 711 | 100 | 699 | 100 | 1,410 | 100 |

*Source*: SFI database.
*Notes*: The numbers do not add up to 100 because of rounding up. The median for all soldiers is four years after deployment and for many-time deployed, five years.

### *Where Have Soldiers with Psychiatric Diagnoses Been Deployed?*

In terms of the veterans' mission experiences, there is a sharp increase in the number of diagnoses around 2000, which is not related simply to an increase in the number of soldiers deployed. Soldiers with mission experience in the former Yugoslavia make up the greatest share of veterans with recorded mental disease. In the later years of the studied period, there is a relatively sharp increase in the numbers of deployed sent to Iraq and Afghanistan.

## Who Received a Psychiatric Diagnosis after Deployment?

Following on from this descriptive overview of the occurrence of psychiatric diagnoses after deployment, we examine the results of a regression analysis of the probability of being diagnosed with a mental illness controlling for a number of possible explanatory factors. Regression analysis explains the probability of diagnosis for 22,944 deployed in 1995–2010. This population does not include the 303 soldiers who died, or the 2,791 soldiers who immigrated or emigrated in that period. The results of the analysis are shown in Table 8.6. For each variable, an estimated odds ratio is given, with an odds ratio of >1 implying that the variable increases the likelihood to be diagnosed and, vice versa, an odds ratio of <1 that it decreases the likelihood.

What emerges is that being registered with a psychiatric diagnosis before deployment is an important risk factor for receiving a diagnosis after deployment. At the same time, there is no statistical interaction between diagnosis before deployment and the other explanatory variables, and we have therefore chosen to include *diagnosis before* as an explanatory variable.

Factors that markedly increase the probability of being registered with a diagnosis are as follows:

- short education;
- spent all or some of childhood in out-of-home care (e.g. foster care);
- grew up in a single-parent family;
- unemployed one year before first deployment;
- repatriated from a mission;
- mission experience in the former Yugoslavia (UNPROFOR and IFOR); and
- more than six years since most recent deployment.

A number of other factors reduce the risk of being registered with a diagnosis:

- ethnic Danish background;
- 18–24 or ≥45 years old. In contrast to Table 8.1, for the 18- to 24-year-olds, once we include the other background variables, the conclusion is a lower risk;
- Sergeant or officer rank (information about the military rank is, however, missing for ca 45% of the deployed); and
- Only 1–2 years since most recent deployment.

A number of variables do not appear to have any effect on risk:

- gender;
- marital status;
- having children;
- only one deployment; and
- missions other than former Yugoslavia.

## Comparison of Deployed and the Control Group

Until now, we have only examined the occurrence of diagnoses among the deployed. In this section, we consider the control group using the same

Table 8.6. Logistic Regression of Probability of Being Registered with a Mental Illness after Deployment.

| **Dependent Variables: Psychiatric Diagnosis after the First Deployment (Yes/No)** | **Probability of Receiving a Psychiatric Diagnosis after Deployment** | |
|---|---|---|
| | **Odds Ratio** | **SE** |
| Psychiatric diagnosis before first deployment | 5.245*** | 1.068 |
| Married or cohabiting | 1.172 | 0.174 |
| Woman | 1.198 | 0.191 |
| Ethnic Danish | 0.597** | 0.137 |
| 18–24 Years | 0.740*** | 0.060 |
| ≥45 Years | 0.654** | 0.133 |
| Education (short) | 1.577*** | 0.120 |
| Education (long) | 0.664** | 0.109 |
| Having a child at home | 0.940 | 0.129 |
| In out-of-home care as a child | 1.959*** | 0.223 |
| Growing up in single-parent family | 1.314*** | 0.106 |
| Unemployed for one year before deployment | 1.766*** | 0.320 |
| One-time deployed | 1.045 | 0.077 |
| Wounded during deployment[a] | 1.004 | 0.488 |
| Repatriated from mission[b] | 3.493*** | 0.786 |
| Sergeant | 0.589*** | 0.101 |
| Officer | 0.480*** | 0.132 |
| Other personnel | 1.478 | 0.446 |
| No information on rank | 1.180 | 0.145 |
| *First mission* | | |
| UNPROFOR | 1.549*** | 0.231 |
| IFOR | 1.398* | 0.258 |
| SFOR | 1.256 | 0.188 |
| KFOR | 0.953 | 0.153 |
| ISAF | 1.189 | 0.243 |
| Iraq | 1.088 | 0.222 |

Table 8.6. (*Continued*)

| **Dependent Variables: Psychiatric Diagnosis after the First Deployment (Yes/No)** | **Probability of Receiving a Psychiatric Diagnosis after Deployment** | |
|---|---|---|
| | **Odds Ratio** | **SE** |
| No. of years since last deployment | | |
| 1–2 Years (i.e. last deployment in 2008–2009) | 0.646*** | 0.092 |
| 6–10 Years (i.e. last deployment 2002–2004) | 1.774*** | 0.213 |
| More than 10 years (i.e. last deployment 1992–1999) | 1.723*** | 0.237 |
| Constant | 0.034*** | 0.010 |
| Total no. of observations | 22,944 | |
| Log-likelihood | −3,785.82 | |

*Source*: SFI.
*Notes*: ***$p < 0.001$; ** $p < 0.05$; * $p < 0.1$. Robust standard error.
[a]Wounded in 1992–1999.
[b]Repatriated in 2005–2009.

principles as in Chapter 7. The birth cohorts 1975–1982 among the deployed are compared with the same birth cohorts in a control group consisting of men who on Armed Forces Day were deemed eligible but were not deployed. The two groups are observed for the period 1995–2010, excluding individuals migrating to or returning from other countries during the period, as well as those who died. Applying these criteria, the analysis covers 6,778 deployed and 104,790 men in the control group. The average age of these groups is almost the same, and the 6,778 deployed have mission experience that is in line with that for all deployed soldiers, that is, with a predominance of missions to former Yugoslavia.

As a whole, there is a smaller range of psychiatric diagnoses among the deployed. The diagnoses that are more common in the control group are organic, including symptomatic, mental disorders (F00–009) and problems with psychoactive substance abuse (F10–19), schizophrenia (F20) and specific personality disorders (F60–69).

The number of psychiatric diagnoses per 1,000 people is shown for the two groups in Figure 8.1 for each year in 1995–2010. The control group has a higher relative occurrence over the whole period, but the level rises sharply among the deployed and in 2010 lies close to that for the control group. Despite the fall in the number of psychiatric diagnoses before deployment because of more stringent military screening, there is a sharp increase in psychiatric diagnoses among deployed at the end of the period. In addition, because we are looking at the

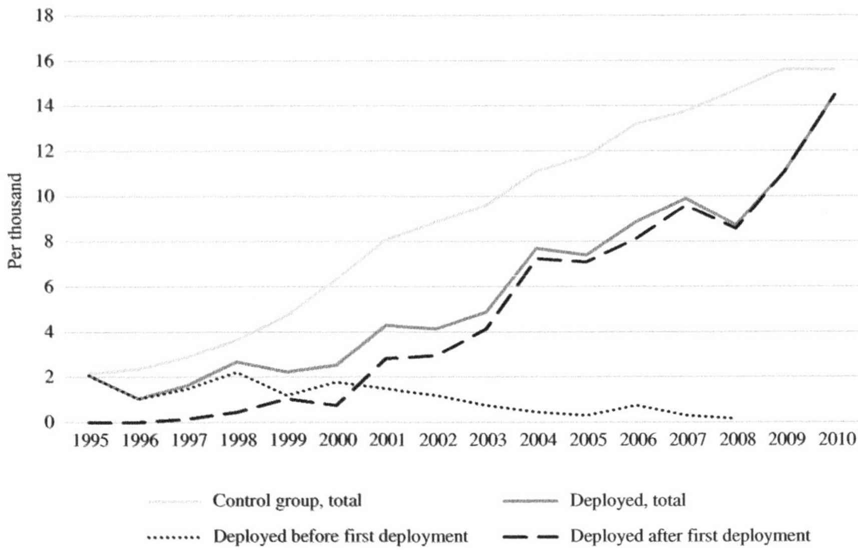


Figure 8.1. Psychiatric Diagnoses during 1995–2010 in Deployed and the Control Group Born in 1975–1982. *Source*: SFI.

period of 1975–1982, these soldiers could not have been deployed before 1992, as the oldest at that time was only 17.

## First-time Deployed in 2002 Compared with the Control Group

As in Chapter 7, we now compare the deployed and the control group before and after 2002. Using our criteria, 924 deployed can be compared with the control group from the birth cohort 1975–1982. The majority were exclusively deployed in former Yugoslavia.

Figure 8.2 shows the share of men with a psychiatric diagnosis in the control group and among the first-time deployed in 2002 for the period of 1995–2010. We also differentiate between those deployed for the first time in that period who had only been on one deployment and those who later went on other missions (one-time deployed vs many time deployed). Three years before deployment in 2002, the level of diagnoses is the same in the control group and among the deployed. But although the frequency of diagnoses increases in the control group, possibly partly explained by the effect of age, this frequency remains very low in 2002 for the deployed. After 2002, some interesting changes appear. For the one-time deployed, the level rises strongly until three years after returning home, and by eight years after deployment, the level is two to three times higher than in the control group. For first-time deployed, for eight years after returning home, the level is lower than for the control group. However, very large differences

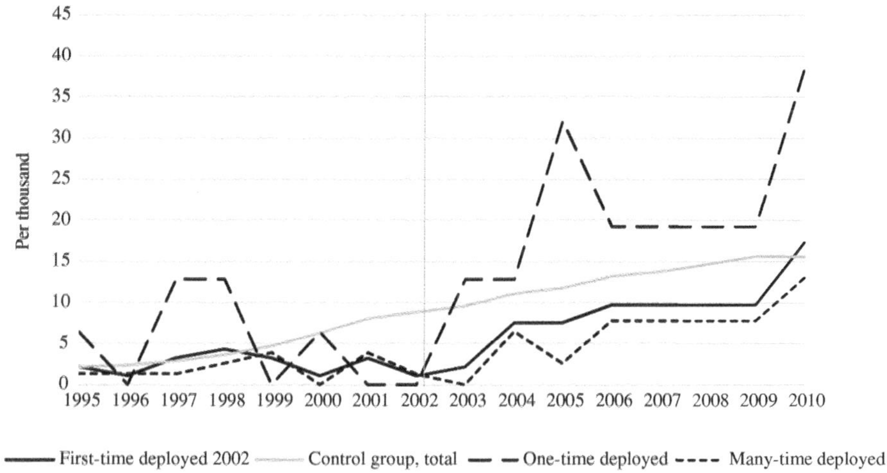


Figure 8.2. Men Born in 1975–1982 with a Registered Psychiatric Diagnosis in 1995–2010, Divided into Those Deployed for the First Time in 2002 and the Control Group and into One-time and Many-time Deployed. *Source*: SFI.

appear for one-time and many-time deployed. In Figure 8.2, we distinguish the one-time and many-time deployed showing that the difference in ages between the groups is not relevant here.

## Contacts with the Psychiatric Health Care Service

Another indicator of mental illness in deployed soldiers is their contact with the psychiatric health service. We analyse the three following indicators:

(1) in-patient treatment in a psychiatric ward;
(2) out-patient visits to a hospital psychiatric department; and
(3) contact with a psychiatric emergency room.

### *Before and after Deployment*

In all, about 5% of the ca 26,000 deployed in the years 1992–2010 had at least one contact with the psychiatric health service. Table 8.7 shows the contacts in all and per person for the three indicators. In particular, among the 813 people who visited an out-patient psychiatric department after returning home, the average is not less than 17 contacts per person. Moreover, contacts may have continued after the observation period, which ended in 2010.

Table 8.7. Contacts Per Person with the Psychiatric Health Care Service in 1995–2010 by Type of Contact and before and after First Deployment.

| | | **Total Number of Contacts** | **Total Number of People** | **Average Number of Contacts** |
|---|---|---|---|---|
| Psychiatric 24-hour admission | Before | 107 | 84 | 1.3 |
| | After | 1,140 | 448 | 2.5 |
| | Total[a] | 1,247 | 507 | 2.5 |
| Out-patient visit to psychiatric ward | Before | 2,014 | 235 | 8.6 |
| | After | 13,710 | 813 | 16.9 |
| | Total[a] | 15,724 | 1,004 | 15.7 |
| Psychiatric emergency room visit | Before | 133 | 95 | 1.4 |
| | After | 1,165 | 519 | 2.2 |
| | Total[a] | 757 | 590 | 1.3 |

*Source*: SFI.
*Notes*: Total of 1,372 individuals.
[a]Before and after numbers do not add up to the year total, as some people were in contact with the psychiatric health service both before and after deployment.

## *The Deployed and the Control Group*

In Figure 8.3, we compare the development in the average number of psychiatric contacts for the first-time deployed in 2002 and for the control group. In the latter group, the number rises steadily up to 2010, probably reflecting an effect of age as well as a general increase in the number of psychiatric patients in the public health care sector during that period. The number of contacts is very low among the deployed in 2002, possibly a result of the screening and self-selection processes which occur up until the time of deployment. Thereafter, the number of contacts rises over 3–4 years after first deployment, reaching the same level as in the control group, after which it falls to about half of that level.

Therefore, there is no doubt that deployment has a marked but short-term effect on the number of psychiatric contacts. In the longer term, Figure 8.3 indicates that the screening before deployment also has an effect afterwards compared with the control group because the deployed on average are psychologically more robust than the control group. When we look at each different type of contact forms, we obtained the same profile as when we aggregate them as shown in Figure 8.3.

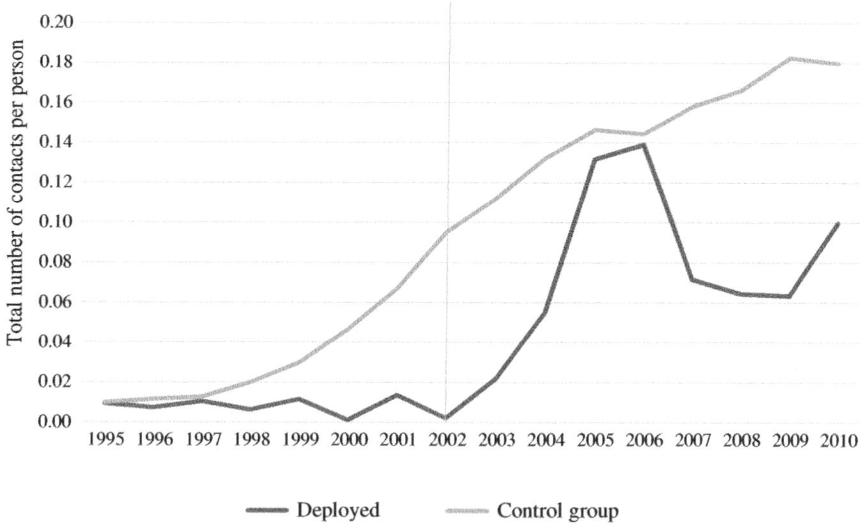


Figure 8.3. Average Number of Psychiatric Contacts in the Period for First-time Deployed in 2002 and the Control Group. *Source*: SFI. *Note*: The vertical line is 2002, the year of deployment.

### *Summary*

In this section, we examined the occurrence of psychiatric diagnoses and contacts with the psychiatric health service among the deployed. We also compared the occurrence of psychiatric diagnoses and contacts among the deployed with that in a control group. The results highlight a number of risk factors for developing psychological problems after a deployment. We find the following results:

**Psychiatric Diagnoses**

- There were 1,410 previously deployed with a registered psychiatric diagnosis in 1995–2010 (corresponding to 5% of all deployed).
- Results show that it is particularly those previously deployed to the former Yugoslavia, who receive psychiatric diagnoses. However, we cannot conclude on the basis of the analyses whether the increasing occurrence of mental illnesses among soldiers deployed to the former Yugoslavia is due to the selection process in the beginning of the period being less stringent, or the special experiences during these missions. Probably, both factors played a role.
- Some of the deployed have a higher risk of having a registered psychiatric diagnosis: These are soldiers who were diagnosed before deployment, were repatriated during a mission in 2005–2009, were between 25 and 44 years at the time of their first deployment, come from a different ethnic background than Danish, had a short education, had been raised in care (foster care), had been raised in single-parent families, were unemployed the year before first deployment, had their most recent deployment at least six years previously, had been deployed as privates and sent on UNPROFOR or IFOR as their first mission.

**Contacts with Psychiatric Health Care Service**

- Among the deployed, there is a general increase in the number of contacts after deployment. However, compared with the control group, the deployed had fewer contacts with the psychiatric health service.

## Medication for Mental Health-related Disease and Substance Abuse

In this section, we compare first the purchase of medications by deployed soldiers before and after the first deployment. These findings are then compared with those in a control group, as in the previous section. Finally, we investigate to what extent previously deployed soldiers have been in treatment for substance abuse. The following questions are addressed:

- How widespread was the purchase of mental health medication among the deployed in 1995–2010?
- How widespread was the purchase of mental health medication among the deployed in 1995–2010 before and after deployment? What are the trends here?
- What were the socio-demographic and military characteristics of the deployed who purchased mental health medication in the period of 1995–2010?
- How widespread was the purchase of mental health medication among the deployed compared with the control group?

### *Mental Health Medication*

To examine the individual's purchase of mental health medication, as another indicator of psychological problems, we use registry data in this section. These data come from the Drug Database (*Lægemiddeldatabasen*), which classifies prescription medicine, according to the ATC system (anatomical therapeutic chemical classification system). We have chosen five groups of medicines of special relevance to mental illness – antipsychotics, anxiety-relieving medicines, sleeping tablets and sedatives and anti-depressives – as these are common medications that are considered in investigations of psychiatric health (Lindegaard & Rosholm, 2010). We have included psychostimulants for alcohol dependency, which also can be used to treat the after-effects of deployment.

As it is not possible to strictly identify the diagnoses by the specific type of medication, in the analysis, we group the seven groups of medicine together as one indicator of mental illness.

### *Purchase of Mental Health Medication among the Deployed*

During 1995–2010, substantially more deployed purchased medication compared with the number with an actual psychiatric diagnosis, 19% vs 5%, respectively. From the end of the 1990s until 2010, the number of deployed who

Table 8.8. One-time and Many-time Deployed Soldiers Who Bought Mental Health Medication in 1995–2010, by Number of Years between Their First Deployment and the First Purchase.

| **Number of Years from First Deployment Until First Purchase of Medication** | **One-time Deployed** | | **Many-time Deployed** | | **Total** | |
|---|---|---|---|---|---|---|
| | *N* | % | *N* | % | *N* | % |
| More than 10 years before | 35 | 1 | 25 | 1 | 60 | 1 |
| 10–9 Years before | 29 | 1 | 43 | 2 | 72 | 1 |
| 8–7 Years before | 52 | 2 | 69 | 3 | 121 | 2 |
| 6–5 Years before | 80 | 3 | 84 | 3 | 164 | 3 |
| 4–3 Years before | 126 | 5 | 129 | 5 | 255 | 5 |
| 2–1 Year before | 142 | 6 | 167 | 7 | 309 | 6 |
| 0–1 Year after | 238 | 10 | 182 | 7 | 420 | 9 |
| 2–3 Years after | 313 | 13 | 304 | 13 | 617 | 13 |
| 4–5 Years after | 304 | 12 | 307 | 13 | 611 | 13 |
| 6–7 Years after | 269 | 11 | 264 | 11 | 533 | 11 |
| 8–9 Years after | 245 | 10 | 245 | 10 | 490 | 10 |
| more than nine years after | 601 | 25 | 613 | 25 | 1,214 | 25 |
| Total | 2,434 | 100 | 2,432 | 100 | 4,866 | 100 |

*Source*: SFI.

*Notes*: Total number of deployed is 26,038 (12,476 one-time deployed and 13,562 many-time deployed). Number of people who purchased mental health medication: 4,856. The median for the number of years after the first deployment to the first purchase occurred is five years for all persons (both one-time and many-time deployed).

purchased medication doubled, and this increase was greater than the increase in the number of deployed.

**When Did the Deployed Buy Mental Health Medication?**

In this section, we examine the health profile in terms of the first purchase of medication in relation to the first mission deployment; the data cover a period from more than 10 years before deployment to the nine years or more after. Table 8.8 shows the distribution of the time of first purchase of medication in relation to the date of the first deployment, for one-time and many-time deployed soldiers.

About 19% of both one-time and many-time deployed bought this type of medicine before their first deployment. In addition, almost 50% in both groups bought medicine for the first time six years or more after their first deployment.

Table 8.9. Purchase of Medication for Mental Illness before and after First Deployment in 1995–2010.

| Purchase of Medication for Mental Illness in Relation to the First Deployment | *N* | % |
|---|---|---|
| Only bought before | 488 | 2 |
| Only bought after | 3,731 | 14 |
| Bought both before and after | 647 | 2 |
| Never bought | 21,172 | 81 |
| Total | 26,038 | 100 |

*Source*: SFI.

**Purchase of Medication before and after the First Deployment**

Table 8.9 shows that 81% of the deployed did not buy medicine in the analysis period, 2% only bought this type of medicine before deployment, 14% only after deployment and 2% both before and after.

As the missions to the individual countries are not evenly spaced over time, relating purchases of mental health medication to the experiences of veterans during a mission is difficult. A very large proportion of the veterans who purchased medication had mission experiences in the former Yugoslavia. The missions themselves, as well as the fact that a significant part of purchases typically fall relatively many years after deployment (see Table 8.8), could explain this finding.

**Who Purchases Mental Health Medication after Deployment?**

The purchase of this type of medication depends on many circumstances and different background factors. We examine the following main questions:

- Is there a relationship between mission experience and purchase of medication?
- Is age at first deployment of significance?
- Are there gender differences in the probability of purchase of medication?

Table 8.10 shows the results of a regression analysis. With regard to the importance of mission experience, we found that deployment to the former Yugoslavia, alone or in combination with other deployments, is associated with a notably higher probability of purchase of medication. Surprisingly, mission experience in Afghanistan, as a peace-enforcing mission, is associated with a significant lower probability. That missions to Afghanistan occurred relatively late in the period could partly explain this finding. While being younger than 25 years is associated with a significant lower probability, being a women carries a significant higher probability of purchase compared with men.

Table 8.10. Logistic Regression of the Probability of Purchasing Mental Health Medication after Deployment.

| **Dependent Variable: Purchase of Medication for Mental Illness after the First Deployment** | **Probability of Buying Medicine for Mental Illness after Deployment** | |
|---|---|---|
| | **Odds Ratio** | **Standard Error** |
| Purchase of medication before first deployment | 10.881*** | 0.921 |
| Married or cohabiting | 0.963 | 0.083 |
| Woman | 1.530*** | 0.135 |
| Ethnic Danish | 0.953 | 0.158 |
| 18–24 Years | 0.731*** | 0.037 |
| ≥45 Years | 1.173* | 0.106 |
| Education (short) | 1.312*** | 0.061 |
| Education (long) | 1.191** | 0.095 |
| Having a child at home | 1.079 | 0.085 |
| In out-of-home care as a child | 1.548*** | 0.130 |
| Growing up in single-parent family | 1.262*** | 0.067 |
| Unemployed the year before deployment | 1.779*** | 0.231 |
| One-time deployed | 1.006 | 0.047 |
| Wounded during deployment[a] | 1.228 | 0.382 |
| Repatriated from a mission[b] | 2.151*** | 0.348 |
| Sergeant | 0.719*** | 0.065 |
| Officer | 0.491*** | 0.061 |
| Other personnel | 0.812 | 0.130 |
| No information on rank | 1.355*** | 0.086 |
| *Mission experience* | | |
| Former Yugoslavia, Iraq and Afghanistan | 1.633*** | 0.219 |
| Former Yugoslavia and Iraq | 1.796*** | 0.252 |
| Former Yugoslavia and Afghanistan | 1.532** | 0.294 |
| Afghanistan and Iraq | 1.170 | 0.126 |
| Former Yugoslavia | 1.155 | 0.155 |
| Iraq | 1.092 | 0.146 |
| Afghanistan | 0.712*** | 0.059 |

Table 8.10. (*Continued*)

| Dependent Variable: Purchase of Medication for Mental Illness after the First Deployment | Probability of Buying Medicine for Mental Illness after Deployment | |
|---|---|---|
| | Odds Ratio | Standard Error |
| No. of years since the latest deployment | | |
| 1–2 Years since the latest deployment (i.e. latest deployment in 2008–2009) | 1.886*** | 0.140 |
| 6–10 Years since the latest deployment (i.e. latest deployment in 2000–2004) | 2.577*** | 0.226 |
| More than 10 years since the latest deployment (i.e. latest deployment in 1992–1999) | 0.057*** | 0.012 |
| Constant | 10.881*** | 0.921 |
| Total number of observations | 22,944 | |
| Log-likelihood | −8,165.59 | |

*Source*: SFI.
*Notes*: ***$p < 0.01$; ** $p < 0.05$; * $p < 0.1$. Robust standard error.
[a]Wounded in 1992–2009.
[b]Repatriated in 2005–2009.

Other factors resulting in a significant higher probability are as follows:

- having purchased that type of medicine before deployment;
- having a short education;
- having been in out-of-home care for all or some of childhood, or growing up in a single-parent family; and
- having been unemployed during the year before deployment.

**Comparison of Deployed and Control Groups**

As previously mentioned, we used a control group of men born in 1975–1982 in comparison with the deployed from the same birth cohorts. Figure 8.4 shows the proportion of deployed and men in the control group who bought mental health medication. The profiles of the two groups are similar but the proportion among the deployed throughout the period studied is lower.

**Soldiers Deployed for the First Time in 2002 in Relation to the Control Group**

As in the previous sections, we compare the purchase of medicine in the control group and with first-timers deployed in 2002. Figure 8.5 is similar to Figure 8.4, but now, the deployed group is restricted to those deployed for the first time in

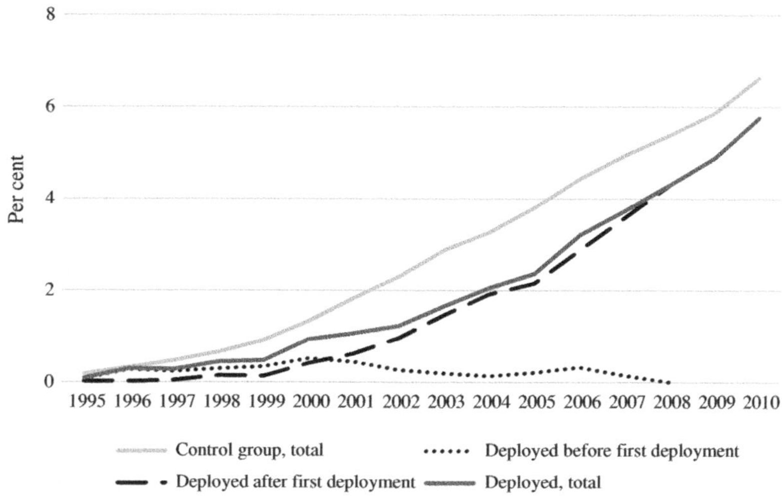


Figure 8.4. Deployed Soldiers and Controls Who Bought Mental Health Medication in 1995–2010, before and after Deployment. *Source*: SFI.

2002. Contrary to Figure 8.4, Figure 8.5 shows that the purchase of medication among the deployed rises sharply beginning three years after first deployment 2010, reaching the same level as that of the control group. Figure 8.5 shows that immediately after the first deployment, a large difference appears with respect to the purchase of medication between the one-time and the many-time deployed soldiers. This difference is so large that the number of one-time deployed in 2002 who purchased medication in 2010 is significantly larger than among the control group.

Finally, we also investigate the purchased medications in so-called defined daily doses (DDD), which makes it possible to compare the amount of the medicine purchased between the two groups. Figure 8.6 illustrates the purchases measured in DDD between 1995 through 2010. For soldiers deployed for the first time in 2002, screening and self-selection resulted in a very low level of purchases up to the year of deployment. Thereafter, especially starting three years after the first deployment, the level of purchases measured in DDD increases markedly compared with the control group. When divided by individual types of medicine, it is in particular the purchase of anti-depressives which increases. This result is in accordance with results presented in Table 8.4 showing an increase for psychiatric diagnoses F32 and F33 from 29% to 36% from before to after deployment.

Considering the present sample, but using matching techniques for the deployed and the controls, Vincent Lyk-Jensen, Weatherall, and Jepsen (2016) estimated the effect of deployment in a difference-in-differences setting controlling

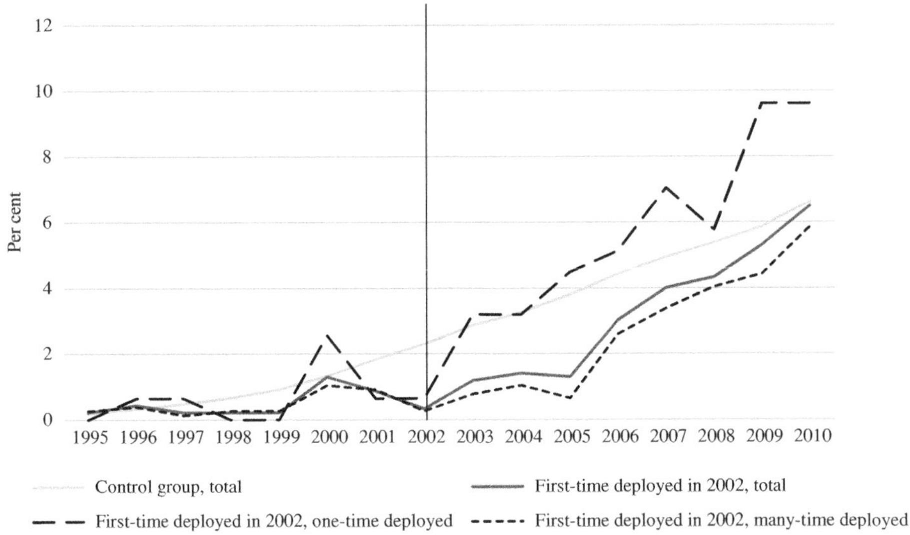


Figure 8.5. Soldiers Deployed for the First Time in 2002 and the Control Group Who Bought Medicine for Mental Illnesses in 1995–2010, Divided into One-time and Many-time Deployed. *Source*: SFI. *Notes*: The vertical line is 2002, the year of deployment. Deployed: 924 observations for each year (one-time deployed and 768 many-time deployed). Control group: 104,790 observations for each year.

for time trends and other omitted variables and found a significant long-lasting adverse effect of military deployment on soldiers' mental health proxied by diagnosis and medication.

## Substance Abuse among the Deployed, 1996–2010

Register-based data are also available concerning substance abuse treatments among both the deployed and the control group. Very few among the deployed have been treated for substance abuse problems, that is, 0.6% of all deployed in 1992–2009. This share is significantly lower than in the control group. There are no signs that deployment results in specific substance abuse problems.

### *Summary*

Analysis of the purchase of mental health medication indicates possible long-term consequences of deployment. It is therefore important to emphasise that it is still too early to draw final conclusions, particularly about those deployed more recently. However, the analyses do indicate the following:

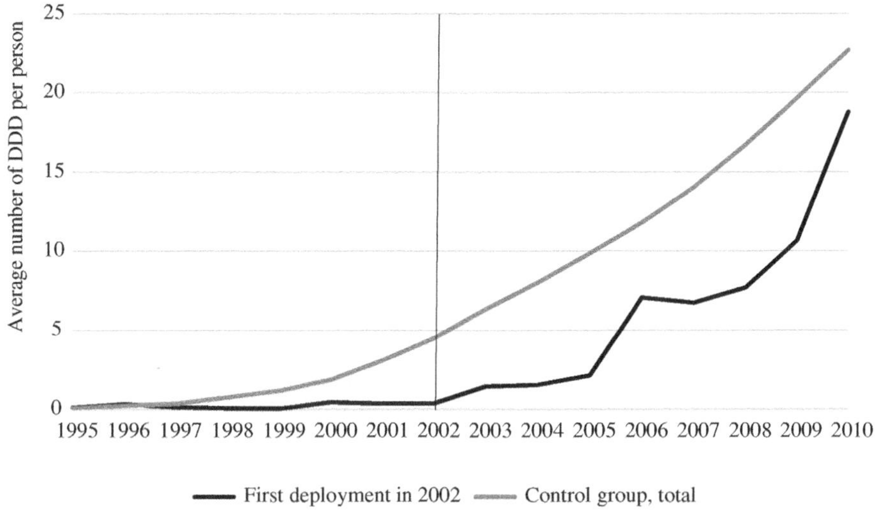


Figure 8.6. Average Number of Daily Doses (DDD) of Medicine for Mental Illnesses among First-time Deployed in 2002 and the Control Group. *Source*: SFI. *Notes*: WHO-defined DDD values for 2010 Deployed: 924 observations for each year. Control group: 104,790 observations for each year.

**Purchase of Medication**

- The risk of purchasing mental health medicine after deployment is higher for the deployed who bought that medication before deployment, were repatriated during a mission, were deployed more than six years ago, were deployed to the former Yugoslavia or Iraq and Afghanistan, former Yugoslavia and Iraq, former Yugoslavia and Afghanistan, or Afghanistan and Iraq, were raised in out-of-home care, were unemployed during the year before deployment, grew up in a single-parent family, had a short or long education, were over 25 years old at the time of their first deployment or were women.
- When we compare first-timers deployed in 2002 from the birth cohorts 1975–1982 with the control group, there is an increase in the amount of medicine purchased for mental illness after deployment, that is, after 2002.

**Substance Abuse**

- Generally, very few of the previously deployed have been treated for substance abuse (0.6% compared with 1.6% in the control group).

**Mental Problems**

- About 17% of the deployed were registered in the National Health Service system after deployment without having been registered before; that is, 17% were registered with a psychiatric diagnosis, or had bought medicine for mental illnesses, or had been treated for substance abuse after deployment, whereas they were never recorded previously.

## Work-related Injuries

In this section, we examine the extent of reported work-related injuries among those previously deployed. In Chapter 4, we surveyed the number of wounded and repatriated soldiers, and we have the opportunity in this chapter to investigate to which extent the previously deployed who reported a work-related accident are the same as the wounded and repatriated, or whether they represent a third group. We have had access to data from the National Board of Industrial Injuries (*Arbejdsskadestryelsen* (ASK)) and the Military Office of Industrial Injuries and Compensation (*Forsvarets Arbejdsskade- og Erstatningskontor* (FAEK)), which provide information on the number of reported work-related injuries among the previously deployed. This study is the first investigation of how widely reported work-related injuries are among previously deployed soldiers.

This section looks at the following questions:

- How many of the deployed have reported a work injury?
- How many have been reported with a work-related injury based on the diagnosis of PTSD?
- Are the deployed with a reported work-related injury in the group of wounded and repatriated whom we have previously investigated?
- How many of the deployed who reported a work-related injury, are in the group of deployed who have been diagnosed with a psychiatric diagnosis, purchased medication for mental illness or treated for substance abuse, as described in the previous sections on mental health diagnoses and medication?

### *Information about Work-related Injuries and Occupational Disease*

In this section, we use two different sources of data – ASK and FAEK – to investigate the occurrence of two types of work-related injuries: accidents, for which a date can be ascertained, and occupational diseases, which often appear after a longer time interval.

For analytical reasons, we only look at work-related injuries registered with ASK in 1997–2009, where the date of the injury coincides with a period of deployment. For the work-related illnesses, we cover all those reported to ASK in 1997–2009, as it is not possible to establish whether the illness started during a deployment. Altogether, this analysis comprises 1,725 reported work-related illnesses. We have also data on the control group from ASK.

FAEK does not deal with cases of work-related illnesses, but only registered work-related injuries. In all, we have data on 3,290 work-related accidents in 1997–2009 that occurred within a period of deployment. There is information on the date of the injury, the country in which the injury happened and the degree of injury. We have taken into consideration the overlap between the two registrations, as 668 people reported a case both to ASK and to FAEK.

**The Number of Reported Work-related Injuries among the Deployed Compared with the Control Group**

Using the same control group as previously described, more deployed (19%) reported at least one work-related injury to the ASK during the period compared with the control group (9%). In relation to registered work-related illnesses, the share is almost the same in the two groups (16% in the control group and 18% among the deployed). Substantially, more of the registered work-related illnesses concern mental illness among the deployed than among the control group.

**Description of Reported Work-related Injuries Linked to a Deployment**

Altogether, 680 work-related injuries were recorded during a deployment, and compensation was offered in 33% of the cases, whereas the cases were dismissed in 21%. In 46% of the cases, no decision has yet been made. From the data, it is possible to establish whether those, whose cases were dismissed, had several mental illnesses and purchased more medicine as a reaction to this. However, there is no evidence pointing to a deterioration of the illness as a result of the dismissal.

An overview of the division of work-related injuries by country and time is shown in Table 8.11. The number in the first year, 1997, is certainly an expression of a registration 'heaping effect'. The Table also shows a shift over time, with most weight placed on injuries occurring in the former Yugoslavia, followed by Iraq and finally Afghanistan. Almost 50% of the work-related injuries registered happened in Afghanistan in the last five years of 1997–2009.

In Table 8.12, we present the degree of injury for 214 of the 680 reported; in all cases, the degree of severity of the injury was at least 5%. In about 70% of the 214 cases, the degree of severity was 5–10%. Only 4% of the reported cases involve a decreased ability to work of 15–75%, resulting in an average compensation of about two million DKK (see Armey, Kniesner, Leeth, & Sullivan, 2018 for an analysis of compensation to American veterans from Iraq and Afghanistan).

**Description of Work-related Illnesses Reported to ASK**

As mentioned earlier, a precise date in relation to deployment cannot be assigned to the occurrence of work-related illnesses. Instead, we look at all work-related illnesses reported to ASK in 1997–2009. The relative distribution over time is shown in Figure 8.7.

Aside from a registration 'heaping' in 1997, the increase is affected by a change from 2005 in the law expanding the definition of work-related illness.

The proportion of reported work-related illnesses considered eligible for compensation is significantly lower than for work-related injuries; only 15% of the cases reported to ASK were judged eligible for compensation, whereas 72% of cases were dismissed. The previously deployed with a recognised work-related illness, are more likely to a have a psychological diagnosis and

Table 8.11. Reported Work-related Injuries among the Deployed in 1997–2009 According to ASK, by Year of Injury and Country in Which the Injury Occurred.

| | Former Yugoslavia | Iraq | Afghanistan | Other countries | Total, % |
|---|---|---|---|---|---|
| 1997 | 95 | 1 | 0 | 4 | 100 |
| 1998 | 100 | 0 | 0 | 0 | 100 |
| 1999 | 87 | 2 | 0 | 11 | 100 |
| 2000 | 96 | 0 | 0 | 4 | 100 |
| 2001 | 84 | 0 | 0 | 16 | 100 |
| 2002 | 83 | 0 | 17 | 0 | 100 |
| 2003 | 78 | 13 | 9 | 0 | 100 |
| 2004 | 43 | 43 | 11 | 4 | 100 |
| 2005 | 31 | 54 | 9 | 6 | 100 |
| 2006 | 16 | 42 | 36 | 5 | 100 |
| 2007 | 14 | 24 | 56 | 7 | 100 |
| 2008 | 11 | 4 | 82 | 3 | 100 |
| 2009 | 9 | 1 | 82 | 8 | 100 |
| In all | 50 | 15 | 30 | 5 | 100 |

*Source*: SFI.
*Notes*: 680 reported work-related injuries that are connected with a deployment, that is, where the date of the injury falls within a period of deployment. Compensation for work-related injuries has not been granted for all the cases.

in many cases to have purchased mental health medication. In relation to mission experience, the deployed who were sent to the former Yugoslavia only, or in combination with other missions, make up a predominant share of those who reported work-related illnesses. However, as the observation period ended in 2009, reports from those deployed to Iraq and Afghanistan can be expected afterwards.

Among the deployed in the observation period, 174 persons reported a case with PTSD as a diagnosis. Of these, compensation was granted in 60% of the cases. As the definition of work-related injuries was expanded in 2005 to include PTSD –the only psychological work-related illness – the study of changes over time is problematic. Again, in terms of mission experience, there is a predominance of deployed with a background in the former Yugoslavia for this diagnosis; however, this diagnosis is made in rather few cases.

Table 8.13 shows the degree of severity of the reported work-related illnesses in ASK. For 85% of the work-related illnesses, the degree is not assessed. For

Table 8.12. Reported Work-related Injuries among the Deployed in 1997–2009 by Degree According to ASK.

| Degree of Severity in Per cent | *N* | % |
|---|---|---|
| 5 | 90 | 13 |
| 8–10 | 60 | 9 |
| 11–15 | 30 | 4 |
| 16–20 | 9 | 1 |
| 21–30 | 7 | 1 |
| 31–99 | 10 | 1 |
| 100–120 | 8 | 1 |
| Reported accidents with no measurement of severity | 466 | 69 |
| Total | 680 | 100 |

*Source*: SFI.
*Notes*: Reported work-related accidents that are connected with a deployment, that is, where the date of the injury falls within a period of deployment. Compensation was not granted for all reported cases of work-related injuries.

the reported work-related illnesses with a given degree of severity, 57% have a value of under 10%.

For the deployed, the average compensation for injuries is around 71,000 DKK, and the average compensation for loss of the ability to work is about 1.7 million DKK. For the control group, the respective amount is 56,000 DKK and ca 1.2 million DKK. Thus, work-related injuries and loss of the ability to work are more serious among the deployed than for the control group.

## Military Office of Industrial Injuries and Compensation (FAEK)

FAEK has registered about 12% of the deployed in 1997–2009 with an accident at work during their period of deployment. Table 8.14 shows that in FAEK, compensation was predominantly not for work-related injuries in the former Yugoslavia but rather for injuries occurring during later deployments to Iraq and Afghanistan.

The shift in the relative importance of the different missions is related to the fact that FAEK was first established in 1997, and knowledge about the institution increased gradually hereafter. The very large increase in accidents among the deployed in conjunction with an increasing engagement in Iraq and Afghanistan is illustrated in Figure 8.8. The low numbers in 2002 may be related to a 30% drop in the numbers of first-time deployed from 2000 to 2001, after which they rose again.

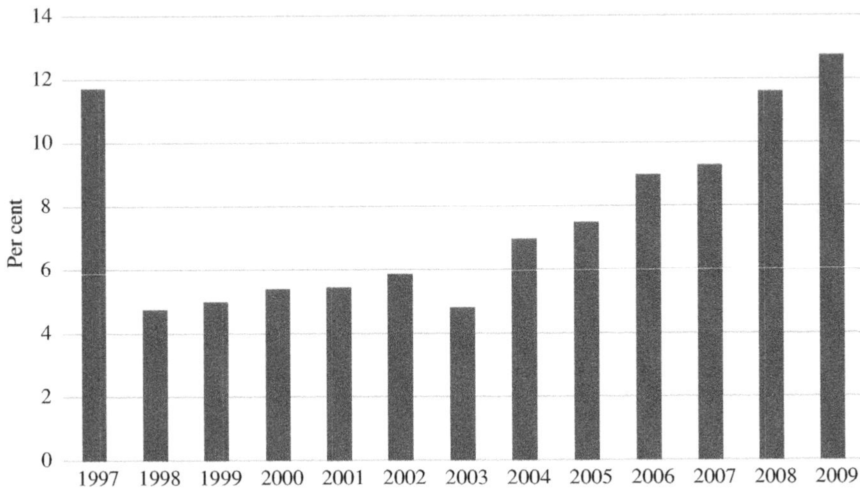


Figure 8.7. Work-related Illnesses Reported to ASK in 1997–2009 among Deployed Divided by Year in Which the Accident was Reported. *Source*: SFI. *Notes*: Total number of reported work-related illness 1,725. All reports for work-related illness among the deployed in 1992–2009. Compensation was not granted for all reported cases of work-related injuries.

Table 8.13. Reported Work-related Illness Recorded at ASK in 1997–2009, by Severity of the Problem.

| **Degree of Severity in Per cent** | *N* | % |
|---|---|---|
| 5 | 80 | 5 |
| 8–10 | 69 | 4 |
| 11–15 | 70 | 4 |
| 16–20 | 36 | 2 |
| 21–35 | 6 | 0 |
| Reported illnesses with no measurement of severity | 1,464 | 85 |
| Total | 1,725 | 100 |

*Source*: SFI.
*Notes*: All reports for work-related illness among the deployed in 1992–2009. Compensation was not granted for all reported work-related illnesses.

As shown in Table 8.15, a considerably smaller proportion of work-related accidents, barely 8%, were assigned a severity rating by FAEK compared with ASK. Another difference is that there is also a smaller share with very high degree of severity in the reports to FAEK.

Table 8.14. Work-related Accidents Registered at FAEK in 1997–2007 by Country in Which the Accident Occurred.

| | *N* | % |
|---|---|---|
| Former Yugoslavia | 1,181 | 42 |
| Iraq | 472 | 17 |
| Afghanistan | 1,091 | 39 |
| Other countries | 65 | 2 |
| Total | 2,809 | 100 |

*Source*: SFI.
*Notes*: Data on the country of injury are taken from military data; according to FAEK and data from the military in general, there are few discrepancies between countries.

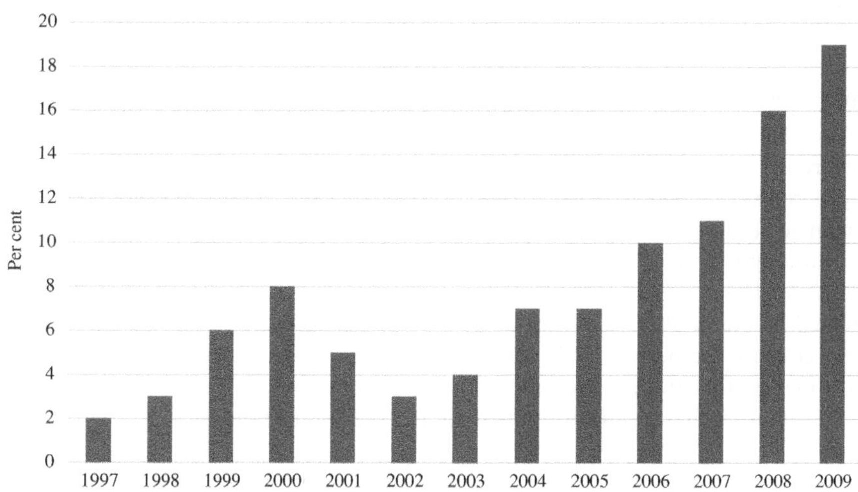


Figure 8.8. Work-related Accidents Registered with FAEK in 1997–2009 by Year in Which the Accident Occurred. *Source*: SFI. *Note*: Total of 2,809 cases in all.

### *Risk of Being Wounded, Repatriated or Reporting a Work-related Injury*

Below, we examine first how many were wounded, repatriated or reported a work-related injury. Second, we show the results from a regression analysis of the relation between the risk of experiencing any of these events and a series of background variables.

In all, 4,659 people, or 18% of the deployed, suffered one or more of these events (i.e. wounded, repatriated or reported a work-related injury). In

Table 8.15. Work-related Accidents Registered with FAEK in 1997–2009 by Degree of Severity.

| **Degree of Severity in Per cent** | *N* | % |
|---|---|---|
| 5 | 90 | 3.2 |
| 6–10 | 57 | 2.0 |
| 11–15 | 28 | 1.0 |
| 16–30 | 18 | 0.6 |
| 31–50 | 8 | 0.3 |
| 51–90 | 5 | 0.2 |
| 91–100 | 7 | 0.2 |
| No measurement of severity | 2,596 | 92.4 |
| Total | 2,809 | 100 |

*Source*: SFI.

2005–2009, 399 soldiers were repatriated, and 48% of these also reported a work-related injury. The same percentage is found for the 123 wounded. However, according to the available data, by far the majority of soldiers (94%) who are registered with either ASK or FAEK, were neither repatriated nor wounded, and the majority of these cases have not been assigned a severity rating.

Although there can be a big difference in the seriousness of the three events, we have chosen to present the results of a regression analysis in which they are treated as the pooled outcomes of a series of background variables. The results only concern the period 2005–2009, as this is the only period for which we have information for all three events (Table 8.16).

The factors that significantly increase the risk are as follows:

- being 45 years old or older;
- having been in out-of-home care for part or all of one's upbringing; and
- having been deployed in the last two years of the analysis period, with a predominance of deployments in Afghanistan.

The factors that indicate a significantly lower risk are as follows:

- having been on only one mission, and
- being in a personnel group other than privates.

### *Summary*

In this section, we have examined the extent of reported and registered work-related injuries among those previously deployed. The extent of work-related

Table 8.16. Logistical Regression of Probability of Being Wounded, Repatriated or Reporting a Work-related Injury in 1997–2009.

| Dependent Variable: Work-related Injuries, Wounded or Repatriated in 2005–2009 (Yes/No) | Odds Ratio | Standard Error |
|---|---|---|
| Married or cohabiting | 0.879 | 0.106 |
| Female | 1.180 | 0.133 |
| Ethnic Danish | 0.746* | 0.126 |
| 18–24 Years old (at latest deployment) | 1.019 | 0.066 |
| ≥45 Years (at latest deployment) | 1.282** | 0.133 |
| Education (short) | 0.947 | 0.055 |
| Education (long) | 0.918 | 0.109 |
| Children living at home | 0.901 | 0.102 |
| In out-of-home care as child | 1.433*** | 0.174 |
| Grew up in single-parent family | 0.922 | 0.062 |
| Unemployed | 1.085 | 0.310 |
| One-time deployed | 0.847*** | 0.051 |
| Personnel Group – Latest Deployment | | |
| Sergeant | 0.673*** | 0.048 |
| Officer | 0.560*** | 0.061 |
| Other personnel | 0.277*** | 0.053 |
| No information on rank | 0.354*** | 0.121 |
| Latest Mission | | |
| KFOR | 1.849*** | 0.221 |
| ISAF | 3.533*** | 0.377 |
| IRAQ | 2.353*** | 0.301 |
| Last Deployment Year | | |
| 2006 | 1.134 | 0.121 |
| 2007 | 1.069 | 0.112 |
| 2008 | 1.400*** | 0.143 |
| 2009 | 1.501*** | 0.150 |
| Constant | 0.128*** | 0.028 |
| Total no. of observations | 10,629 | |
| Log-likelihood | −4,817.39 | |

*Source*: SFI.

*Notes*: ***$p < 0.01$; ** $p < 0.05$; * $p < 0.1$. Robust standard error. The sample contains both one-time and many-time deployed. The socio-demographic characteristics are linked to the year of the first mission regardless of age, which refers to the last mission. Reported injuries at work include those registered with ASK and FAEK.

injuries is interesting as it contributes to give an overall picture of the consequences of deployment on international missions. In Chapter 4, we described the wounded and repatriated soldiers, but in this section, we found that veterans who report a work-related injury form a more diverse group than just the wounded and repatriated. We have based our analyses on data from the Industrial Injuries Board (ASK) and the Military Office of Industrial Injuries and Compensation (FAEK). The following conclusions were made:

- 17% of previously deployed, or 4,448 veterans, reported a work-related injury to ASK (in 1992–2009) or FAEK (in 1997–2009).
- If we include the wounded and repatriated, 18% of the deployed (i.e. 4,659 veterans) who were wounded, were repatriated (data only for 2005–2009), reported a work-related injury (not all injuries were subject to compensation) or had registered a work-related injury at FAEK.
- 22% of the deployed who were wounded, repatriated or reported a work-related injury, have been registered with a psychiatric diagnosis, have purchased medication for mental illness or have been in treatment for substance abuse following their latest deployment.
- 1,725 work-related illnesses were reported, and 18% of the cases dealing with reported work-related illnesses involved psychological problems.

In addition, we compared the deployed with a control group and found the following:

- A larger share of the deployed (19%) than the control group (9%) had a work-related injury reported to ASK in 1992–2009.
- Among the deployed, a larger share of work-related illness was reported to ASK, based on psychological diagnoses (18%), compared with the control group (5%).

We investigated the characteristics that are correlated with the risk of being wounded, being repatriated or reporting a work-related injury in 2005–2009. We found that the risk is:

- lower among the ethnic Danish veterans and greater among those who were raised in out-of-home care, or who were older than 44 at their latest deployment;
- greater for those whose latest deployment was ISAF, Iraq or KFOR with 'Other missions'; and similarly, the risk is greater for those who were deployed in 2008–2009 compared with 2005; and
- lower for sergeants, officers and other personnel (compared with privates) and for the one-time compared with the many-time deployed.

Looking at all formerly deployed soldiers suffering physical or psychological injuries in 1992–2009 based on the analysed data, this adds up to 31% of the deployed. However, the severity of the injuries varies greatly in this group of affected soldiers. Most of those who have been registered with a work-related injury at FAEK or ASK did not have permanent problems.

## Analysis of Mortality

In this section, we examine mortality among veterans. The analysis focuses particularly on mortality after deployment. We survey the previously deployed who died in 1992–2010 and undertake a probability estimation for those dying after deployment. In Europe and North America, after the World War II and the Vietnam war, it was discussed whether veterans had a higher post-deployment/post-war probability of dying compared with the general population of non-veterans. On the one hand, international studies have shown that veterans of the Vietnam war and the World War II were more likely to have poor health and a high mortality rate (Cook, Riggs, Thompson, Coyne, & Sheikh, 2004; Hearst, Newman, & Hulley, 1986). On the other hand, other studies have shown that mortality among those previously deployed is not greater than that among various comparison groups (Conley & Heerwig, 2009). Høier-Madsen, Jørgensen, Sørensen, and Stokkebye (2010) investigated the risk of death during a mission among Danish soldiers in 1992–2008. They found a mortality rate of 0.08 during deployment and an increasing survival rate among those wounded (see Vedtofte, 2016 for a study of suicides among Danish veterans in the period 1992–2014; Shen, Cunha, & Williams, 2016 for a study of suicides among American veterans).

### *Analysis of Mortality of Deployed Soldiers*

Of the 26,038 soldiers deployed in 1992–2009, a total of 303 had died up to 2010. As there were only eight women among the dead, the focus in this section is on the 295 men who died after deployment up to 2010. The section uses both descriptive analysis of the veterans who died and results from a statistical analysis of the risk of death following deployment.

Figure 8.9 shows the trend in number of soldiers and veterans dying between 1993 and 2010, divided up into those who died during or after deployment. The increasing time trend reflects partly an increase in the number of those deployed over time, partly that the veterans became older and were exposed to an age-related increased risk of death and finally that the missions changed in character from peacekeeping to peace-enforcing, with an increasing probability of being engaged in combat situations.

In all, 54 men died during deployment, most of whom in battle. Out of the 295 men who died during or after deployment, about half (48%) of the 295 died from natural causes, 17% because of accidents and 13% by committing suicide.

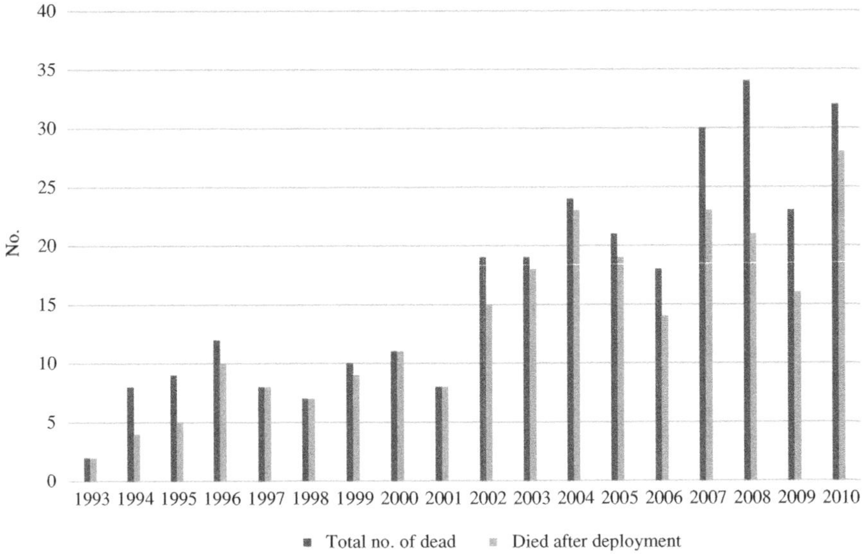


Figure 8.9. Deployed Men Who Died in 1992–2009 by Year, Assessed as the Total Number of Dead and Those Dying after Coming Home. *Source*: SFI.

Focusing on those who had died up to and including 2010 in relation to those who are still alive, there are several differences in socio-economic and health background factors. Significantly, more men 45 years or older died, compared with 18- to 24-year-olds. Other background factors are difficult to interpret in a partial comparison because they vary considerably with age. However, this hardly applies to the relation that the share of dead is significantly higher for those who have received at least one psychiatric diagnosis.

In the same way, it is difficult in a partial analysis to get a complete overview of the correlation between risk of death and selected military characteristics. For example, we found a significantly smaller proportion of dead among the soldiers who were privates, which is probably related to the fact that they are the youngest group. Likewise, it is very difficult to evaluate the proportion of dead in terms of mission type in relation to analysis period, which reflects that the missions have changed character and destinations over time. We go one step further than pure partial correlations by carrying out a logistic regression, in which we seek to explain how different background variables influence the mortality risk among the deployed after returning home. Although that gives us more information than a pure description, it is important to underline that the regression does not establish any causal relation between the risk of dying after returning home and various background factors. In addition, the observations only go up to 2010. Those deployed on later missions can therefore only be followed for a relatively

Table 8.17. Logistic Regression on the Probability of Dying after Deployment among Veterans in 1992–2009.[a]

| Dependent Variable: Die after Deployment (Yes/No)[b] | Odds Ratio | Standard Error |
|---|---|---|
| 18–24 Years (25–44 years) | 0.558*** | 0.107 |
| ≥45 years (25–44 years) | 2.121*** | 0.436 |
| Former Yugoslavia and Iraq and Afghanistan (former Yugoslavia) | 0.108*** | 0.056 |
| Former Yugoslavia and Iraq (former Yugoslavia) | 0.166*** | 0.068 |
| Former Yugoslavia and Afghanistan (former Yugoslavia) | 0.051*** | 0.051 |
| Iraq (former Yugoslavia) | 0.116*** | 0.046 |
| Afghanistan (former Yugoslavia) | 0.084*** | 0.034 |
| Other countries (former Yugoslavia)[c] | 0.328*** | 0.086 |
| One-time deployment | 2.244*** | 0.350 |
| At least one psychiatric diagnosis | 1.678*** | 0.397 |
| At least one purchase of medication for mental illness | 3.133*** | 0.492 |
| Years since last deployment | 0.759*** | 0.015 |
| Married or cohabiting | 1.053 | 0.215 |
| Short education | 1.620*** | 0.272 |
| Long education | 1.044 | 0.205 |
| Child living at home | 0.253*** | 0.048 |
| Private | 0.166*** | 0.036 |
| No. of observations | 22,035 | |
| Log-likelihood | −989.8302 | |

*Source*: SFI.
*Notes*: Died before 31 December 2010. Does not include immigrants or emigrants or those who died during deployment. ***$p < 0.01$; **$p < 0.05$; *$p < 0.10$.
[a]Method described in Chapter 3.
[b]Reference categories are given in parentheses.
[c]A combination of missions in Afghanistan and Iraq.

short period. With these reservations in mind, Table 8.17 shows the results of the regression analysis.

The results point to a series of factors that increase the probability of death significantly, as well as a number of factors that decrease the probability. We summarise some of these factors below.

Factors that significantly increase the mortality risk:

- 45 years or older;
- single mission;
- at least one psychiatric diagnosis, and purchasing medication for psychological problems at least once; and
- a short education.

Factors that significantly decrease the mortality risk:

- 18–24 years of age;
- several mission experiences in comparison with only having been deployed to the former Yugoslavia;
- increasing number of years since the last deployment;
- children at home; and
- rank of private.

**Age**

We now investigate the relationship between age and cause of death. Figure 8.10 shows the respective causes of death by age for the four age groups. As seen, there is wide variation and in the youngest group, most died during deployment. Thereafter, as expected, the number of those dying from natural causes increases

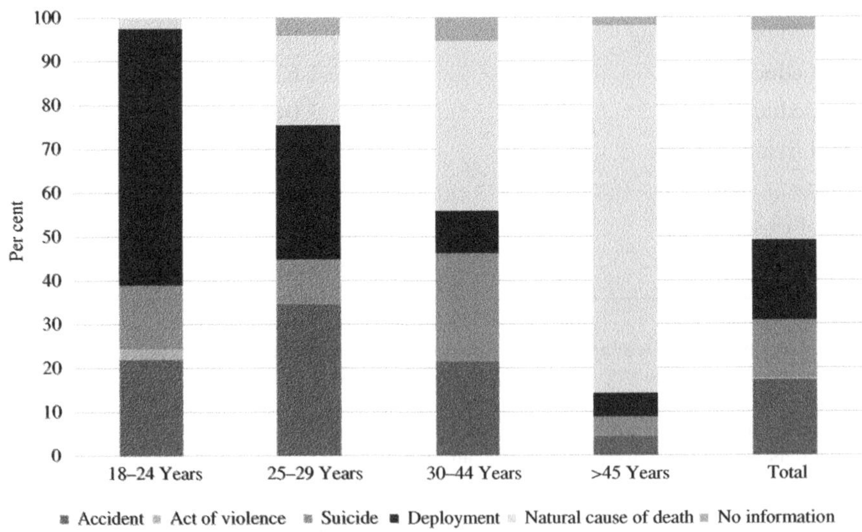


Figure 8.10. Men Deployed in 1992–2009 by Cause of Death, Divided into Age Groups and Times of Death. *Source*: SFI. *Notes*: Died before 31 December 2010. In all, 295 people died. Includes those dying during deployment.

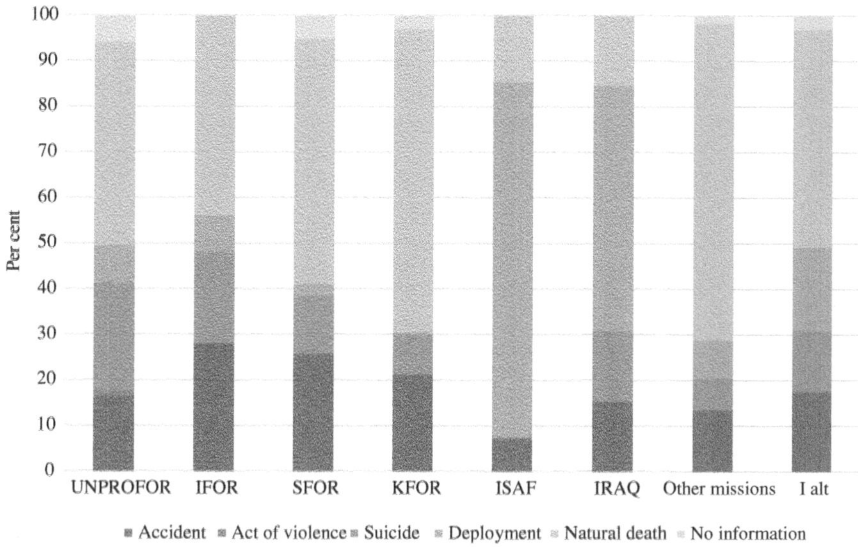


Figure 8.11. Men Deployed in 1992–2009 Who Died, by Cause of Death and the Latest Mission. *Source*: SFI. *Notes*: Died before 31 December 2010. In all, 295 people died. Includes deaths during deployment, UNCRO is included under UNPROFOR.

with age and is greatest for the age group 45 years or older. It also appears that the predominant causes of death among 25- to 29-year-olds are suicide and accidents.

**Missions and Destinations**

A corresponding division of causes of death in relation to the most recent deployment is shown in Figure 8.11. Although the time factor here plays a role in the interpretation, there is no doubt that there is a large difference between missions in relation to the respective causes of death. The proportion who died during deployment is particularly large for those deployed to Afghanistan, but also constitutes over half of those deployed to Iraq. In contrast, a large share of deaths in the former Yugoslavia was suicides.

**Number of Deployments**

In chapters 4 and 6, we found that among the repatriated and wounded, there is generally a higher proportion of many-time deployed. In Figure 8.12, we examine whether there is also a relatively higher share of many-time deployed soldiers among those who died.

Figure 8.12 shows that there is not a relatively higher number of one-time deployed among the dead than among those still alive. When interpreting this result, one should take into consideration both self-selection – that the soldiers themselves want to be deployed again – and the Military screening of those

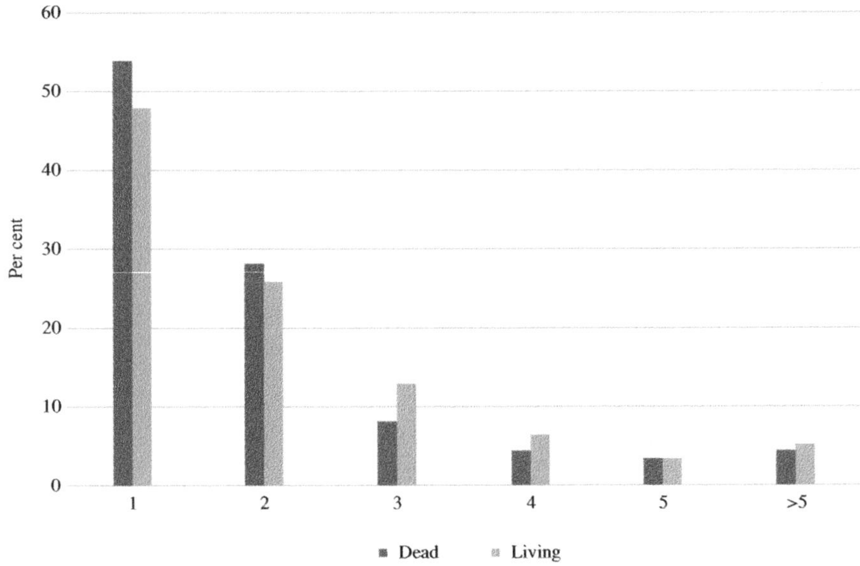


Figure 8.12. Men Deployed in 1992–2009, by Number of Deployments for Those Still Alive and Those Who Died. *Source*: SFI. *Notes*: Dead and living on 31 December 2010. Total: 24,745 men. Includes deaths during deployment.

judged eligible for a new deployment. Both can lead to a tendency to select the psychologically strongest for re-deployment.

**Number of Years Since the Most Recent Deployment**

The regression analysis in Table 8.17 shows that risk of death becomes less, the longer the time that has elapsed since the most recent deployment. However, the estimated coefficient of the variable 'number of years since most recent deployment' does not give any information about the time profile concerning the association between risk of death and the number of years since coming home. The time profile is shown in Figure 8.13, in which the men deployed in 1992–2009 who died after returning home are categorised by the number of years since the most recent deployment. Figure 8.13 clearly shows that stressful experiences during a mission can influence the deployed, so that the risk of dying is greatest 2–4 years after returning home, after which the numbers fall to a low level.

**Health**

In the regression, we found that the variables 'at least one psychiatric diagnosis' and 'at least one purchase of mental health medication' had significant coefficients, whose size indicated that both variables had an increased effect on the risk of death. Of those who died, 13% had at least one contact with the psychiatric health care system, and 5% had more than three contacts.

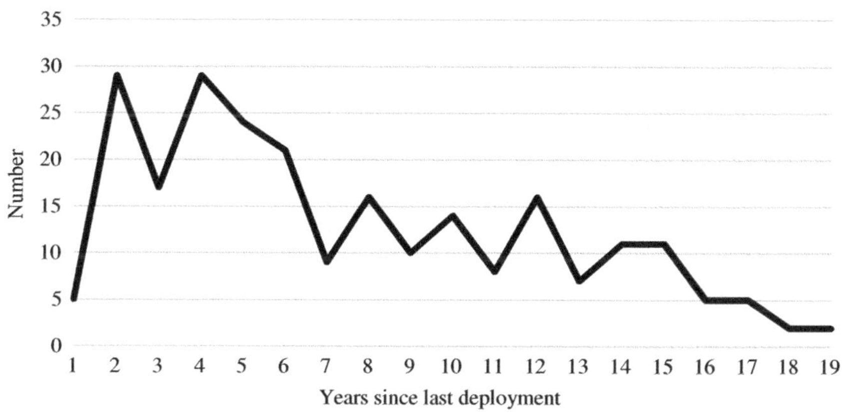


Figure 8.13. Men Deployed in 1992–2009 Who Died After Returning Home, by Number of Years since the Most Recent Deployment. *Source*: SFI. *Notes*: Died before 31 December 2010. Total dead: 241. Excludes deaths during deployment.

### *Over- or Submortality (Standard Mortality Rate)*

Until now, we have focused on mortality among the deployed. In this section, we introduce a control group and compare the mortality between these two groups. We use the standard mortality rate (SMR), which is calculated by relating the actual number of dead in a chosen group ($D_u$) to the expected or estimated number of dead. The expected number of dead is the product of the standard mortality (number of dead per 100,000) in the control group from the general population ($S_b$) and the number of people in the chosen group ($P_u$):

$$\text{SMR} = \left(D_u/(S_b{*}P_u)\right){*}100$$

An SMR value over 100 indicates that there is an over-mortality in the chosen group, here the deployed, whereas a value under 100 indicates a diminished mortality. We use the same control group of men born in 1975–1982 who were declared eligible for military service. In the control group, 0.7% died before the end of 2010. The respective proportion for veterans is 0.4%.

If the veterans had the same mortality quotient as the control group, the number of veterans who died should be 80% higher than the actual numbers found. Note, this is only in relation to deaths after returning home and does not include deaths while on missions. The SMR calculations support the hypothesis that the deployed are generally physically and mentally stronger than the men in the control group. Nonetheless, the calculations should be considered with the reservation that the data are only available up to 2010 and therefore only to a limited extent cover death after the returning home for participants in the most recent missions.

### *Summary*

There is great variation between the dead in relation to socio-demographic, health-related and military characteristics.

The probability of dying after deployment among veterans is correlated with personal, health-related and military characteristics of the most recent deployment. The probability of dying after deployment is greater if:

- the deployed has been registered with a psychiatric diagnosis or purchased mental health medication;
- the deployed is a one-time deployed soldier who was sent to the former Yugoslavia; and
- the deployed is more than 45 years old, has a short education or has no children at the time of the most recent deployment.

The mortality calculations show that there is a submortality among veterans compared with the control group for the years 1975–1982 in the period from 1992 to 2010, if those who died during deployment are excluded.

## Conclusion

The objective of this chapter was to examine the psychological health profile of Danish soldiers who have been deployed on international missions. The main conclusions of the chapter are as follows:

- In all, after deployment about 17% of the 26,000 soldiers deployed from 1992 to 2009 were registered with a psychiatric diagnosis, bought mental health medication or were treated for substance abuse without previous registration for this.
- When we compare deployed soldiers born between 1975 and 1982 with a similar control group consisting of over 100,000 men who were deemed as eligible for military service at the Armed Forces Day (draft day) but who were not deployed, we find that the deployed generally have fewer psychiatric diagnoses or contacts with the psychiatric health care system. In addition, fewer have purchased medication for mental illness, and fewer have been treated for substance abuse. We also find that the deployed have a lower mortality rate than the control group.
- At the time of deployment, the occurrence of mental illness is lower among the deployed than the control group, but about three years after deployment, a fairly marked increase occurs compared with the relatively constant increase seen in the control group. The result of this is that, over a few years, the levels in the two groups are the same. In addition, the deployed report more psychological work-related illness than the control group and in general more work-related injuries.
- It is especially those previously deployed to the former Yugoslavia in the beginning of the 1990s who are registered with psychological problems, although those repatriated (sent home) from missions in Afghanistan and Iraq in 2005–2009 were also registered with psychological problems after deployment.

Chapter 9

# Perspectives

In recent decades, Danish soldiers have been deployed on international missions of very different character, from peacekeeping (PK) to peace-enforcing (PE) missions involving actual combat situations. At the same time, there have been great changes in the society which the soldiers have to integrate into, on their return home.

In this study, we have focused on some of these important areas. Data available for the study have made it possible to compare the situation for soldiers deployed on international missions with developments after returning home. The study has confirmed that in general, the Danish veterans manage well and that they represent a heterogeneous group. It is therefore an important perspective to consider that the results of the study should be viewed in the light of the differences in the background of the veterans and that their return home has taken place in a society undergoing change. There have been changes in both attitudes in the general public about participation in international missions and policies concerning veterans.

One of the important perspectives in the study is that the veterans throughout handle everyday situations well in relation to their jobs and families. The same positive perspective can be found in the financial situation, with soldiers having stable finances. Finally, it is an important perspective that veterans commit fewer crimes than a comparative control group.

The area that the study has identified as very important in a long-term perspective concerns the psychological after-effects of having been deployed. Veterans who have returned home with severe physical injuries will be affected in the long term. It is also important to emphasise that the problems and challenges in this area are manifold. The missions have changed in character over the 20 years the investigation covers, and PK and PE missions can create different types of psychological and physical injuries that can stretch over many years.

The severity of psychiatric diagnoses, purchase of mental health medication and mortality was less among the veterans than in a comparative control group. To a certain extent, this underrepresentation is connected to the selection process that takes place before deployment: self-selection, as well as screening by the military. While we observe a considerable deterioration in the veterans' psychological well-being after returning home, the indicators of their psychological health show them on a level with the control group. In the study, it was only possible to follow the development for a longer period for a limited number of veterans. An important perspective is therefore to maintain focus on the situation in this area in the long term.

This focus applies not least to a group of veterans no longer in the military who participated in missions many years ago. They risk becoming 'invisible' as they are no longer employed in the military and were deployed before various support options became available to veterans. For these soldiers, there is a serious focus on the after-reactions of deployment. These 'invisible' veterans no longer in the military were deployed as privates to the former Yugoslavia in the 1990s. Generally, the deployed on missions in the late 1990s and those repatriated from Iraq and Afghanistan have a greater probability of being registered with psychiatric diagnoses or of purchasing mental health medication. While it is important to take into account this group of veterans, it is also important to highlight that, nonetheless, most of the veterans in this study manage a sustainable and well-functioning life.

In comparison with other countries, Denmark has a shorter experience with participation in more recent military missions. It can therefore be difficult to compare the results of this study with international knowledge, as many of the studies, for example in the United States, are based on veterans of the Vietnam war and the war in the Gulf in 1991, making it possible to follow up the soldiers over a longer period. In this study, analyses of mental health indicate possible long-term consequences of deployment. It is therefore still too early to draw conclusions about the more long-term consequences for the younger generation of soldiers, as psychological problems can appear many years after deployment and we could only follow developments up to 2010.

In recent years, especially after Denmark became engaged in the wars in Iraq and Afghanistan, the number of offers of support for veterans increased sharply. However, we still do not know what effect these offers have had on possible after-reactions. On the one hand, veterans with indications of mental illness can be difficult to contact after deployment. On the other hand, the increased focus on psychological after-effects may make it easier to communicate and get help.

From 2010, several initiatives were put into place, forming the basis of an independent veterans' policy in Denmark. From the results of this study, it is an important perspective to maintain ambitions for a veterans' policy and especially to concentrate on possible long-term consequences that deployment may have for some veterans.

# References


Angrist, J., & Pischke, J. S. (2008). *Mostly Harmless Econometrics*. Princeton, NJ: Princeton University Press.

Armey, L., Kniesner, T. J., Leeth, J. D., & Sullivan, R. (2018). *Combat, Casualties, and Compensation: Evidence from Iraq and Afghanistan*. IZA DP No. 11785. IZA, Bonn, Germany

Atkinson, M. P., Guetz, A., & Wein, L. M. (2009). A Dynamic Model for Posttraumatic Stress Disorder Among U.S. Troops in Operation Iraqi Freedom. *Management Science*, *55*(9), 1454–1468.

Bache, M. (1998). DIB-soldat eller ej? (DIB Soldier or Not?). *FCL Publikation*, 146.

Bell, C., Gorin, D., & Hogarth, J. M. (2009). *Does Financial Education Affect Soldiers' Financial Behavior?* Federal Reserve System Community Affairs Research Conference draft 06-12-09. Federal Reserve Board, Division of Consumer & Community Affairs.

Bouffard, L. A. (2003). Examining the Relationship between Military Service and Criminal Behavior during the Vietnam Era: A Research Note. *Criminology*, *41*, 491–510.

Brænder, M. (2016). Adrenalin Junkies: Why Soldiers Return from War Wanting More. *Armed Forces and Society*, *42*(1), 3–25.

Caforio, G. (Ed.). (2013). *Soldiers without Frontiers: The View from the Ground. Experiences of Asymmetric Warfare*. Acireale, Roma: Bonanno Editore.

Canan-Sokullu, E. S. (2012). Domestic Support to Wars: A Cross-case and Cross-country Analysis. *Armed Forces & Society*, *38*(1), 117–141.

Cesur, R., Sabia, J. J., & Tekin, E. (2013). The Psychological Costs of War: Military Combat and Mental Health. *Journal of Health Economics*, *32*(1), 51–65.

Conley, D., & Heerwig, J. A. (2009). *The Long-term Effects of Military Conscription on Mortality: Estimates from the Vietnam-era Draft Lottery*. NBER Working Paper No. 15105.

Cook, J., Riggs, D. S., Thompson, R., Coyne, J. C., & Sheikh, J. I. (2004). Posttraumatic Stress Disorder and Current Relationship Functioning among World War II Ex-prisoners of War. *Journal of Family Psychology*, *18*, 84–114.

Danish Health Authority (Sundhedsstyrelsen). (2010). *Center for Forebyggelse. Narkotikasituationen i Danmark* (Drug Situation in Denmark). København.

Danish Health Authority (Sundhedsstyrelsen). (2011). Den nationale sundhedsprofil 2010 – Hvordan har du det? (The National Health Profile 2010 – How Are You?). Retrieved from http://www.sst.dk

Danish Government. (2010). *Anerkendelse og støtte – Veteranpolitik* (Recognition and Support). Copenhagen. Retrieved from http://www.fmn.dk/temaer/veteraner/veteranpolitik/Documents/Veteranpolitik.pdf

Doyle, M., & Peterson, K. A. (2005). Re-entry and Reintegration: Returning Home after Combat. *Psychiatric Quarterly.*, *76*(4), 361–370.

Dubisch, J. (2009). Forget the War, Remember the Warrior. *Anthropology News*, May 10.

Eighmey, J. (2006). Why Do Youth Enlist? Identification of Underlying Themes. *Armed Forces and Society*, *32*(2), 307–328.

Ekholm, O., Kjøller, M., Davidsen, M., Hesse, U., Eriksen, L., Illemann Christensen, A., & Grønbæk, M. (2006). *Sundhed og Sygelighed 2005 i Danmark & Udviklingen siden 1987 (Health and Illness 2005 in Denmark and Development since 1987)*. Copenhagen: Statens Institut for Folkesundhed.

Engelhard, I. M., van den Hout, M. A., Weerts, J., Arntz, A., Hox, J. J. C. M., & McNally, R. J. (2007). Deployment-related Stress and Trauma in Dutch Soldiers Returning from Iraq. *British Journal of Psychiatry*, *191*(2), 140–145.

Galovski, T., & Lyons, J. A. (2004). Psychological Sequelae of Combat Violence: A Review of the Impact of PTSD on the Veteran's Family and Possible Interventions. *Aggression and Violent Behavior*, *9*, 477–501.

Gerber, D. A. (1994). Heroes and Misfits: The Troubled Social Reintegration of Disabled Veterans in the Best Years of Our Lives. *American Quarterly*, *46*(4), 545–574.

Gilroy, C., & Williams, C. (Eds.). (2006). *Service to Country. Personnel Policy and the Transformation of Western Militaries*. Cambridge, MA: The MIT Press.

Hageman, I., Pinborg, A., & Andersen, H. S. (2008). Complaints of Stress in Young Soldiers Strongly Predispose to Psychiatric Morbidity and Mortality: Danish National Cohort Study with 10-year Follow-up. *Acta Psychiatrica Scandinavica*, *117*(2), 148–155.

Hearst, N., Newman, T. B., & Hulley, S. B. (1986). Delayed Effects of the Military Draft on Mortality. *The New England Journal of Medicine*, *314*(10), 620–624.

Hedlund, E. (2011). What Motivates Swedish Soldiers to Participate in Peacekeeping Missions: Research Note. *Armed Forces and Society*, *37*(1), 180–190.

Heurlin, B. (2006). *The New Danish Model: Limited Conscription and Deployable Professionals* (chap. 6, pp. 157–178). In C. Gilroy & C. Williams (Eds.), *Service to Country. Personnel Policy and the Transformation of Western Militaries*. Cambridge, MA: The MIT Press.

Hines, L. A., Gribble, R., Wessely, S., Dandeker, C., & Fear, N. T. (2015). Are the Armed Forces Understood and Supported by the Public? A View from the United Kingdom. *Armed Forces and Society*, *41*(4), 688–713.

Hoge, C. W., Auhterlonie, J. L., & Milliken, C. S. (2006). Mental Health Problems, Use of Mental Health Services, and Attrition from Military Service after Returning from Deployment to Iraq or Afghanistan. *Journal of the American Medical Association*, *295*(9), 1023–1032.

Hoge, C. W., Castro, C. A., Messer, S. C., McGurk, D., Cotting, D. I., & Koffman, R. L. (2004). Combat Duty in Iraq and Afghanistan, Mental Health Problems, and Barriers to Care. *The New England Journal of Medicine*, *351*(1), 13–22.

Humensky, J. L., Jordan, N., Stroupe, K. T., & Hynes, D. M. (2013). How are Iraq/Afghanistan-Era Veterans Faring in the Labor Market. *Armed Forces & Society*, *39*(1), 158–183.

Høier-Madsen, K., Jørgensen, H. O., Sørensen, J. L., & Stokkebye, J. (2010). Skader og død hos udsendte danske soldater (Injuries and Death among Deployed Danish Soldiers). *Ugeskrift for Læger*, *172*, 128–132.

Jacobson, I. G. M., Ryan, A. K., Hooper, T. I., Smith, T. C., Amoroso, P. J., Boyko, E. J., Gackstetter, G. D., Wells, T. S., & Bell, N. S. (2008). Alcohol Use and Alcohol-related Problems Before And After Military Combat Deployment. *Journal of the American Medical Association, 300*(6), 663–765.

Jonasen, R. (2009). Fra "battlemind" til "homemind" (From Battlemind to Homemind). *Militært Tidsskrift (Military Journal)*, *1*, 40–46.

King, A. (2011). *The Transformation of Europe's Armed Forces: From the Rhine to Afghanistan*. Cambridge, MA: Cambridge University Press.

Kold, K., & Sørensen, H. (2013a). *Psychological Stress*. In Caforio (Ed.), *Soldiers without Frontiers: The View from the Ground. Experiences of Asymmetric Warfare* (Ch. 4, Part II, pp. 233–254). Acireale, Roma: Bonanno Editore.

Kold, K., & Sørensen, H. (2013b). *Denmark*. In Caforio (Ed.), *Soldiers without Frontiers: The View from the Ground. Experiences of Asymmetric Warfare* (Ch. 2, Part III _Country chapters, pp. 289–298). Acireale, Roma: Bonanno Editore.

Kristiansen, L., Ekholm, O., Grønbæk, M., & Schurmann Tolstrup, J. (2008). *Alkohol i Danmark – Voksnes Alkoholvaner og Holdning til Alkoholpolitik (Alcohol in Denmark – Alcohol Habits and Attitudes to Alcohol Politics in Grown Ups)*. Copenhagen: Statens Institut for Folkesundhed.

Larson, G. E., Highfill-McRoy, R. M., & Booth-Kewley, S. (2008). Psychiatric Diagnosis in Historic and Contemporary Military Cohorts: Combat Deployment and the Healthy Warrior Effect. *American Journal of Epidemiology*, *167*(11), 1269–1276.

Le Roux, B., & Rouanet, H. (2010). *Multiple Correspondence Analysis*. London: SAGE.

Lindegaard, H., & Rosholm, M. (2010). *The Effect of Changing Mental Health on Unemployment Duration and Destination States after Unemployment*. Social Science Research Network (SSRN). Retrieved from https://ssrn.com/abstract=1672026

Lyk-Jensen, S. V., & Glad, A. (2018). Why Do They Serve? Changes and Differences in Motives of Danish Soldiers Deployed to Peace-Keeping and Peace-Enforcing Missions. *Defence and Peace Economics*, *29*(3), 312–334.

Lyk-Jensen, S. V., Weatherall, C. D., & Jepsen, P. W. (2016). The Effect of Military Deployment on Mental Health. *Economics and Human Biology*, *23*, 193–208.

MacCoun, R., Kier, E., & Belkin, A. (2006). Does Social Cohesion Determine Motivation in Combat? An Old Question with an Old Answer. *Armed Forces & Society*, *32*(4), 646–654.

Noonan, M. E., & Mumola, C. (2007).*Veterans in State and Federal Prison, 2004. Bureau of Justice Statistics Special Report*. Washington, DC: US Department of Justice, Office of Justice Programs.

Petersson, M. (2011). Defense Transformation and Legitimacy in Scandinavia after the Cold War: Theoretical and Practical Implications. *Armed Forces and Society*, *37*(4), 701–724.

Roberto, J. R., Hyams, K. C., & Wessely, S. (2005). Screening for Psychological Illness in Military Personnel. *JAMA*, *293*, 1257–1260.

Rona, R. J., Jones, M., French, C., & Wessely, S. (2004). Screening for Physical and Mental Illness in the British Armed Forces. I: The Acceptability of the Programme. *Journal of Medical Screening*, *11*, 148–153.

Rutledge, M. S., Sanzenbacher, G. T., & Crawford, C. V. (2016). The Labor Supply of Disabled Veterans: 1995-2014. Working paper no. CRR WP 2016-8. Center for Retirement Research at Boston College.

Schulker, D. (2017). The Recent Occupation and Industry Employment Patterns of American Veterans. *Armed Forces & Society*, *43*(4), 695–710.

SFI. Rapport 10:21. (2010). Kofod, J., A.F. Benwell and A.A. Kjær. *Hjemvendte soldater. En interviewundersøgelse* (Home Coming Soldiers. An Interview Study). Copenhagen: The Danish National Institute of Social Research.

SFI. Rapport 11:25. (2011). Lyk-Jensen, S., C.D. Weatherall, J. Heidemann, M. Damgaard and A. Glad. *Soldater før og under udsendelse*. En kortlægning (Soldiers before and during Deployment. A Mapping). Copenhagen: The Danish National Institute of Social Research.

SFI. Rapport 12:01. (2012). Lyk-Jensen, S., A. Glad, J. Heidemann and M. Damgaard. *Soldater efter udsendelse. En spørgeskemaundersøgelse* (Soldiers after Deployment. An Interview Study). Copenhagen: The Danish National Institute of Social Research.

SFI. Rapport 12:09. (2012). Lyk-Jensen, S., J. Heidemann and A. Glad. *Soldater – før og efter udsendelse. En analyse af motivation, økonomiske forhold og kriminalitet* (Soldiers – before and after Deployment. An Analysis of Motivation, Economic Incentives and Criminality). Copenhagen: The Danish National Institute of Social Research.

SFI. Rapport 12:24. (2012). Lyk-Jensen, S., J. Heidemann, A. Glad and C. D. Weatherall. *Danske hjemvendte soldater. Soldaternes psykiske sundhedsprofil før og efter udsendelse* (The Health Profile of Soldiers – before and after Deployment). Copenhagen: The Danish National Institute of Social Research.

Shen, Y. C., Cunha, J. M., & Williams, T. V. (2016). Time-varying Associations of Suicide with Deployments, Mental Health Conditions, and Stressful Life Events among Current and Former US Military Personnel: A Retrospective Multivariate Analysis. *The Lancet Psychiatry*, *3*(11), 1039–1048.

Skomorovsky, A., & Bullock, A. (2017). The Impact of Deployment on Children from Canadian Military Families. *Armed Forces & Society*, *43*(4), 654–673.

Synnott, A. (2009). *Re-thinking Men. Heroes, Villains and Victims*. Farnham: Ashgate.

Sørensen, H. (2010). *The Intention of Inventing a New Retention Policy for the Danish Armed Forces*.In Tresch and Leuprecht (Eds.), *Europe without Soldiers? Recruitment and Retention across the Armed Forces of Europe* (Ch. 15, pp. 259–269). Montreal: McGill-Queen's University Press.

Teachman, J., Anderson, C., & Tedrow, L. M. (2015). Military Service and Alcohol Use in the United States. *Armed Forces & Society*, *41*(3), 460–476.

Thomsen, D. Y., Jonassen, R., Berntsen, D., Johannessen, K. B., Hoxer, C. R., Pedersen, C. H., Bach, P., Klausen, H. B., & Bertelsen, M. (2010). *Study of the Psychological Subsequent Effects on Soldiers Deployed to Afghanistan from February to August 2009*. Copenhagen: Military Academy.

Treadwell, J. (2010). Counterblast: More than Casualties of War?: Ex-military Personnel in the Criminal Justice System. *The Howard Journal of Criminal Justice*, *49*(1), 73–77.

Tresch, T. S., & Leuprecht, C. (Eds.). (2010). *Europe without Soldiers? Recruitment and Retention across the Armed Forces of Europe*. Montreal: McGill-Queen´s University Press.

Van Gennep, A. (1960 [1909]). *The Rites of Passage*. Chicago, IL: University of Chicago Press.

Vedtofte, M. S. (2016).*Selvmord blandt veteraner: 1992-2014. (Suicide among Veterans: 1992-2014)*. Ringsted: Veterancentret.

Wadsworth, S. M., & Riggs, D. S. (Eds.). (2014). *Military Deployment and Its Consequences for Families, Risk and Resilience in Military and Veteran Families series*. New York: Springer.

Wessely, S., Unwin, C., Hotopf, M., Hull, L., Ismail, K., Nicolaou, V., & David, A. (2003). Stability of Recall of Military Hazards over Time. *British Journal of Psychiatry*, *183*, 314–322.

Winslow, D. (1999). *Canadian Warriors in Peacekeeping: Points of Tension in Complex Cultural Encounters (DCIEM-CR-1999-125)*. Toronto: Defence and Civil Institute of Environmental Medicine.

Yager, J. (1976). Postcombat Violent Behaviour in Psychiatrically Maladjusting Soldiers. *Archives of General Psychiatry*, *33*, 1332–1335.

# Index

Printed and bound by CPI Group (UK) Ltd, Croydon, CR0 4YY

13/09/2026

14961059-0005